ANDREW F. JONES

Yellow Music

MEDIA CULTURE AND COLONIAL MODERNITY IN

THE CHINESE JAZZ AGE

Duke University Press

Durham and London

2001

© 2001 DUKE UNIVERSITY PRESS

All rights reserved

Printed in the United States of America

on acid-free paper ∞

Designed by C. H. Westmoreland

Typeset in Palatino with Quadraat display

by Tseng Information Systems, Inc.

Library of Congress Cataloging-in-

Publication Data appear on the last

printed page of this book.

CONTENTS

This book is the product of the collective efforts of colleagues and friends both near and far-flung, and could not have been written without their help. Lydia H. Liu, my doctoral adviser and colleague at the University of California, was instrumental to the formation of this project, which began its life as a doctoral thesis in Berkeley's Department of East Asian Languages and Cultures. Theodore Huters and David Lloyd also played essential roles in seeing the dissertation through to the end, both as members of the dissertation committee, and as sympathetic interlocutors and careful and critical readers of my written work. Leo Ou-fan Lee, whom I like to think of as an unofficial member of the committee, steered me toward the study of the cultural history of the Republican era during my sojourn as exchange scholar at Harvard University in the spring of 1995.

The bulk of the research for this project was undertaken in 1995 and 1996 with the financial assistance of Mellon Fellowships in the Humanities, and it was facilitated by research institutions, colleagues, and friends in three Chinese cities. I am especially grateful to Liang Maochun, Wang Yun, and the staff of the Music Research Library of the Institute of Culture and Arts in Beijing for the pleasant and productive days I spent working in their archives. I am obliged to Zhu Tianwei and Yang Yuanying of the Beijing Film Archive and Professor Chen Shan of the Beijing Film Institute for providing valuable advice and access to archival materials and movies. Thanks also are due to Guo Yiqing, who arranged for the delivery of several packages of research material from Beijing after I had already left.

I benefited enormously from the professionalism and expertise of the staff at the Shanghai Municipal Library, both in Xujiahui in 1995 and in the library's palatial new surroundings on Huaihai Road on a subsequent research trip in December 1998. Wang Zhigang and his students at the Shanghai Institute of Drama hosted a researcher from afar with generosity and style.

In Hong Kong, I am deeply indebted to Paul Fonoroff for allowing me to make use of his unique collection of prewar film journals and popular cultural ephemera. Without his help, my efforts to trace the cultural history of this period would have been greatly impoverished. I also have bene-fited immensely from Wong Kee-chee's expertise and guidance. For those interested in the history of Chinese popular culture, his heroic efforts to preserve the legacy of Chinese popular music on compact disc will be much appreciated for years to come. It was also Mr. Wong who kindly arranged for me to interview the legendary and extraordinarily lively Pathé recording artist, Yao Li. Mr. Law Kar, film critic, historian of Chi-nese cinema, and one of the principal organizers of the Hong Kong Inter-national Film Festival, has been unstintingly generous with his time, his vast fund of knowledge, and his collection of books, magazines, and video-tapes.

A supplementary research trip undertaken in December 1998 to col-lect documents and photographs at the Shanghai Municipal Library was funded by a Fritz Faculty Research Grant from the China Studies Program at the University of Washington's Jackson School of International Studies.

In the United States, I am grateful to the staffs of East Asian collec-tions at Berkeley, the University of Washington, Stanford University, and Harvard's Yenching Library. On a number of occasions Wen-Hsin Yeh has given me the opportunity to present my work-in-progress to the sympa-thetic and Shanghai-savvy audiences at the Center for Chinese Studies at Berkeley. I also am grateful for the organizers and audiences of related conference presentations at the Department of History at the University of Illinois (Urbana-Champaign) and the Interdisciplinary Humanities Cen-ter at the University of California, Santa Barbara. My students at Berkeley and the University of Washington also have read and commented on my work in the context of undergraduate lecture courses and graduate semi-nars. Their energy and intellectual curiosity have sustained my scholarly efforts over the course of the past few years.

The following friends and colleagues at Berkeley, the University of Washington, and elsewhere also have expedited the project's completion in a number of ways over the years, either by lending me materials and ref-erences, intellectual stimulation, or an ear: Tani Barlow, Eileen Chow, Dai Jinhua, Prasenjit Duara, Poshek Fu, Gail Hershhatter, Adam Kern, David Knechtges, Gregory Lee, Li Tuo, Kathryn Lowry, Nikhil P. Singh, John Treat, Frederic Wakeman, Steve West, and Yingjin Zhang.

A revised version of chapter 2, "The Gramophone in China," appears in Lydia H. Liu, ed., *Tokens of Exchange: The Problem of Translation in Global Circulations* (Durham, N.C.: Duke University Press, 1999). An earlier formulation of aspects of the analysis presented in chapters 3 and 4 appears as "The Sing-Song Girl and the Nation: Music and Media Culture in Republican China," in Kai-wing Chow, Kevin Doak, and Po-shek Fu, eds., *Constructing Nationhood in Modern East Asia* (Ann Arbor: University of Michigan Press, 2001).

I deeply appreciate Ken Wissoker's editorial insight and support of this project. He and his staff at Duke University Press have made the process of bringing this book to its readers a real pleasure.

Finally, numerous close friends and relatives were instrumental to the successful completion of this project and for ensuring that the process was a happy one. Cherry Chan and her family gave me a home in Hong Kong during the year in which I did the bulk of the research for the project, for which I will always be grateful. He Yong and David Smith hosted me on numerous occasions in their Beijing *hutongs,* and Lucan Way shared his dacha in Sonoma. Nicole Huang and Eric Allina have been constant sources of advice and encouragement. And, as ever, I am deeply grateful for the love and support of my parents, to whom this book is dedicated.

Listening to the Chinese Jazz Age

In 1935 a young trumpet player named Buck Clayton arrived in Shanghai with his jazz orchestra for an extended engagement at the elegant Canidrome Ballroom. For Clayton—who would go on to jazz fame as a member of the Count Basie Orchestra—the sojourn in Shanghai represented the "happiest two years" of his life, during which he felt he "finally" received the sort of respect and recognition that had been denied him in his native country because of his color.[1] Clayton's journey to Shanghai had been precipitated by brisk trans-Pacific traffic in recorded music. Gramophone records of the music of Duke Ellington and other artists had already reached Chinese shores, spurring on a rage for black bands in the city's nightclubs and dance halls.[2] Thus, Clayton's orchestra, which hailed from Los Angeles, was billed as the "Harlem Gentlemen," despite the fact that none of the band members had ever ventured east of Kansas City.

The city in which Clayton found himself (according to an American composer and arranger named Claude Lapham who wrote about his journeys in Asia for the jazz trade journal *Metronome*) was a "seventh heaven for the jazz musician," a "Paris of the East" that far outstripped the real Paris in terms of "the appreciation of jazz."[3] Indeed, Shanghai's reputation as the "jazz mecca" of Asia had already made it the destination of choice for aspiring Japanese jazz musicians, who worked the cabarets of the Hongkew district while studying the music firsthand with globetrotting American musicians like pianist Teddy Weatherford.[4] And it was Weatherford, in his capacity as a booking agent for the owners of the Canidrome, who was responsible for arranging Clayton's journey in the first place.

In his first few days in Shanghai, Clayton was struck by both the sheer density of the crowds that funneled through the streets of Shanghai's International Settlement and their remarkable diversity. "Companies from all over the world did business in Shanghai, and you could see all kinds of nationalities—Indians, French, Russians, Americans, and people from all

Buck Clayton in the International Settlement, Shanghai, circa 1934.
Courtesy of the Institute of Jazz Studies, Rutgers University.

Buck Clayton and his Harlem Gentlemen performing at the Canidrome Ballroom. Courtesy of the Institute of Jazz Studies, Rutgers University.

corners of the world."[5] In the ensuing months, Clayton learned to drink vodka from White Russian refugees, watched South American athletes play jai alai (on which spectators placed wagers), and explored the city's seemingly infinite array of nightclubs, dance halls, and cafés with friends drawn from the ranks of American military units stationed in the city.

Clayton and his band members became beneficiaries of the same sorts of colonial privileges enjoyed by other foreigners in Shanghai (and routinely denied them back home). These privileges were based in part on the strength of the dollar relative to local currency; Clayton and his band members took to ordering handmade suits "like we were millionaires" and cultivating decidedly patrician pursuits like horseback riding.[6] Clayton's enjoyment of these sartorial and equestrian pleasures, however, was matched by a sharp awareness of the other side of the colonial coin, as embodied by the desperate poverty of many local Chinese.

The Chinese population exceeded all others. . . . They were everywhere—
in the streets, on the sidewalks, in alleys . . . some of them hardly wore any
clothes at all and others had on tattered rags. . . . I would see sometimes
twenty or thirty coolies pulling a big huge heavy cart that in America
would be pulled by a truck or horses. These people seemed to be really
nothing but human horses and all they would be paid for at the end of the
day was just enough to get a couple of bowls of rice and a place to sleep.
I don't know how they did it.[7]

These same poor people, Clayton adds wryly, could not afford even
to *look* at the Canidrome Ballroom where his orchestra was the headline
act. The Canidrome (the name derived from the greyhound racecourse to
which the ballroom was attached) catered to wealthy Chinese and a diverse crowd of foreign businessmen, colonial bureaucrats, diplomats, and
military officers.[8] So elite was the club's patronage, in fact, that China's
"first lady," Madame Chiang Kai-shek, attended the orchestra's first performance at the club with her sister Elsie Soong, who went on to take private lessons in tap dancing from Clayton's trombone player, Duke Up-
shaw. The American provenance of Clayton's Harlem Gentleman, in short,
had immediately catapulted them to the pinnacle of Shanghai's popular
musical pyramid, above the "Filipino bands, Russian bands, East Indian
bands, and of course the oriental bands" that also purveyed jazz and other
kinds of dance music in less prestigious venues.[9]

Their identity as *African* Americans, however, soon landed them in trouble with their fellow expatriates in Shanghai. The first intimation of the
kind of homegrown American racism that would eventually cost the band
its cozy position at the Canidrome is also an object lesson in the tangled
colonial hierarchies into which Clayton and his band had been placed by
their presence in Shanghai. Almost a month after having arrived at the
Canidrome, Clayton and several members of the band were assaulted by a
contingent of American marines. Riding in rickshaws and shouting racial
epithets, the soldiers hurled bricks at Clayton and his sidemen. A melee
ensued, from which the musicians emerged more or less victorious, if not
unscathed. What distinguished this incident from the sort of racialized
violence with which Clayton was all too familiar in the United States was
that it took place in a colonial setting characterized (as are all such settings)
by the systematic oppression of the "natives."

When it was all over the Chinese onlookers treated us like we had done something that they had always wanted to do and followed us all the way home cheering us like a winning football team. I guess they figured it was something that should have been done a long time before, because I remember one time I saw a marine fall off his bicycle and he promptly got up, went over to a Chinese coolie and kicked him in the ass and then got back on his bicycle and rode on off.[10]

It was also an American marine who sucker-punched Clayton one night as he introduced a new act recently imported from the United States, the Hollywood Blondes. The blow was landed (in full view of the nightclub's elegant patrons) in retribution for the ostensible crime of having looked at a white woman; a nasty brawl resulted. This was the first salvo of an elaborate campaign, spearheaded by a group of American club owners and booking agents, to eject the Harlem Gentlemen from their position at the Canidrome. A telegram from a group of white Southerners threatened the Chinese owners of the club with a hail of machine-gun bullets if Clayton should appear onstage at the ballroom, and a lawsuit was brought against the band for damages resulting from the earlier brawl. Despite Municipal Police protection and the failure of the lawsuit in the courts of the International Settlement, the Canidrome elected to break off the band's engagement, and Clayton found himself "stranded half way around the world" without sufficient funds for the trans-Pacific passage home to Los Angeles.

Desperate for cash, Clayton soon found work leading a smaller ensemble in a substantially less elegant setting: the Casa Nova Ballroom. This nightclub, owned by a half-American, half-Chinese businessman and populated with the sort of low-class Russian hostesses and taxi dancers who were an integral part of Shanghai's seamy nocturnal demimonde, catered less to foreigners and the native elite than to the Chinese urban petit bourgeoisie (*xiao shimin*).[11] And it was for this reason that Clayton—who eventually left China just two weeks before the Japanese attack on Shanghai in July 1937 that heralded the advent of World War Two—spent the remainder of his sojourn playing not only American jazz but also Chinese popular music. "We found that on this new job we were obliged to play Chinese music so we began to learn how. I sketched out some of the most popular Chinese songs at the time and after a few rehearsals we were playing it like we had been doing it a long time. It wasn't too much different from our music except the Chinese have a different scale tone, but as long as it could be written in on the American scale it could be played."[12]

Some of the Chinese songs that Clayton was compelled to learn after his ejection from the Canidrome were almost certainly penned by Li Jin-hui, an educator and composer to whom the creation of a hybrid genre of American jazz, Hollywood film music, and Chinese folk music known in Chinese as "modern songs" (*shidai qu*) is usually credited.[13] Li's controversial brand of popular music—often dismissed and excoriated by its critics as "yellow" or "pornographic" music (*huangse yinyue*)—and the urban media culture with which it was closely associated is a primary focus of this musical, cultural, and historical study of China's jazz age. As such, the book offers an account of the rise of both "yellow music" and a new form of left-wing mass music (*qunzhong yinyue*) expressly designed to counter Li Jinhui's musical idiom in the urban media marketplace of Republican China; and in so doing, to serve as a musical means of national mobilization against Euro-American colonial domination and Japanese militarism in the decade preceding 1937.

Throughout the book, this relatively circumscribed focus opens onto larger topical and temporal horizons. In explicating the genres that make up the Republican musical field, as well as the emergence of the mass media (cinema, radio, and print) through which these genres were disseminated, I also provide a genealogy for this complex sonic and technological landscape. Readers will come away from the book with an introduction not only to the history of Chinese music in the wake of its nineteenth-century encounter with the missionaries and militaries of the imperial West, but also with new perspectives on the emergence of Chinese media culture in the early twentieth century. The portrait I paint here of the interwar period—in which yellow music and anticolonial mass music rub sonic shoulders and contend for a measure of dominance within a newly constituted media marketplace—also serves to adumbrate the divisions, and perhaps more important, the secret historical affinities between the commodity culture of Hong Kong and Taiwan (a culture forged from the forced removal of Shanghai's culture industry to China's colonial and neocolonial peripheries in 1949) and the experiments in revolutionary culture undertaken in Mao's China that characterize Chinese cultural history in the postwar period.

But as I propose in this introduction (and as the story about Buck Clayton already has suggested), this book does not concern itself exclusively with China. Nor is it necessarily a study of music per se, much less of Chinese music. The methodological and substantive implications of these counterintuitive assertions are perhaps most economically suggested by several questions that underlie the book's intellectual trajectory. Is it possible to speak of jazz music in China without first considering the trans-Pacific circulation of gramophone records and musicians that enabled its presence there in the first place? How do we account for Li Jinhui's appropriation of an African American musical form? How did this new cultural form play into the politics of nation-building and anticolonial resistance in Republican China? What might Clayton's translation of Li's Chinese music back into "American" suggest about the relationship between the two? And, finally, what does the transaction itself tell us about the status of national music in an age in which culture is rendered increasingly portable by the global diffusion of new media technologies?

CULTURAL HISTORY AND COLONIAL MODERNITY

Every piece of writing contains, amberlike, traces of the reasons why it has not been written before. In setting out to write the story of Li Jinhui and the Chinese popular music he helped to create, I did not expect to encounter Buck Clayton. But the questions that his presence in the historical record necessitate shed new light not only on the world that these two men shared, but also on the practice of Chinese cultural history and the problematic status of China (as a determinate and reified object of study) within that disciplinary formation. Clayton's account of his years in Shanghai alerts us to the folly of trying to understand Chinese jazz as an example of Western influence on Chinese musical forms. Nor can the "Chinese" in "Chinese jazz" be relegated to the realm of the merely adjectival and understood as a modifier of what remains an essentially African American musical genre. For, as the story of Clayton's slide down the ladder of Shanghai nightlife suggests, Chinese popular music in the 1930s was less an achieved form than a musical, technological, financial, linguistic, and racial transaction conducted within the boundaries of the complex colonial hierarchies peculiar to that time and place. This is why listening to the Chinese jazz age, and in particular to the cacophony of its multiply colonized treaty ports, ought to provide insight into both Chinese modernity and the "colonial core" of Euro-American modernity as well.[14] We need, in other words, to ask why Buck Clayton's "life seemed to begin in Shanghai," to hear the "China" in American jazz just as distinctly as the "America" in Chinese popular music, and to identify the ways in which both are implicated in the global unfolding of colonial modernity.[15]

These are, however, precisely the cross-cultural and cross-disciplinary problems that have led scholars in both China and abroad to neglect this vital aspect of Republican era cultural history.[16] For Mainland Chinese scholars of music history, yellow music is indelibly tainted by its "deep-seated coloniality," by its association with the ideologically unorthodox commercial media culture that took shape in China's colonial treaty ports in the years before the Communist victory in 1949.[17] Nor is this inattention new. Since its mass-mediated appearance on the Chinese musical scene, yellow music was condemned by nationalist and leftist critics alike as a "decadent sound" (*mimi zhi yin*) capable of seducing citizens away from the pressing tasks of nation-building and anti-imperialist resistance. Indeed, this ideological taint—and the complex and oftentimes conflictual relation between nationalist discourse and mass culture of which it is a symptom—is one of the recurring motifs of this history. A second and less immediately obvious theme is the extent to which this disdain has blinded critics and historians to the close mutual intertwinement of yellow music with the officially sanctioned leftist mass music that has come to be seen as its historical and ideological "other."

Dismissed until recently in the Chinese academy on ideological grounds, yellow music has also fallen victim to neglect in the Anglo-American context, in part because it slips through a number of disciplinary cracks. Ethnomusicologists tend to focus their scholarly efforts on those aspects of Chinese musical culture in which China's *difference* from the West is most pronounced, including various forms of traditional, regional, and folk musics. As Sue Tuohy points out in a pioneering study of Chinese film music of the 1930s, a similar dynamic is also at work in accounts of Republican era movies written by scholars of Chinese cinema that consistently stress the "incongruity" of the seemingly foreign sounds on the soundtrack (be they nondiegetic recordings of European classical music or renditions of jazzy Chinese popular music) with the Chinese "realities" onscreen.[18] Literary and cultural critics—discussed in greater detail in chapter 3—have found it difficult to reconcile the hybrid and commercial character of the music with narratives of Chinese modernity that take the nation-building project of the new literary elites associated with the May 4th Movement of 1919 as their ideological and historical fulcrum. And those scholars who have been willing to devote their attention to Chinese popular culture often focus on the realm of the immediately contemporary, partly because of difficulty in gaining access to historical materials, and partly because of a certain tendency—born of the cold war era practice of journalistic and social scientific "China-watching"—to interpret such phenomena solely in terms of late-breaking sociopolitical events in the People's Republic.[19]

A deeper and perhaps more daunting problem—and one that directly underlies the ways in which these disciplinary boundaries fail to overlap—has to do with the constitution of area studies as such, especially in regard to modern East Asia. The institutionalization of area studies programs in the Euro-American academy has led to the creation and maintenance of scholarly fiefs, complete with borders that serve to delimit their geographical (and epistemological) horizons. All too often, these institutional and ideological arrangements have reified the geographical region in question and avoided the complexities and inequities of the global historical processes in which these localities are necessarily involved. As Tani Barlow has convincingly argued, "the occlusion of colonialism" as a category for analysis so characteristic of postwar Chinese studies is the inevitable result of such an institutional arrangement, precisely because a narrow focus on one area precludes engaged analysis of the intertwining of capitalist modernity and imperialism on a global scale.[20]

It is in this specific sense that the historiographical category of "colonial modernity" becomes useful, for it alerts us to the necessity of grounding our analyses of modern Chinese cultural production in a rigorously transnational frame—in a manner responsive to both the irreducible specificity of the local and the immense complexity of the global. At the same time as it opens the writing of modern Chinese cultural history to ostensibly "foreign" interlopers, media technologies, and artistic forms, such a historiography also sidesteps reductive models which hold that these interactions are entirely one-sided. By placing previously segregated analytical domains into productive tension, this model steers us away from a vision of modern Chinese cultural history as a mechanistic or merely reflexive reaction to imperialist encroachment. In emphasizing the temporal simultaneity of these processes, moreover, it short-circuits notions of Chinese modernity as a belated or even as yet incomplete project, as a futile foot race in which a backward China is condemned to forever pursue—and never overtake—the West. Instead, we need to look at the ways in which both (and indeed all) parties have been and continue to be inextricably bound up in a larger and infinitely more complex process whereby "national cultures . . . [are] rearticulated within the new global framework" of colonial modernity.[21]

THE PROBLEM OF TECHNOLOGY

The trope of "Western technology" is perhaps one of the most important impediments to the creation of an adequately materialist history of the emergence of media cultures in the colonial world. In a groundbreaking study of the means by which Euro-American anthropologists have constituted their ethnographic objects of study as "other," Johannes Fabian argues that differential relations of power are often understood (and reinforced) in ethnographic writing by way of recourse to tropes of temporal difference: the Western observer of foreign cultures inhabits the modern present, while the natives that he or she observes are consigned to a primitive past. This "denial of coevalness" is not limited to narrowly ethnographic discourse.[22] It is instead, a constitutive feature of imperialist historiographies that posit a binary division between advanced civilizations and backward tribes, between those who possess history and those who do not. And it is precisely because the notion of advanced technology has so often been pressed into service as a bulwark of this binary system that any study of the emergence of technologically mediated cultures in the non-West should be wary of how this trope distorts our understanding of modernity in the colonies.

Michael Taussig provides an interesting commentary on the way in which devices such as cameras and gramophones come to serve as emblems of both Western technological superiority and native incomprehension. In his book, *Mimesis and Alterity,* Taussig draws on a rich trove of ethnographic representations that focus our attention not only on the fascination that these devices hold for the natives—one classic example being the celebrated scene in Robert Flaherty's 1922 film *Nanook of the North* when a mystified Eskimo tries to eat the 78-rpm record in which (according to the film's inter-title) the "white man 'cans' his voice"; but also on (2) the less immediately obvious but ultimately more productive question of just "why Westerners are so fascinated by Others' fascination with this apparatus?"[23] As Taussig points out, this fascination serves in large part to obscure the history of the reception of these machines in the West itself. "Vis à vis the savage, [Western colonizers] are the masters of these wonders that, after the first shock waves of surprise upon their invention and commercialization in the West, pass into the everyday. Yet these shocks rightly live on in the mysterious underbelly of the technology—to be eviscerated as 'magic' in frontier rituals of technological supremacy."[24] Historically determinate technologies, in other words, are naturalized as a necessary attribute of "Western civilization," and machines slip unremarked into the domain of an implicitly racialized sense of culture.

The discursive echoes of these powerful and profoundly ahistoricizing "frontier rituals" still suffuse contemporary scholarship on non-Western media cultures. In most scholarship on the history of Chinese cinema, for instance, film is insistently labeled as a foreign technology to which traditional Chinese forms of visuality and performance culture must be uncomfortably assimilated. Paul Clark's *Chinese Cinema: Culture and Politics Since 1949,* to cite one widely recognized example, hinges on a description of the ways in which Chinese filmmakers have sought to "Sinify" what Clark almost invariably characterizes as a "foreign medium."[25] More recent work on the early history of cinema in China has focused on how the "Shanghai film industry [took steps] to help Chinese audiences adapt to or 'domesticate' the alien entertainment form (that is, Western shadowplay)."[26] In pointing out such tropes, I do not deny that the cinematic apparatus was invented in the West, nor that it was often associated by its Chinese users with a Western geographical and historical point of origin. However, I do want to note the way in which this sort of usage obscures the foreign quality of this technology in the West itself in the years following its invention. Just as in China, traditional Western dramaturgical and visual culture was forced to adapt itself to the exigencies and possibilities of a novel medium. Perhaps more significantly, this shock took place nearly simultaneously in both Europe and Asia, Paris and Shanghai. The Lumière brothers' epochal unveiling of their new Cinématographe took place on December 28, 1895, in the basement of the Grand Café in Paris. The first demonstration of cinema in China took place just eight months later, on August 11, 1896, at the Xuyuan teahouse in Shanghai.[27] Technology, in short, traveled roughly at the speed of the steamships that plied colonial trade routes. This fact alone–one which seems surprising only in light of the sort of imperial historiography mentioned earlier—

ought to call into question the empirical validity of any attempt to cast the culture of the colonial periphery in terms of its belated modernity vis-à-vis the metropole.

It also exposes the essentialist fallacy inherent in attributing to film (or any other technological medium) a point of origin located not simply in geography and history, but in discourses of ethnicity and/or national character. Throughout the first few decades of the twentieth century—decades that witnessed the rapid development of a thriving film industry and cinematic culture in urban China—the movies presented themselves to Chinese viewers not as an ineffably and unalterably foreign cultural form, but as a technical apparatus, a system of distribution and exhibition, a mode of spectatorship, and a set of cultural products dominated by foreign financial and ideological interests. In the words of one Chinese commentator writing in 1932 in a guide to life in modern Shanghai:

> going to the movies does not mean catering to the foreign, but Chinese movies are really not as good as foreign movies. This is undeniable in industrially backward China. . . . If a Chinese film costs two or three hundred thousand *yuan,* it is called a big production. But in America's Hollywood, the headquarters of world film-making, frequently a film would cost tens of thousands and even millions of dollars. With such discrepancy of capital, the distance of achievement is likewise large.[28]

We find a similar approach in the film actor and historian Zheng Junli's 1936 appraisal of the development of Chinese film, "A Brief History of Modern Chinese Cinema."[29] Zheng's essay, surely among the most comprehensive and valuable of its kind dating from the Republican period, directly grapples with the question of the medium's origins outside China. But his portrait of the struggle of Chinese producers and artists to create a viable national cinema focuses on questions of economic and structural inequity. How do Chinese production companies cope with the foreign monopoly on the film exhibition business? How does fierce competition with Hollywood result in the development of new Chinese genres? Some of his conclusions throw a fresh and surprising light on problems of derivation and agency in the emergence of a distinctly Chinese media culture. He argues, for instance, that precisely those types of Chinese-made films which claimed the mantle of "Chineseness" and resistance to Europeanization—that is, the martial arts and period costume dramas of the mid- and late 1920s—resulted from the strenuous efforts of Chinese producers to emulate the huge popularity of such Douglas Fairbanks swashbucklers as *Robin Hood* (1922).[30]

As these contemporary accounts nicely suggest, scholarly insistence on film as a "foreign" medium serves only to recast what is first and foremost a problem of political economy—the concentration of the means of mechanical reproduction in the hands of the colonial powers and transnational capital—in terms of cultural difference.[31] In addition to being ahistorical, this move implicitly reproduces something very like the "frontier rituals of technological supremacy" that Taussig identifies in the still relatively unexplored discursive territory at the confluence of area studies and cultural studies.

In pointing out the dangers of such procedures, I do not mean to deny the importance of local culture as an analytical category. The arrival in China of media technologies such as the cinema and the gramophone did, of course, result in a fundamental dislocation of certain indigenous forms of cultural production and cultural authority, particularly for the landed Confucian literati whose dominance had been culturally constituted through command of the classical literary tradition. This local development, however, must be read against the backdrop of the larger historical and spatial context within which it unfolds.

Friedrich Kittler, a German media theorist, has written eloquently of the "terror" elicited by these novelties in Europe as they began to displace the traditional authority of writing in the waning years of the nineteenth century, an era he terms the "founding age of technological media."[32] This sense of threat was compounded in China by the exploitative economic arrangements and imperialist violence (both real and symbolic) that often accompanied the diffusion of media technologies.[33] Indeed, in positing an axial age of media technology beginning in 1880, Kittler fails to point out how and to what extent the explosive development of the new culture industries made possible by the camera and the gramophone were, from the start, complicit with colonial expansion. In turn, their diffusion throughout the colonized world was a primary factor in the dramatic acceleration of the globalization of culture taking place in the late nineteenth century.

As is detailed in chapter 2, "The Gramophone in China," the trade in phonographic records that eventually expedited Buck Clayton's journey to China was transnational from its inception in the late 1890s when such newly minted corporations as the Victor Talking Machine Company, the Gramophone Company, and the Compagnie Phonographique Pathé-

Frères began to fan out across the globe in search of new sounds and new markets.

The story of one such agent, F. W. Gaisberg, whose 1902 journey throughout Asia yielded more than 1,700 recordings of "native" music for the Gramophone Company, is chronicled here. Interestingly, this operational mode closely mirrored that of the Lumière brothers several years earlier; the Lumières, within a year of the invention of their cinematic apparatus in 1895, had dispatched camera operators to the United States, Latin America, Russia, the Middle East, and Asia in search of new footage for metropolitan filmgoers and to establish footholds in local exhibition territories. Given the confluence of their activities with the high tide of global imperialism, the peregrinations of phonographic and cinematographic agents followed the trajectories and trade routes traced across the globe by the operations of colonial capital.

The development of a new brand of mass-mediated urban popular music in China (as well as the preservation and promotion of a number of different forms of regional and folk musics) is closely bound with the presence of these globetrotting companies in Shanghai's International Settlement. In these pages I focus primarily on the corporate history of the multinational company Pathé Asia (Dongfang baidai changpian gongsi), a subsidiary of Pathé-Frères, which served as the most important incubator of both yellow music and (ironically, given its composers' explicitly anticolonial agenda) leftist mass music. Not inconsequentially, Pathé's factory in Shanghai was a center for the production and distribution of both Chinese popular music and an astonishing variety of Southeast Asian musics. Studying Pathé Asia and the larger enterprise of colonial phonography in which it took part, then, not only situates Chinese popular music in the context of an emergent turn-of-the-century transnational economy unfolding in China's treaty ports but also helps to historicize the theoretical speculation on the nature of globalization and transnational culture that has increasingly dominated academic and journalistic discourse in our own time.[34]

FROM COLONIAL PHONOGRAPHY
TO PHONOGRAPHIC REALISM

One of the tasks of this book, then, is to trace the historical career of sound recording in China; and in so doing, explicate the process by which colonial phonography was appropriated as a means of anticolonial resistance in the Republican period. This task is complicated by the unfortunate fact that the products of these colonial phonographers—black amber on which traces of the sound world of early twentieth-century China were miraculously inscribed—are extremely difficult to find. In the United States we take the preservation (and astonishingly easy availability) of our popular musical heritage for granted. For example, each of the scores of records that Buck Clayton made with the Count Basie Orchestra after his return to the United States from Shanghai have been preserved, and the vast majority of these are available on digitally remastered compact discs.

Sadly, such is not the case in China. While the multinational entertainment conglomerate EMI-Hong Kong (a corporate descendant of Pathé Asia) has undertaken a compact disc reissue series aimed at restoring the legacy of Chinese "modern song" for contemporary listeners, the majority of releases were made in the immediate postwar period from 1945 to 1949. Recordings dating from before the outbreak of Sino-Japanese hostilities in 1937 (the period considered in this study) have yet to be released. This is doubtless because the ravages of the Sino-Japanese War and the Communist revolution have left so few of the original, and notoriously brittle, shellac discs intact. Until recent years, moreover, the ostensibly deleterious and "decadent sounds" of prerevolutionary "yellow music" have been seen as unworthy of serious consideration, let alone preservation and academic study. As journalistic reports reveal, the extent of this neglect is nothing short of devastating. The Shanghai branch of China Records, the state holding company that annexed Pathé Asia in 1952, has acknowledged that a substantial percentage of the more than 80,000 recordings in its vaults have been damaged beyond repair by years of improper storage. These recordings represent some 75 percent of China's pre-1949 output, including more than seventy different types of regional opera and folk song, as well as an estimated 4,000 masters made during the heyday of modern song.[35] The two best remaining sources for recordings of this popular musical legacy are archival sound films of the era and private collections, both of which are necessarily fragmentary.

This practical quandary, coupled with my own lack of musicological expertise, partly governed my approach to the topic at hand. I am much less interested in providing musicological (or even textual) analysis of Chinese popular music in the Republican era as such than in exploring the discursive and social formations through which it was produced, understood, and deployed as an agent of cultural struggle and ideological contention throughout the interwar period. In this book, then, I listen closely to both the music still available and the voices (as recorded in sound films and described in newspapers, journals, and memoirs) of those who were involved in the music's production and (perhaps more important) its polemicization. Indeed, as I suggest in the context of discussions of both Li Jinhui's pathbreaking popular musical performances in the late 1920s and later leftist repudiations of his work in the wake of the Japanese military annexation of Manchuria in 1931, public discourse about popular music becomes a privileged means for Chinese cultural critics, political polemicists, filmmakers, and musicians to discuss many of the most pressing issues of the day: modernity and antifeudal struggle, shifting gender roles, class inequality, and the politics of national salvation.

This volume is concerned with textual analysis of these debates and with the historical processes in which the debates were embedded. It rejects a narrow focus on just one or two popular musical genres to the exclusion of various regional, folk, traditional, and imported musical forms. Instead, I situate the emergence of modern song within the hierarchized "music-historical field" of the Republican period.[36] That field, in turn, cannot be understood in isolation from the forces of imperialist encroachment and nationalist resistance of which it was a product. In chapter 1, I review both the colonial diffusion of Western music in China via missionaries and the military in the nineteenth century as well as the ways in which these new forms were appropriated and harnessed to China's nation-building project in the early twentieth century. These efforts—which often existed in an agonistic relationship to native and popular musical forms—culminated in the efforts of a group of May 4th era musical reformers to institute a modern musical regime in China and, in so doing, lay the groundwork for a new (and essentially Europeanized) national idiom with which China might represent itself on the international stage. Finally, with the deepening national crisis of the 1930s, music increasingly became both a means for the rearticulation of China's national culture in global (and thus implicitly colonial) terms, and a powerful medium for mass mobilization.

As such, music was often conceptualized by both May 4th intellectuals and leftist musicians as a technology of social control and political mobilization. This technological troping, as chapter 1 suggests, is linked to the late nineteenth-century deployments of military bands and Christian hymns as adjuncts of colonial conquest; it also is tied to May 4th discourses that attribute to Western music technological superiority (in terms of harmonic structures, orchestration, and the engineering of musical instruments) over its indigenous counterpart. Within the cultural Darwinist scheme of these musical reformers, in other words, Chinese music becomes an outmoded and underutilized technology of nation-building in desperate need of major overhaul. Technology, then, emerges as an ambiguous emblem of the postcolonial reconstruction of national culture.

Not incidentally, the burgeoning of this notion of music as a technology coincides with an unprecedented mass mediation of music in China (and indeed, throughout the world). By the 1930s, recorded music was for the first time able not only to reach, but also to create a mass audience in Chinese cities, particularly in the string of treaty ports opened to European and American colonizers in the nineteenth century as entrepôts for trade and military operations along China's eastern seaboard.

I have touched on the role of transnational record companies in the development of Chinese popular music. Throughout the book I also pay rigorous attention to the ways in which this new hybrid form was forged of the discursive, operational, and commercial interaction of new media technologies such as wireless broadcasting, sound cinema, and mass-circulation magazines in urban China. Indeed, part of my argument is that the Chinese jazz age and its particular "structure of feeling" (to borrow Raymond Williams's suggestive phrase) is a direct product of this convergence of various media in the Shanghai culture industry of the interwar period.

This interactivity becomes particularly salient in chapter 4, in which I examine the aesthetics of a new mode of leftist musical production that rose in the 1930s as a means of infiltrating the culture industry with new sonic images of anticolonial resistance, social revolution, and national unity. This aesthetic and political practice—which I label phonographic realism—was pioneered in part by a remarkable leftist musician named Nie Er, best-known as the composer of China's national anthem; it takes the form of an uneasy fusion of Hollywood film music, Tin Pan Alley pop, Chinese folk song, and Soviet mass music. Through this new genre, leftist musicians and their cinematic collaborators sought to simultaneously appropriate and displace Li Jinhui's "yellow music" and the mass-mediated sing-song girls who had become the focus of Shanghai's culture industry by the 1930s.

The historic significance of this emerging leftist current within the

Shanghai culture industry has long been acknowledged. Indeed, Nie Er has been hailed as a revolutionary culture hero since his untimely death in 1935, and the tradition of leftist mass music that he helped to spawn was later enshrined as a vital component of postrevolutionary cultural orthodoxy in the People's Republic. From 1949 until 1979, in fact, the triumph of phonographic realism in revolutionary China was unequivocal. "Yellow music" was banned outright on the Mainland in the early 1950s, and the producers and sing-song girls who had dominated the field (including Pathé-EMI Records and its stable of starlets) banished to Taiwan and the British Crown Colony of Hong Kong. Throughout the 1950s and 1960s, Hong Kong became a sort of Shanghai manqué—the epicenter of modern song and the Mandarin musical cinema.[37] It was only in the late 1970s, with the advent of China's gradual reinsertion into transnational financial and cultural circuits, that Li Jinhui's musical legacy—in the person of Taiwanese chanteuse and EMI recording artist Teresa Teng (Deng Lijun)—began to reclaim audiences in the cities and towns from which it had originally sprung.[38]

The close examination of the genealogy of this musical and political divide enables, even necessitates, a rethinking of some of the verities of modern Chinese cultural history. Specifically, I argue that it is in the blinding light of Nie Er's post-1949 canonization and the concomitant vilification of Li Jinhui that the term "phonographic realism" takes on its real heuristic value. In chapter 3, I show that rather than being diametrically opposed to the nationalist ideals of May 4th era Chinese intellectuals—as both those same intellectuals and scholars of modern China who have since replicated their dismissive take on the realm of the "popular" have always maintained—Li Jinhui's contributions to the development of a new urban media culture were, in fact, underwritten by the same nation-building project. The notion of phonographic realism, in turn, underscores the ways in which leftist cultural production was implicated in the same (ostensibly compromising) mechanisms as yellow music. Nie Er's music, despite its filiation with May 4th-derived discourses of realist representation and social engagement, was recorded by the same colonial conglomerate, reflected a similar aesthetic of colonial bricolage in its cobbling together of Soviet, Hollywood, and indigenous aesthetics, and catered by way of a similarly sophisticated understanding of the commercial interactivity of the mass media to the same urban audiences as the music of Li Jinhui. Nor was the influence unidirectional. As discussed in the concluding chapter 4, recording technology, because of the ways in which it was seen to transcend the snares of bourgeois subjectivism, became an important trope in the watershed debates on the politics of realist representation that took place in Chinese literary circles in the late 1920s and early 1930s. The notion of phonographic realism, then, points us toward new ways of writing modern Chinese cultural history, for it accounts more fully and more accurately for the complexity and mutual imbrication of elite literary culture and emergent media cultures than previous historiographic models.

The advent of phonographic realism in the 1930s, finally, supplies the book with a provisional end point to the historical trajectory that begins with the introduction to China of colonial phonography by companies such as Pathé-Frères in the waning years of the nineteenth century. The efforts of leftist musicians in the 1930s to create an anticolonial mass music from within the circuitry of Shanghai's newly emergent culture industry marks an epochal, if equivocal, cultural shift. In harnessing Li Jinhui's sing-song girls and promotional networks to their own political and aesthetic ends, they also were able to articulate an immanent critique of colonial phonography and its monopolization of the means of mechanical reproduction. They became knowing Nanooks, wilfully ingesting recording technology as a means of "canning" a new (and perhaps equally problematic) master's voice: that of a strategically imagined national collectivity.

FROM CHINESE "NOISE" TO "CHINESE" MUSIC

This book follows one final historical and thematic trajectory in attempting to puzzle out the status of national music (and, indeed, national culture) in postcoloniality. Earlier, I put forward the claim that this book is not really about *Chinese* music at all. This claim has to do with my understanding of the colonial processes through which the modern Chinese musical field was constituted in the late nineteenth and early twentieth centuries. Chinese music is usually described by nineteenth-century Euro-American listeners as unintelligible noise. In accounts written by figures as diverse as the late-Romantic composer Hector Berlioz and the Gramophone Company's pioneering mobile recording engineer F. W. Gaisberg, Chinese music is almost invariably likened to the sound of yowling cats, or it is simply denied the epistemological status of music at all. One aim of this study—one that touches on some central questions in cross-cultural comparative analysis and postcolonial discourse—is to trace the contours of the trajectory through which Chinese music entered into a relationship of commensurability with that of the West.[39] What changes did Chinese music undergo between the advent of sound recording in China around 1900 and the outbreak of war in 1937 in order to facilitate its translatability into Euro-American terms? How was Buck Clayton able to transcribe and play the music of Li Jinhui?

Part of the answer to this question is found in chapter 2, in which I chronicle China's incorporation into global gramophone culture. A second aspect of the question is addressed in chapter 1, where I discuss the program of musical modernization undertaken by Chinese musicians of the May 4th era. These reformers, in retooling Chinese musical forms, musical education, and perhaps most importantly musical notation along Western lines, not only profoundly altered the nature of modern Chinese music and musical life, but also irrevocably altered the ontological status of traditional and regional musics as well. When Chinese music—or at least the pentatonic melodies with which Chinese music is usually associated—entered the symbolic universe of Western harmony and Western notation, that is, it ceased to exist save as a signifier of "Chineseness" self-consciously deployed as a marker of national identity. Chinese music—whether in the guise of the new national music of the native elite, the yellow music of Li Jinhui, or the phonographic realism of leftist cultural workers of the 1930s—becomes modern Chinese music only when its "Chineseness" comes in quotes.

CHAPTER ONE

The Orchestration of Chinese Musical Life

As to the Chinaman's voice, nothing so strange had ever struck my ear. Imagine a series of nasal, guttural, moaning, hideous tones, which I may without too great exaggeration compare to the sounds a dog makes when after a long sleep it stretches its limbs and yawns . . . to give the name of *music* to what they produce by this sort of vocal and instrumental noise is, in my opinion, a strange abuse of the term. — Hector Berlioz[1]

A full-scale orchestra is another thing altogether. It comes at you with all the grand bombast of a May Fourth Movement, transforming each individual's voice into something quite different from what it was at the start. The whistling and scraping on every side becomes one's own voice, and you are shocked by the depth, volume, and resonance of the sound you are making. It's a little like the moment after you wake up in the morning: someone calls your name, and unsure whether the voice is someone else's or your own, you feel a vague kind of terror. — Eileen Chang [Zhang Ailing], "On Music"[2]

Imagine tuning the streamlined Bakelite knobs of a wireless radio to the ether above Shanghai circa 1937. As the vacuum tubes begin to amplify signals broadcast from that distant world, what sorts of sounds emerge? What would you hear as you move up and down the dial, sampling from the sonic world of Republican China? The crash of gongs, the plucked strings of a *sanxian*, the rhythmic recitation of drum song, the hypnotic drone of chanted sutras, the sharply nasal syllables of Peking opera? The warble of a Chinese sing-song girl? The lilt of Hawaiian steel guitar? The propulsive swing of big band jazz? Advertisements? Anthems? String quartets? Scholarly lectures? Official pronouncements? Symphony orchestras? In the cacophony of a multiply colonized metropolis of more than 3 million inhabitants, in which well above sixty radio stations operated by the mid-1930s, the answer would surely be all of the above, and much more.

How would we go about not simply listening but making sense of these diverse sounds? For a contemporary Chinese listener in Shanghai, this tour across the dial would almost certainly have evoked a complex cluster of associations, with each snippet of sound triggering a seemingly instinctive knowledge of both its particular historical, demographic, and ideological significance—Chinese or foreign? High class or low? Conservative, decadent, or progressive?—and the musical and extramusical codes governing its production and consumption. Our imaginary listener, in short, would have understood what kinds of pleasures each sort of music afforded, what those pleasures might mean, and what place each station occupied in relation to the musical field as a whole.[3] As later born listeners, we are not as immediately privy to such knowledge (or to the sounds themselves), and our grasp of the ways in which this sonic tapestry mattered to people living at that time will of necessity remain fragmentary and incomplete.

We can, however, begin to reconstruct the historical and ideological contours of the Republican musical field. In this chapter, I set out to do just that by way of two parallel analytical motions across the dial of the Republican sound world. The first motion is diachronic in nature. I begin by tracing the historical trajectory that lies between the mid-nineteenth-century world of Berlioz—in which a yawning gap still remains between Chinese and Western musical practice—and that of the early twentieth, when reformist intellectuals attempt an unprecedented orchestration of Chinese musical life in the wake of the May 4th movement—an orchestration dedicated to harnessing music to the imperatives of nation-building. What links these two end points is a complex and variegated series of encounters between indigenous, Euro-American, and Japanese musical practices that will forever alter the status, the function, and the meaning of Chinese music in the modern age.

My second motion across the dial involves a synchronic look at the Republican musical field in the wake of that historic transformation. This survey is conducted through a set of interrelated questions. What were the political and cultural stakes of musical modernization? Which sorts of music were valorized, and which sorts were devalued? How did the institutional arrangements for the production and dissemination of music and musical knowledge set in place by May 4th reformers function, and what purposes did they serve? How did contemporary musicians and critics discuss music, and what do their writings tell us about the world (musical and extramusical) in which they lived? I conclude the chapter by "listening in" on a 1933 radio broadcast, "The Power of Music" (Yinyue de shili), delivered by one of the primary architects of China's musical modernization and a central figure in the history recounted here, Xiao Youmei—that, in positing music as a means of constructing a powerful nation-state, throws these questions into sharp relief.

MUSIC AS TECHNOLOGY

In the course of our efforts to reconstruct the Republican musical field, many of our commonplace assumptions about the nature of music obscure more than they reveal. The first, and perhaps most dangerous of these assumptions is that music is a universal language. Strictly speaking, it is neither universal nor a language.[4] In this context, however, I am less interested in the philosophical or musicological truth-value of this claim than its ideological function, with the way in which it obscures the mutual imbrication of music, imperialism, and modernity not only in China, but in every place in which local musical practices were transformed by encounters with Euro-American militarists, merchants, and missionaries in modern times. In an era when Western music gradually supplanted indigenous forms on a global scale, as Richard Kraus notes, "the international-language metaphor proved comforting to both conquerors and subjects alike."[5] The forcible translation of indigenous musical idioms into universal terms—a process that began in China in the early nineteenth century with the advent of Western imperialist encroachment into China and that continues to the present day—is an inescapable component of the musical field to be explored in this chapter.

A second misconception is that of music as a pure form, which floats unfettered above the realm of political struggle. The provenance of this claim to autonomy, of course, is distinctly modern, arising from the dialectical tension between romantic individualism and the rise of bourgeois economic control over musical production in nineteenth-century Europe. In China, the historical and political context of music was fundamentally different. That context—here termed colonial modernity—rendered these sorts of claims beside the point. As early as the late nineteenth century, music was explicitly and inextricably tied to the imperatives and exigencies of China's nation-building project. Musicians, cultural critics, and educators promoted music as a means of national mobilization, resisting Western imperialism, and fighting Japanese aggression. Musical modernization, moreover, was conducted not under the auspices of the bourgeoisie, but of the nationalist state. Even the group of urban professional musicians who were responsible for constructing China's modern musical establishment—whose story is the focus of this chapter—were far less concerned with the artistic autonomy of music than its political and social instrumentality.

For this reason, the notion of music as technology becomes an extremely useful interpretive frame, one that sheds new light on the role of both imperialism and nationalism in the formation of the modern Chinese musical field. By technology, I indicate several different analytical trajectories. Perhaps the most straightforward sense is that of music as a technology of power, a practical tool with which different groups and classes at different times have sought to demarcate real and ideological territory, mobilize support, and silence dissenting voices. In the words of Jacques Attali, a French political economist and theorist of the intertwining of music and power, "the technology of listening in on, ordering, transmitting, and recording noise . . . is the ability to interpret and control history, to manipulate the culture of a people, to channel its violence and hopes."[6]

Attali's critique is largely restricted to the role of music in European societies, especially with the deployment of music as a form of social control in modern states. As such, his work might have benefited from closer attention to how music has been implicated in the power dynamics of transcultural contact. The history of imperialist encroachment into China (and many other places) is littered with examples of the deployment of music as a technology of power. Lord Macartney's notorious diplomatic mission to the Qianlong emperor in 1793 included an ensemble of five German musicians, presumably intended as a means of overawing their Chinese hosts. Soldiers of the imperial armies in China were inevitably accompanied by brass bands. The hymns and harmoniums of Protestant missionaries in China's interior were as much a part of the colonial enterprise as gunboats or printing presses.

These technologies for the "appropriation and control" of noise, in turn, were adopted by Chinese insurgents, warlords, educators, and nationalists.[7] In the 1850s, Hong Xiuquan used Protestant hymns (with new Chinese lyrics) as a means of rallying support for his millennial Taiping rebellion.[8] By the 1860s, choral singing and brass bands, introduced by foreign military advisers, had become a standard means of drill instruction and morale-building in the Qing army. These practices were later adopted by warlord armies, nationalist military units, and Communist guerrillas in the 1920s and 1930s. In the years preceding the 1911 overthrow of the Qing, finally, choral singing was incorporated into the curriculum of new-style schools as a means of propagating a variety of revolutionary and nationalist ideologies and enforcing collective discipline.[9]

The second way in which the notion of technology comes into play is bound up with the colonial diffusion of Western music. With the coming of the May 4th Movement of 1919, a new generation of musicians and educators, many of whom had either been exposed to Western music in China or studied it in Europe and Japan, began to build a modern musical infrastructure in China. For these musical reformers—who shared with their May 4th counterparts an iconoclastic faith in science and Social Darwinism—European music represented both an alternative musical culture and a set of manifestly superior technologies for the organization and use of sound. Musicians and critics like Xiao Youmei and Wang Guangqi believed that Chinese music was an outmoded product of "a thousand years of stagnation," a tradition "at a standstill," defined primarily in terms of what it ostensibly lacked: a tempered scale, functional harmony, counterpoint, orchestration, standardized notation, and the engineering prowess embodied by Western instruments like the piano.[10]

In this chapter, I argue that these musicians' and critics' work was technocratic in nature. On the one hand, they labored to disseminate Western musical techniques, institutionalize music education, and set standards for musical practice and performance. On the other, they strove to study, catalog, and ultimately rationalize (along scientific lines suggested by the West) Chinese traditions. For example, efforts were made to re-engineer Chinese instruments to specifications demanded by the formal logic of Western harmony and notation.

To what end were these technocratic reforms carried out? *Techne* in service of what sort of *kratos*? Perhaps the single most important goal was to place musical activity in service to the construction of a modern nation-state. In reviving Chinese musical culture, reformers like Xiao Youmei (the president of the Shanghai National Conservatory of Music) believed they also would revitalize its citizenry. "Good music" was to be used as a means of mobilizing nationalist sentiment; "bad music" was to be silenced for the good of the nation. Indeed, in Xiao's 1933 broadcast, "The Power of Music," music becomes a technology through which specialists work to channel the affective life of the masses in directions beneficial to the nationalist cause. Music, in effect, is posited as a powerful form of micropolitics, a disciplinary regime with which the state might minister to the emotional lives of its subjects. This "sonic regime," in turn, would be implemented and presided over by elite technocrats like Xiao himself, with the financial support of the Nationalist (KMT) government.

At the same time, Xiao and his contemporaries argued, the institution of such a modern sonic regime would allow for the creation of a distinctly Chinese musical idiom, a national school that would represent (and even enact) China's emergence as a modern nation on the international stage. This effort, of course, was influenced by the emergence of avowedly nationalist idioms in Russia, Eastern Europe, France, and other nations and regions in the late nineteenth and early twentieth centuries and by a conviction that "unless a school has a national character, it cannot be of international value."[11] Although the precise form of China's contribution to world music remained a matter of considerable debate, it was generally agreed that China's representative on the world musical stage must of necessity feature the insertion of carefully selected elements of indigenous musical culture into European-derived harmonic structures. Unsurprisingly, however, this project was beset by a familiar postcolonial predicament: How do you attain the universal while at the same time preserving what is distinct about local culture?

There is another sense in which these efforts were tangled in the snares of postcoloniality. It is no secret that musical taste and musical attainments often serve as markers of class distinction and as a form of symbolic capital. This particular form of cultural capital was caught up in colonial economies of status and power in the treaty ports of Republican China. May 4th era musicians lived in a social world in which these economies ensured that Western European art music was both hegemonic and "highclass." Inasmuch as the cultural capital and institutional power of this "native elite" derived from its members' specialized training in Western musical techniques, their efforts to establish a modern sonic regime were characterized by an agonistic relationship to both "native" and popular cultural forms.[12]

This antipathy was further justified by way of the elite's nationalist politics. While certain elements of rural folk music could be rehabilitated and used as essentialized markers of local difference in a new national school, the modern songs of the urban petit bourgeoisie were thought to be tainted by both their commercial vulgarity and their cultural hybridity. And although certain forms of mass music (anthems, military marches, and the like) could be harnessed to the task of national mobilization at political rallies and on parade grounds, the decadent sounds that filled the record stores, the airwaves, and the dance halls were seen as incitements to political indiscipline. As is argued in this chapter and throughout the book, this conflict—between a polyvocal culture of consumption and a univocal sonic regime, between music as a medium of social control and a commodified popular culture expedited by new media for the dissemination of music (the gramophone, the wireless, and the cinema)—plays a profound role in shaping the contours of the musical field in the Republican era.

DIVERGENT TRADITIONS

By 1937, the sort of "vocal and instrumental noise" that the French Romantic composer Hector Berlioz derides in the epigraph to this chapter had been drowned out by the orchestral salvos of Western music. This inundation was already well under way in 1852, the year in which Berlioz described his impressions of a concert of Chinese music he had attended one night in London. But as his refusal to even dignify the foreign sounds he had heard that evening as *music* indicates, a seemingly insurmountable divide still separated European and Chinese musical practices.[13]

That divide can be accounted for, in part, in musicological terms. Chinese melody is predominantly characterized by pentatonicism, as opposed to the chromaticism of the Western tradition in which Berlioz was schooled. The use of microtones, anathema in European orchestral music before the twentieth-century avant-garde, is not uncommon in traditional Chinese music. China's traditional vocal techniques, moreover, tend toward the high-pitched and nasal, as opposed to the open-throated vocal production characteristic of the West. Finally, Chinese music—particularly the refined traditions associated with literati culture and its preferred musical instrument, the *qin*—evinces a remarkable sensitivity to timbre and tone color that is lacking in the West. Chinese music, in turn, lacks the

complex harmonic language and the polyphony that are defining charac-
teristics of European art music.

Just as striking, perhaps, were the extramusical dimensions of this divide. Grand generalizations about Chinese musical practice and performance, of course, are dangerously prone to inaccuracy. This musical culture was ancient, variegated, and dynamic, and, contrary to the assertions
of May 4th era reformers, it continued to develop and thrive up to and
after the moment of Western incursion. Even so, a few (necessarily reductive) comments are in order, if only to help illuminate the changes that
did take place as a result of Western encroachment and the program of
musical modernization implemented in the 1920s and 1930s.

In Europe, notation has played a decisive role in musical practice since
the fourteenth century. In China, notation never attained the same sort
of hold on musical life, despite the existence of several different forms of
written music.[14] Part of the reason for this characteristic lies in the relative
importance of oral transmission (as opposed to written composition) in
traditional Chinese musical pedagogy. Another factor, as Kraus suggests,
was the absence of a bourgeois discourse of artistic originality in premodern China.[15] In Europe, the notion of composition as intellectual property
both necessitated and spurred on the development of standardized notation. Whatever the reasons, this contrast in musical practice had profound
ramifications both in terms of the technical development of music in each
respective culture, and the colonial encounter of these cultures in the nineteenth and twentieth centuries.

Max Weber pointed out that standardized notation allowed for the development of exactly those "rationalized" aspects of Western music that
impressed Chinese musicians as representing its superiority over "backward" indigenous forms: polyphony, functional harmony, and sophisticated orchestration.[16] At the same time, the "hegemony of notation"—and
its inability to represent or even account for the microtones, subtleties of
accent, phrasing, and tone colors that characterize Chinese and other non-
Western musics, as well as popular genres like jazz—"erected a block in
the Western ear against the inner complexities of non-Western musics."[17]
And it is this block, in part, that contributed to the sort of "discriminatory
deafness" that we see in Berlioz's reaction to Chinese music—a deafness
that is replicated when May 4th musicians trained in the European idiom
turn their attention to urban folk music and the Sinified jazz in the 1920s
and 1930s.[18]

A second divergence relates to the social standing of musicians. According to traditional schema, music in China was divided into two basic
types: refined (*yayue*) and common (*suyue*). *Yayue* was cultivated by the
imperial court for use in rituals of state power. It was also the province
of literate scholar-officials, for whom performance was an amateur, if
extremely cultivated, pursuit. The social standing of professional performers of *suyue*—a category that might include itinerant musicians, courtesans, and operatic actors—was extremely low. This outcast status was
attributable to their associations with the seamy, commercial pleasures of
the urban demimonde. With the reformation of Chinese musical life along
Western lines in the first half of the twentieth century, these divides play
out in interesting ways. On the one hand, the creation of an entirely new
occupational category—the professional musician—becomes an important aspect of the May 4th era project of musical modernization.[19] On the
other, the lingering taint of the popular musician's (particularly the female
vocalist's) traditional association with unorthodox pleasures remains, reinforced by a new emphasis on her lack of formal (that is, Western) musical
training.

A third division has to do with the social contexts in which music is
performed. The "central institution of bourgeois musical life" in Europe
was the concert. This was not always the case. The development of concert
halls and symphony orchestras reflected profound changes in both the real
and the symbolic economy of music in the eighteenth and nineteenth centuries. At the same time that music was commodified, it also was reified—
shorn from the diverse social contexts in which it had previously flourished (rural fairs, city streets, the salons of nobility) and listened to silently
as art. "The artist," as Jacques Attali notes, "was born at the same time as
his work went on sale."[20] This movement into the concert hall was paralleled by the enshrinement of music as an object of scientific study in the
conservatory, and the development of musical curricula in the schools.

The situation in China was different. Until the nineteenth century, music
was integrated into various aspects of social life. It was a component of
solemn Confucian ritual at the imperial court, a medium of intellectual
and emotional exchange between literati, an element of religious ritual,
an integral aspect of operatic performance, and a diversion among many
other diversions at temple fairs and rural market festivals. In urban contexts, music had long been commodified, but its consumption in the tav-
erns and brothels of the pleasure quarters was not conducted with the

sort of hushed reverence characteristic of the European concert hall.[21] As will be discussed in more detail, performative contexts—and the different modes of listening they necessitate—are not without ideological significance. Musical modernization (and eventually the diffusion of mass media like the gramophone and the wireless) exercised a profound effect on the social context of musical performance and consumption. These changes, in turn, played an important role in shaping the musical field in Republican China.

MUSIC AND IMPERIALISM

European music first arrived on Chinese shores with the Jesuit missionaries to the imperial courts of the late Ming and Qing dynasties. Matteo Ricci presented a harpsichord to the imperial court in 1601, trained at least four eunuchs in its use, and composed eight Chinese songs in hopes of proselytizing the court.[22] During the reign of the Qing's Kangxi emperor (1669–1722), the Jesuits Grimaldi and Tome Pereira entertained the court with both harpsichord and organ music. Pereira and a third member of the order, Theodorico Pedrini, also contributed a section on European notation and harmony to an imperially sanctioned compendium of music theory, the *True Meaning of Pitch Temperament* (*Lülü zhengyi*).[23] The Portuguese missionary Y. P. Perci next installed an organ inside a Jesuit cathedral built in Beijing in 1670.[24] European music also reached the Qing court by way of diplomatic missions; Lord Macartney's famous retinue of ninety-five diplomats, scientists, soldiers, and Chinese language teachers, which visited Beijing in 1792 in hopes of establishing trade relations, included five German musicians who performed for the Qianlong emperor.

It was not until the outbreak of the Opium Wars in 1839, however, that European music began to spread its influence among the populace. The diffusion of European music beyond the confines of the imperial court in Beijing took place by way of three conduits: Protestant missionaries, soldiers, and new-style schools.[25] This pattern was by no means unique to China. It played itself out on a global scale, irrespective of different degrees of territorial colonization.[26] The introduction of Western music in Japan (which was not territorially colonized) and China (which was partially colonized by several of the colonial powers) was strikingly similar. In both cases, modern schools (founded on Western educational principles and explicitly intended as a means of self-strengthening in the face of the imperialist threat) helped to diffuse this music still further.[27]

The first book of Protestant hymns to be rendered into Chinese was published by the noted American Methodist missionary and translator Robert Morrison in 1818.[28] This early effort was followed by a flood of hymnals, published both in simple classical Chinese and in various local dialects, with and without musical notation, throughout the nineteenth century.[29] The most successful and widely circulated of these efforts at proselytization through music was the *Blodgot and Goodrich Hymnal* (*Songzhu shige*), first printed in Beijing in 1872. The influence of these song-texts was felt far beyond the major cities (Beijing, Hankou, Ji'nan, Nanjing, Suzhou) and coastal ports (Tianjin, Qingdao, Shanghai, Ningbo, Fuzhou, Xiamen, and Guangzhou) where missionaries and traders concentrated their efforts. One remarkable example of this influence was the use of modified Protestant hymns to sway peasant insurgents to the cause of the Taiping rebellion in the 1850s. The anthem of the Taiping's heavenly kingdom, in fact, was an adaptation of the "Old Hundred," a hymn that the movement's chief ideologue, Hong Xiuquan, had learned as a student of a Baptist missionary preacher from Missouri who was stationed in Guangzhou, I. J. Roberts (1802–71).[30] More recent research suggests that similar song-texts made inroads even among various minority groups in remote regions of southwest China.[31] Nor should this be surprising, considering that by 1877, sixty-three different sorts of hymnals had been distributed throughout the country, some in editions as large as 20,000 copies.[32]

Hymns, of course, accompanied a variety of religious rituals performed by Protestant congregations and mission schools. They were sung collectively by the congregation or the student body, often accompanied by piano or harmonium. Their diffusion throughout China, in addition to introducing new musical instruments and unfamiliar harmonic and melodic forms, also ushered in the very notion of collective singing. This development was pivotal. As Isabel Wong points out, Taiping-era hymns represent the most important single precedent for "the use of mass songs as a modern political and didactic tool, whether or not conscious imitation can be documented."[33] Choral singing came to play a central role in nationalist indoctrination in modern schools in the late Qing and early Republican era. As will be discussed in chapter 4, mass singing became a preferred means through which leftist musicians enacted collective rituals of resistance to imperialist domination and Japanese aggression throughout the 1930s and 1940s.

European and American imperialists in China (and elsewhere) arrived with a hymnal in one hand and a gun in the other. The armies that cleared the way for British narcotics merchants such as William Jardine to expand their illicit business in China during the Opium Wars of 1839 and 1842 marched to the music of brass bands. The same was true of the American, British, and French forces that occupied Guangzhou and Tianjin in 1858 during the Arrow War and Beijing in 1860. When the Qing moved to establish a modern army in the 1860s, German military advisers introduced choral singing as an instructional tool. In the wake of the Sino-Japanese clashes of 1894 and 1895, the Qing military (under the leadership of Yuan Shikai) organized its own brass band. By 1911, when the Qing fell, "the warlord armies that salvaged pieces of its authority all had brass bands, just as their officers copied the gaudy uniforms of the imperialist armies."[34]

As early as the 1880s, finally, the foreign communities in Beijing and Shanghai maintained their own brass bands, which were well-known to local inhabitants.[35] With the growth of the expatriate community in the first decade of the twentieth century, the Shanghai Public Band expanded to become the first (and reputedly the best) symphony orchestra in East Asia. Interestingly, local brass bands sprang up around the same time and were incorporated into funeral and marriage processions in the treaty ports and some rural areas; in many overseas Chinese communities, this tradition has been preserved to the present day.[36]

SCHOOL SONGS

A third path for the diffusion of Western music in China was cleared not by foreign imperialists, but by Chinese nationalists. Indeed, the history of choral "school songs" (*xuetang yuege*) both underscores the intimate relationship between music and nationalism in modern China and serves to remind us of the complexity of the history of imperialism in East Asia. Colonial modernity was not simply a matter of China and the West; the introduction of Euro-American culture into China was often mediated by way of Japan, which had set out on its own program of colonial expansion as early as the 1890s following the success of the Meiji reforms.[37]

The reform movement that roiled the Qing court in the years preceding the turn of the century was a direct response to the aftermath of the Sino-Japanese War of 1894–95, when the Qing were forced to surrender by treaty Taiwan and portions of Manchuria to Japan. In the wake of this Treaty of Shimonoseki, a number of Chinese reformers sought to reformulate Chinese education along lines suggested by Meiji Japan. Music was an important part of this effort, and its introduction into the public school curriculum was championed in contemporary newspapers and journals by no less a figure than Liang Qichao.[38]

In 1904, Liang and a group of like-minded intellectuals, who were studying Japanese models of modernization firsthand in Tokyo, formed a Music Research Society (Yinyue jiangxi hui).[39] The Meiji government had introduced choral singing and music education into the public schools as early as 1879 with the aid of an American educator, Luther Whiting Mason, and a Japanese musician, Izawa Shūji. This institutionalization of music education, in turn, triggered the development for classroom use of an intensely nationalist genre of school songs called *shōka* (literally, "choral songs"). These songs consisted of Japanese texts set to largely Euro-American melodies. Their musical settings reflected the influence of missionary hymns and military bands, the means by which most Japanese had been introduced to Western music. The first collections of *shōka* were published by the Japanese ministry of education, but through the efforts of a number of popular composers, the genre went on to gain wide currency throughout Japan. Ironically, songs urging Japan onto victory in its imperialist campaigns against China in 1894–95 became an integral part of the *shōka* repertoire.[40]

Liang and contemporaries like Shen Xingong set out to duplicate these efforts. Indeed, their work bears the direct and unmistakable imprint of Japanese models. Shen's first collections of Chinese school songs (which have subsequently come to be known as *xuetang yuege*) were titled *shōka* songbooks (*changge ji*). Many of the songs, moreover, simply replaced the original Japanese lyrics with Chinese ones, while retaining their original Euro-American melodies.

With the establishment of the Republic in 1911, school songs found a new champion in the prominent reformist educator Cai Yuanpei. Trained in Germany, fond of Western classical music, and hostile to indigenous operatic forms, Cai encouraged the integration of these school songs into the newly nationalized school curricula.[41] With the songs themselves came instruction in a number of Western instruments (piano, harmonium, organ, and violin), as well as textbooks introducing students to Western notation and music theory. The advent of school songs marked the first time in which systematic education in Western music had been undertaken in Chinese schools; indeed, singing classes were mandatory for every student enrolled in primary school throughout the country. These songs and classes also served to familiarize Chinese with a range of heretofore unknown aspects of Western musical practice: public concerts and composition using Western notation.

School songs served several different ideological ends. Intellectuals like Liang Qichao and Cai Yuanpei saw music as a means of "aesthetic education" (*meiyu*), a method by which the intellectual and moral "quality of the citizenry" could be elevated to advance the nationalist cause.[42] School songs also served to enforce collective discipline. Sally Borthwick, a historian of educational reform in China, describes the use of these songs in "rituals of unity" enacted within the school community.[43] Her argument is illustrated by a fascinating print from a 1907 issue of the *Xingqi huabao* (Revival pictorial) portraying a primary school choir. The students are separated into two columns. Three students stand at the front of the stage, each playing a military snare drum, while one student stands to the rear and provides harmonic support for the choir with a harmonium. The mixture of military and missionary influences could hardly be clearer.

Perhaps the most significant function of these songs, however, was the dissemination of progressive and nationalist ideologies. In keeping with their didactic purpose, the songs were short and rudimentary. Their melodic content was mostly diatonic, although efforts were made to write pentatonic melodies as well. Lyrics were rendered in the simplified classical idiom typical of the journalistic writing of the day. Songs extolled scientific method, hygiene, and discipline. Other songs called for the liberation of women (one song was authored by the famed feminist revolutionary Qiu Jin) and an immediate end to the practice of foot-binding. A substantial number of these compositions, finally, were patriotic anthems that lamented the humiliations visited on the nation by Western imperialism and Japanese aggression and urged Chinese citizens to mobilize and resist.

In the years after 1911, these sorts of tunes spread well beyond the confines of new-style schools. Indeed, because of the explosive growth of the same treaty port publishing industry that had allowed Liang Qichao's educational agenda to reach its intended audience by means of newspapers and pictorial magazines in the first place, they quickly became a mass medium.[44] The composer Shen Xingong alone was responsible for at least three series of mass-produced songbooks: the *School Songbook* (*Xuexiao changge ji*, 1907, 3 vols.), the *New Expanded School Songbook* (*Zhongbian xuexiao changge ji*, 1911–, 6 vols.), and the *Republican Songbook* (*Minguo changge ji*, 1911–, 4 vols.).[45] In the years preceding the May 4th Movement, school songs also came to be sung at political rallies and other civic gatherings, serving as a powerful means for the expression of nationalist aspirations.[46]

MUSIC AND THE MAY 4TH MOVEMENT

Against this historical backdrop, intellectuals attempted an unprecedented orchestration of Chinese musical life in the wake of the May 4th Movement of 1919. My invocation of this movement is important in several ways. The intensive modernization of Chinese music roughly coincided with the burst of political, intellectual, and social ferment for which the movement is named. Many of the luminaries of May 4th era literature and culture, moreover, were active in promoting new music. Among others, they included Cai Yuanpei, Zhao Yuanren, and Feng Zikai. More important, musicians like Xiao Youmei and Wang Guangqi shared with their literary compatriots a commitment to modern science, enlightenment ideals, and, perhaps most centrally, the nation-building enterprise. These goals were undergirded by an iconoclastic dismissal of traditional Chinese culture. These musicians also shared an almost heroic sense of themselves as authors of an epochal cultural transformation. Just as Lu Xun had resolved to awaken the souls of his countrymen with his pen, May 4th musicians would elevate the spirits of the masses with a conductor's baton.

This project, of course, was not achieved overnight. Nor did its intellectual and political character remain static and unchanging. From 1919 to 1927, musicians focused on establishing new channels for music education, research, and publishing. Much of this activity was centered around Beijing University and was either academic or amateur in nature. As in the literary world, the period was characterized by intellectual ferment and vigorous debate. In 1927 the center of gravity shifted south to Shanghai for reasons of political and economic exigency. At the same time, the task of modernizing Chinese music increasingly came under the auspices of the Nationalist government. The next five years saw an unprecedented expansion of music education, publishing, performance, and other kinds of activity.

The Japanese annexation of Manchuria and subsequent attack on Shanghai in early 1932 mark an important turning point in modern Chinese cultural history. The national crisis triggered by Japanese military aggression precipitated a heightened politicization of musical (as well as literary) endeavor. Music professionals splintered into factions: the left, the humanist center, and those who had thrown in their lot with the increasingly reactionary policies of the KMT. This last group, which included Cai Yuanpei and Xiao Youmei, had come to represent the musical establishment in China.

MUSICAL MODERNIZATION, 1919–1927

How did May 4th era reformers go about disciplining Chinese musical life? The first systematic attempts at creating a modern musical infrastructure in China began in 1916 at the behest of Cai Yuanpei. Cai, who had recently been installed as the president of Beijing University, organized a series of "music reform groups" dedicated to introducing Western music to Chinese students and reformulating traditional Chinese music along "scientific" lines. These groups consolidated in 1919 to form the Beijing University Music Research Group (Beijing daxue yinyue yanjiu hui), which consisted of some 200 musicians, including ten foreign instructors. In 1921 the group became the first modern music department in China and was renamed the Institute for the Promotion and Practice of Music at Beijing University (Beijing daxue yinyue chuanxi suo). Departmental activities included instruction in Western and Chinese musical instruments and music theory, performances of Western music, academic research, and the publication of a professional journal, the *Music Magazine* (*Yinyue zazhi*). In addition, the department organized training sessions for primary and secondary school music teachers. Inspired by the example of Beijing University, five colleges opened their own music departments from 1920 to 1925, and dozens of urban high schools offered an expanded range of classes on music and musical activities.[47]

Publishing was a significant aspect of this modernization project. In addition to Beijing University's *Music Magazine* (founded in March 1920), five other music-related periodicals were established before 1927. These periodicals covered a wide variety of topics: the role of music in educational reform (*Aesthetic Education*), information for music education professionals (*The Music Teacher's Companion*), profiles of Western composers and proposals for musical reform (*Musician's World*), theory and new composition (*Music Quarterly*), and news and views of general interest to amateur musicians and listeners (*Music Wave*).[48] In addition, a flood of books on music from 1920 to 1927 included both textbooks and more theoretical volumes.

Most of this material was in the mainstream of May 4th intellectual currents. Leafing through the pages of the *Music Magazine,* we see humanistic and philosophical treatises on music, a translated essay on romantic theories of musical genius, and reflections on the relationship between music and gender. Many of the articles reflect an interest in Western musical technique and technology. They include introductions to key elements of Western musical culture (harmony, instrumentation, and the like), and translated treatises on acoustics and the "material foundations of music."[49] Comparisons of Chinese and Western musical culture (in which China always seems to emerge the worse for wear) abound.[50] Nationalism is also a dominant concern. There are reflections on Chinese "national character" (*guomin xing*) as expressed through music and a series of articles suggesting likely candidates for China's national anthem.[51] If any single theme runs through the magazine, it is the renaissance of China's national music. While there are debates about the extent to which Chinese music should Westernize, the consensus favors the jettisoning of traditional music in favor of modern Western models. In cases where traditional music (usually referred to as "national music," or *guoyue*) is to be revived, its reform must be undertaken on the basis of Western musical knowledge.[52]

The periodical literature was complemented by a raft of book-length publications by scholars like Xiao Youmei, Wang Guangqi, and Feng Zikai. Xiao, who had served as Sun Yat-sen's personal secretary after the Revolution of 1911 and gone on to study music at the Leipzig Conservatory of Music in Germany, promoted the wholesale adoption of Western music through a host of reference works, textbooks, and academic treatises published from 1920 to 1937. His work was supplemented by that of Wang

Guangqi, an ardent patriot, Beijing University law student, and disciple of progressive intellectuals such as Cai Yuanpei, Li Dazhao, and Chen Duxiu. In 1920, he went to Germany to study politics, and in 1923 he turned to the study of music. During his subsequent years at Berlin University, Wang wrote a series of treatises calculated to introduce Western musical culture to Chinese readers in a systematic way.

Wang was startlingly prolific. From 1923 through 1934 he produced no fewer than seventeen books, many of which reveal the intellectual and political preoccupations of his era. His influential *Musical Life of the Germans* (*Deguoren zhi yinyue shenghuo*, 1923) suggested that German wealth and power were attributable in part to the richness of its musical culture, and he called on the Nationalist Party to promote a musical "renaissance" in China. The very title of his *Theory of the Evolution of European Music* (*Ouzhou yinyue jinhua lun*, 1924) reflects the saturation of much May 4th-era writing with the discourse of Social Darwinism. Predictably, it laments the evolutionary backwardness of Chinese music and recommends a healthy infusion of Western elements to effect the creation of a revitalized national music. Yet another study, *Research on Musical Systems East and West* (*Dongxi yuezhi zhi yanjiu*, 1926), sets up a comparison between a formerly great but now stagnant China and a modern, vital Europe so characteristic of the intellectual discourse of the era, and identifies music as a key to the birth of a new "Young China" (Shaonian Zhongguo).

This music publishing boom was rounded out by Feng Zikai, a pioneering cartoonist and arts educator. Feng wrote five books on music for popular audiences, including *Beginner's Guide to Music* (*Yinyue rumen*, 1926) and *Music and Life* (*Yinyue yu shenghuo*, 1929). According to Wang Yuhe, Feng's writing on music (directly based on a series of middlebrow Japanese books) enjoyed considerable success and was "instrumental in the popularization of modern musical knowledge."[53]

CHINESE MUSIC IN THE MAY 4TH ERA

What was the fate of indigenous music amid this rush toward Westernization and modernization? Traditional and folk music were not entirely supplanted by Western forms. But the context in which they were performed was fundamentally altered by the May 4th movement. Loyal to the past, conservative literati fought to preserve serious instrumental music and the performance traditions of the sophisticated operatic form known as *kunqu*.[54] Their work, loosely associated with the National Essence movement in literature, took place outside the university at the margins of the May 4th mainstream of music professionals. Amateur groups of this nature included the Heavenly Cadence Society (Tianyun she), the Chinese Music Research Society (Guoyue yanjiu she), and the Great Unity Society (Datong she).

Even the activities of these groups (all of which were founded in 1919 and 1920), however, reflected the hegemony of Western musical theory and the assumption that Chinese music was somehow backward and in need of reform. Indeed, the slogan under which such organizations labored—"revive national music" (*fuxing guoyue*)—revealed the extent to which the discourse of scientific progress (and Chinese stagnation) had carried the day.[55] They arranged Western-style performances of Chinese music, set traditional music to Western notation, and made efforts to improve the design and manufacture of Chinese musical instruments. This last venture is particularly interesting, for it reveals the extent to which Western music had impressed itself on Chinese listeners as constituting a superior technology. The deficiencies of Chinese instruments as perceived by May 4th era musicians are neatly summarized by a prominent Western-trained musician of the 1930s, Ying Shangneng.

> In days gone by, China had her own great music. But judging from what we find of it nowadays, nothing remains to remind us of its past glory. This sorry state of affairs is to a large extent to be accounted for by her musical instruments. Most of them are still quite crude and simple: they do not admit of the development of highly finished techniques. Then again, no standard pitch can be found among them. No two flutes made by the same hand can be made to play in unison harmoniously. The scale steps are also found to vary. Among different instruments, the variations mentioned are still further marked. Moreover the tone qualities of the musical instruments are none too pleasing. The 7-chord *ch'in* has hardly any sound at all. No wonder, therefore, in the annals of Chinese music, there is no Beethoven or Schubert.[56]

These problems prompted a number of attempts at revised musical engineering. In reformulating the *sheng* (an instrument constructed of bamboo pipes), for instance, researchers from the Great Unity Society used thirty-two pipes instead of the original thirteen. This modification allowed the *sheng* player to create harmonic effects by changing keys.[57] In other words, part of the work of these societies consisted in making indigenous traditions conform to Western harmony and tonality.

At the very moment that Chinese music became an object of study, classification, and rationalization along Western lines, it also came to signify Chineseness. The new national music, as conceived by May 4th era music theorists, would utilize indigenous musical elements (such as pentatonic melodies) as markers of ethnicity within a predominantly Western harmonic structure. In a manner suggested by European composers like Bartók and Sibelius, this "ethnic" material would ideally be culled from folk sources. This project dovetailed with that of the Folksong movement at Beijing University. In 1918 a group of intellectuals led by Liu Fu began to collect folk songs in an effort to rediscover the unvarnished voice of the Chinese people. These songs, after having undergone a process of collation, study, and revision, were thought to be the ideal basis for a new national vernacular language.[58]

This predominantly literary project was mirrored in the musical sphere by the work of Liu Fu's brother, the musician Liu Tianhua, who joined the faculty of Beijing University's music department in 1922. In undertaking the collection of instrumental folk music, Liu expanded the scope of the Folksong campaign initiated by his brother. This music, in turn, was set in Western notation, and incorporated into Liu's own compositions, which self-consciously fused Western musical structure with folk-derived melodies. Liu also experimented with indigenous Chinese instruments—for instance, by applying violinistic techniques (tremolo and vibrato) to the *erhu* (a bowed instrument with two strings).[59] In 1927 he founded the Society for the Reform and Advancement of Traditional Music (Guoyue gaijin she) to encourage similar work. Liu's sympathy for traditional forms was shared by another luminary of the New Culture movement, Zhao Yuanren. Zhao, a gifted linguist and sometime composer of art songs, tried to create a uniquely Chinese musical idiom, one based on Sinified harmonies, pentatonic melody, and a sensitivity to the distinctive tonal character of Chinese song-texts.[60]

Liu and Zhao's approach, however, remained on the periphery of musical discourse. Indeed, musicians in the mainstream harbored a certain hostility to folk forms, especially as they continued to be practiced by modern men and women. Xiao Youmei, asked to compare the music of the modern West with traditional Chinese forms, gave voice to this attitude in a 1937 interview.

Our so-called traditional music can be divided into two types: (1) *Yayue,* or our ancient ritual music and; (2) *Suyue* (including *Kun*-style opera and the instrumental music of Beijing opera, and so on). Modern Western music is about fifteen hundred years ahead of the former, and seven or eight hundred years ahead of latter. *Yayue* is merely a historical artifact, while *suyue* exerts a powerful negative influence over the masses of common people even now.[61]

The historical subtext of Xiao's comment is the fact that these "evolutionary throwbacks," rather than falling victim to modern "cultural selection," had continued to exist alongside the "sonic regime" of which Xiao was a principal architect. As Wang Yuhe details in his authoritative history of modern Chinese music, traditional and folk music underwent a series of radical changes in the Republican era.[62] These changes were, in a sense, after-effects of imperialist encroachment. The explosive growth of China's urban economy (and particularly that of treaty ports like Shanghai) resulted in mass migrations of peasants to the cities of China's eastern seaboard. With these movements came the gradual urbanization of a number of traditional forms, most notably folk songs, various regional operas (including *pingju, yueju,* and *shenqu*), as well as traditional balladry and narrative songs (such as drum songs and Suzhou *tanci*).

Urbanization entailed a process of commodification and professionalization. Folk forms began to be performed in urban theaters, and folk musicians banded together in professional organizations. With the growth of mass media like gramophone records and wireless broadcasting, moreover, urbanites were able to listen to recordings of *tanci, pingju,* and *shenqu* and a range of folk music (alongside modern songs and various sorts of Western music). Participation in this urban context inevitably resulted in a certain degree of cross-pollination of musical forms. *Tanci* songs (popularly known as *kaipian*) were wedded with radio advertising pitches and nationalist slogans.[63] Cantonese folk musicians began to incorporate guitars, banjos, and saxophones into their regional music.[64] Popular musicians set pentatonic melodies drawn from urban folk traditions atop jazzy harmonies. Despite (or perhaps because of) the popularity of this newly urbanized music, "serious" musicians were careful to draw a line between rural (and thus "pure") folk traditions worthy of study and reform and these "degraded" and "vulgar" hybrid forms.

THE MUSICAL ESTABLISHMENT, 1927–1932

From 1927 until 1932 the scope of musical modernization continued to expand. The period witnessed the opening of a host of new schools and music departments as well as the establishment of new professional groups and amateur music societies. It spawned a new crop of magazines and books devoted to disseminating modern musical knowledge. Perhaps most significantly, in the wake of the success of the KMT's Northern Expedition and consolidation of political control, the musical activities of May 4th era reformers began to receive government support and sanction.

However, the period began with a serious setback. In 1927 the Institute for the Promotion and Practice of Music at Beijing University was closed because of a lack of financial support from the warlord government of Zhang Zuolin. At roughly the same time (November 1927), the Shanghai National Conservatory of Music (Guoli yinyue yuan) was opened at the behest of Cai Yuanpei (who had become a KMT official in Nanjing) with generous government funding.[65] Xiao Youmei was installed as the director of the new school, and its curriculum and teaching methods were largely modeled on those of his alma mater, the Leipzig Conservatory of Music. The Shanghai faculty included many of the leading Western and Japanese-trained musicians and composers of the day (including Xiao himself, Huang Zi, and Qingzhu) as well as faculty members drawn from Shanghai's European community and visiting professors from as far afield as Russia and France.[66] The conservatory overwhelmingly emphasized Western music; of 110 advanced students in 1937, just two chose to study traditional Chinese instrumental music![67] This figure is even more significant when we realize that the Shanghai Conservatory was far and away the most prestigious and influential institution for music education in Republican China. As such, its graduates "came to dominate the musical life of the intelligentsia of the treaty ports and to be regarded as authorities for acceptable musical standards and behavior" throughout the country.[68]

In addition to classes, the conservatory sponsored twenty-seven books on music published by the Commerical Press as well as two separate periodicals: an academic journal, *Sounds: The Bulletin of the National Conservatory of Music,* and a more popular *Music Magazine,* published in collaboration with the Liangyou (Young Companion) publishing company. The school also sponsored a number of concerts, recitals, and other musical activities throughout Shanghai. These diverse events were patronized by the class from which the school also drew many of its students: Shanghai's petit bourgeoisie. For this elite group, Western musical culture and its accoutrements (for instance, pianos in the domestic parlor) were markers of modernity and class privilege.[69] Chinese music, in turn, was seen as low-class and vulgar.

The celebrated Shanghai author Eileen Chang in her 1942 essay "On Music" provides an illuminating window into the affective dimensions of this particular set of power relations. Recalling her childhood experience of Western orchestral music in the Shanghai of the 1930s, she writes: "When my mother took me to concerts, she would admonish me over and over again before we arrived, 'You absolutely cannot make a sound or say a word during the concert. Don't let them say that Chinese people are disorderly.' "[70] For the native elite (of which Chang's family was certainly a part), concertgoing was both an emblem of modernity and, paradoxically, a suitably bourgeois and distinctly equivocal gesture of resistance against colonial domination. The lesson that Chang's mother teaches her daughter is that Chinese "noise" must submit to modern, Western discipline, if only as an article of national pride.

The Shanghai Conservatory was not the only school engaged in the propagation of Western musical discipline. The decade's first two years saw a number of music schools established throughout the country, the most notable being the Guangzhou Conservatory of Music (Guangzhou yinyue yuan) founded by the composer Sitson Ma in 1932.[71] In addition, dozens of colleges and universities, including Yanjing University, Hujiang University, the University of Shanghai, Lingnan College, Huanan College, Jinling Women's College, the National College of Fine Arts in Hangzhou, Peiping Women's College of Arts and Sciences, Central University, and others, established new departments of music. These institutions spawned a variety of choral groups and school bands, a development complemented by expanded musical curricula in high schools and primary schools.

The expanded infrastructure of China's music education led to an explosion of music publishing and amateur music societies. Thirteen new music periodicals appeared from 1928 to 1934, many of them mouthpieces for amateur and scholarly societies.[72] An amateur symphony orchestra and choral and instrumental groups (including the Shanghai Songsters and the Chinese Harmonica Association) were established in Shanghai during this period. Similar activities took place in Hankou, Beijing, Nanjing, and Tianjin.

The most politically influential of these new organizations, however, took root in the provinces. In 1932, Cheng Maoyun, a KMT official and the composer of the Nationalist Party anthem, established the Jiangxi Committee for the Advancement of Musical Education (Jiangxi tuixing yinyue jiaoyu weiyuan hui). This organization operated out of the Jiangxi bureau of education and was funded by the KMT. Locally, the committee maintained its own orchestra and choir, organized concerts and recitals, and promoted the dissemination of patriotic school songs. Its primary mission, though, lay in enforcing standards of musical quality and crusading for the elimination of "vulgar" folk and popular music. Indeed, one project undertaken by the committee involved detaining blind, itinerant folksingers in order to teach them new (and presumably less objectionable) material![73] The committee also exerted influence on a national level through its monthly magazine, *Music Education*. This official publication played a crucial role in the political struggles that began to rage around music in the wake of the deepening of China's national crisis in 1932, serving as a mouthpiece for both conservative advocates of the KMT's increasingly repressive cultural policies, and (in the years directly preceding the outbreak of the Sino-Japanese War in 1937) leftist insurgents.

The crisis of 1932, initially sparked by the Japanese annexation of Manchuria, marked a turning point in the May 4th project of musical modernization. It took the Japanese attack on Shanghai's Zhabei district in the spring of 1932, however, to bring the gravity of China's plight home to the intellectuals, writers, and cultural workers clustered in the multiply colonized metropolis. In music, the attack resulted in an unprecedented politicization of musical production and activity. Composers, regardless of their ideological camp, threw themselves into composing patriotic anthems and military marches. Much of this output reflected the influence of school songs and brass band music. At the same time, many grander goals of the May 4th project—the creation of a national school, for instance—began to lose some luster. These ideals were replaced by a heightened interest in music as a technology of power, as an instrument for the mass mobilization of nationalist sentiment.

While the majority of music professionals embraced nationalism, not all of them were willing to support the Nationalist Party. Indeed, this crisis marked the factionalization of Chinese music. By 1932, three distinct groups can be discerned: the cultural left, the humanist center, and the KMT right. A musical left had begun to coalesce as early as 1930 with the founding of the League of Left-wing Writers (Zuoyi zuojia lianmeng hui). By 1933, leftist musical activists had begun to form cells for the study of Soviet and proletarian music. Some of them had also begun to participate in the production of popular music and sound films. Many of these musicians lacked formal Western musical training; several, in fact, were dropouts from the Shanghai Conservatory.[74] For this reason, they may have lacked the sense of investment in the musical establishment shared by their elite counterparts within the academy.

In the center stood a group of music professionals unwilling to commit themselves to either side of the political fray. Qingzhu, a composer and influential music theorist based at the Shanghai Conservatory, is representative of this group. He and others like him were committed, broadly speaking, to humanism and musical cosmopolitanism. While they shared with their colleagues a nationalistic concern for the fate of China (and sporadically pitched in by writing patriotic songs), they maintained a faith in individualism and the autonomy of artistic creation. Qingzhu, in particular, was a romantic apostle of the sacrality of secular music, a man who saw music as "the highest expression of the inner world of man."[75] Just as music rose above political struggle, he asserted, it also crossed linguistic and cultural boundaries with impunity.[76] In the highly charged political context of 1932, though, Qingzhu's emphasis on the aesthetic and spiritual autonomy of music seemed obsolete at best.

A powerful and established figure like Xiao Youmei had more in common with the left-wing music movement than a figure like Qingzhu. Xiao and Cheng Maoyun—both of whom were closely affiliated (ideologically and financially) with the KMT—shared with the left an interest in the power of music to mobilize the masses. The difference between these men and their leftist counterparts, of course, was that this power was to be harnessed not by the revolution, but by the nation-state.

THE POWER OF MUSIC

I want to turn (or more accurately tune) to Xiao's seminal statement on the relationship between music and political power in Republican China, one that is revealing not only of the project of a musical modernity orchestrated by the state but also of the pitfalls of such an approach. "The Power of Music" was originally delivered on November 15, 1933, over the Great China Wireless Broadcasting Station (XHHU) as part of a "Popular Schol-ars" lecture series sponsored by the Shanghai Municipal Bureau of Edu-cation. The transcript of Xiao's address was reprinted in three separate magazines from 1934 to 1936: the official *Music Education, Yisheng* (a mass-market publication devoted to cinema and music and loosely affiliated with the leftist music movement), and the popular *Music Magazine*, pub-lished by Liangyou in conjunction with the Shanghai Conservatory.[77] As such, we can assume that Xiao's address reached an unusually large and diverse audience. The almost three-year interval between the initial broad-cast and its republication in 1936, moreover, suggests that the issues ad-dressed by Xiao retained much of their relevance for some time. As such, the broadcast merits detailed examination.

The speech itself is remarkable, for it represents a distillation of many of the themes discussed in this chapter. Xiao's address partakes of the dis-dain for traditional Chinese and urban popular music typical of his class (Western-educated music professionals) and his era. At the same time, it argues for the social and political instrumentality of music. Nor is this argument merely rhetorical. The speech is a carefully crafted plea for con-tinued government support of the modernization project of which Xiao was a principal architect. To argue that music has an important role to play in the construction of the (anticolonial) nation-state is, of course, nothing new. Indeed, as has been shown in this chapter, it had been a fundamental aspect of Chinese discourse on music from at least the turn of the century onward. Xiao's vision of music here, however, is far more expansive (and frightening). In exulting in the power of music to orchestrate the emo-tions (and discipline the bodies) of the masses, his vision of a new "sonic regime" is more than a little reminiscent of fascism in its (to borrow Walter Benjamin's succinct characterization) insistent aestheticization of politi-cal activity.[78]

Xiao's speech begins with a seemingly innocuous explanation of the fundamental building blocks of musical expression: rhythm, harmony, and melody. These very categories, of course, reflect Xiao's bias toward Western music theory, and he concludes with a standard refrain: Chi-nese music has stagnated for one thousand years and lacks the refinement and power of its Western orchestral counterpart. Having established the parameters of good (Western) and bad (Chinese) music, Xiao begins to enumerate the ways in which different sorts of music affect the emotions of listeners. The first eight effects seem straightforward; indeed, they read like a catalog of the human emotional spectrum.

1. Gentle, tranquil music is able to soothe one's mind and help you fall asleep. Lullabies are an example of this category of music.
2. Happy and energetic music is able to refresh the spirits of its listeners. When small children hear this sort of music they are likely to jump up and down in a most lively fashion. This sort of music is quite prevalent in the West, so much so that it would be difficult to single out one piece as an example.
3. Noble and dignified music is able to inspire courage and elevate the spirit. Military marches belong to this category.
4. Tragic music makes the listener feel sad, and can even make them cry. Dirges and elegies belong to this category.
5. Melancholy music depresses people who listen to it.
6. Joyful music makes people feel happy and delighted.
7. Elevated, noble and serious music is capable of washing people's thoughts clean, elevating their aims, and ensuring that their actions are serious and noble.
8. Mournful music gives vent to human grief.[79]

These eight points are hardly surprising. Certain types of music evoke certain emotional responses. Other types of music can profoundly influence the moral development of the individual as well. But a significant and dangerous assumption is expressed in these deceptively simple statements. Xiao portrays these emotional effects as being essentially Pavlovian—immediate, instinctive, automatic. Xiao's theory, in other words, leaves absolutely no room for the agency of the listener. Musical input directly conditions emotional output; music is conceived as a technology with which one might program the soul.

The assumptions that underlie Xiao's argument to this point are not much different from the commonplaces of Confucian musical discourse with its emphasis on the crucial role of music in both regulating the polity and effecting ethical instruction (*jiaohua*) in individual subjects.[80] Xiao's list continues, however, with some suggestions for the practical application of this remarkable technology in distinctly modern institutional contexts. The first application is medical, the second penal. Both derive their authority from European precedent.

9. Music can also be used to treat illness, or lighten the suffering of those afflicted by illness or injury. During the Great War in Europe, most of the countries involved played special music in their hospitals for wounded soldiers to alleviate their pain. They also played music during amputations.

10. In recent years, European law courts have also experimented with using music to reform criminal minds. Every morning they play a special sort of music and make convicts listen to it. After a certain amount of time has passed, the criminals begin to feel remorse and resolve to change their ways. Many of these prisoners really have turned over a new leaf and gotten back on the right track once they have served out their sentences and been released from prison. Magistrates can also use music to their benefit. In one place there was a murder case. A suspect was arrested, but even after protracted investigation, he refused to confess. The magistrate, unable to find sufficient evidence to prosecute him, used music to help conclude the case. He locked the murderer in a dark room. In the middle of the night, he played sad music through the wall of an adjacent cell, accompanied by the sound of grief-stricken weeping. After a few days of this treatment, he continued the interrogation of the murderer, who had been so moved by the music that his conscience had been reawakened, and he gave the judge a complete confession. An incident like this truly reveals the power of music.[81]

It would be difficult *not* to read a passage of this nature in light of Foucault's work on the nature and development of modern disciplinary and penal systems.[82] Music is envisioned here as a powerful mechanism for the maintenance of the regime, a means by which the state heals bodies broken in its service, and breaks the spirits of those who step beyond the behavioral boundaries it has imposed. Music is both punitive (an instrument of torture) and productive (a labor-saving device); it compels confession *and* molds criminals into citizens loyal to the social order.

But the scope of this instrumentality, Xiao continues, is by no means limited to the individual citizen.

The most readily apparent power of music is that musical rhythm is capable of conducting the great masses, of unifying the movements of the entire nation.

In the West, they often sing an anthem before and after mass rallies. These rally songs have strong, simple rhythms and lyrics appropriate to the occasion. Once the anthem is sung, the spirit of cooperation is greatly increased.

The influence of these sorts of songs on the masses is like the working of gravitational force on the globe; as they sing, people will unwittingly begin to move *en masse* in the same direction. When an army of men march across the land without feeling any fatigue, when tens of thousands of men charge at the enemy singing a military song, and feel no pain—these are concrete examples of this effect.[83]

Here, the invasive micropolitics of the previous passage give way to an unmistakably fascist aesthetic, as evidenced by Xiao's decidedly cinematic vision of orchestrated crowds moving in lockstep, evoking the massive political rallies that figured so prominently in the practical and ideological programs of Hitler and Mussolini.[84] This aesthetic is coupled with an exaltation of military action reminiscent of the work of the Italian proto-fascist theorist of the avant-garde, F. T. Marinetti.[85] While we may bristle at the notion of saddling a canonical May 4th figure with such a highly charged (and denunciatory) term, it is important to remember that fascism was very much in the air in 1933. Adolf Hitler had just come to power, and Benito Mussolini's accomplishments in Italy were regarded with grudging respect, even by some in the liberal democracies of the West. China, finally, was faced with military invasion by a powerful militaristic regime in Japan, increasingly dominated by a crypto-fascist right wing. The genocidal totalitarianism of these regimes had not yet become apparent to contemporary observers, but their sheer efficacy in terms of political and military mobilization (and perhaps even the modernist allure of their political aesthetic) must have seemed attractive to anticolonial nationalists in China. Chiang Kai-shek maintained close links with the Third Reich until at least 1936, and his armies were trained and supplied by German advisers. At the time of Xiao's speech, moreover, the advent of Chiang's New Life Movement in February 1934 (inspired in part by National Socialism and implemented by Blueshirt activists modeled on the Brownshirts of Nazi Germany) was only months away.[86] Mass rallies of the sort that Xiao praises here were a prominent feature of that movement. Madame Chiang Kai-shek's New Life Movement Association, for instance, appointed Xiao's colleague at the Shanghai Conservatory, Zhao Meibo (Chao Mei-pa), to serve as a conductor of mass singing at political rallies under New Life auspices.[87]

Indeed, as the remainder of Xiao's speech makes clear, the question of who would "conduct the great masses" is key. By 1933 the emergent leftist music movement (treated in detail in chapter 4) had already appropriated many of the techniques of mass musical mobilization that Xiao describes. While leftists took many of their cues from Leninist political theory (and were far more willing to use emergent communications technologies to their own advantage) considerable tactical overlap occurred between leftists and their rightist counterparts.

This subtext of political struggle informs Xiao's next rhetorical move: a plea that the government entrust the task of musical mobilization to the technocratic elite that he represents. This plea begins with a reminder of just how seriously various European governments take the business of music education. Xiao pointedly praises the recent creation of a national ministry of music in Hitler's Germany, which he implicitly offers as a model for similar efforts in China. He situates this argument with reference to China's own dynastic history. The most "powerful and prosperous" dynastic regimes (Xiao cites the Zhou and Tang as prime examples) were precisely those in which music was taken the most seriously by the imperial court. With musical decline came dynastic decline. Having established this parallel (one that is not incidentally, given the studied neotraditionalism of the Nationalist New Life ideology, a truism of traditional Confucian musical criticism), he asks:

> Why, then, aren't we moving as quickly as possible to eliminate bad music with lewd lyrics and lewd tunes, and introduce good music in its stead? If we fail to do so, there will be very little hope of reforming the souls of the people of our nation. The power of music is an awesome one: not only good music, but also bad music, can be used to powerful effect. Bad music can also be very powerful indeed. People who are used to listening to sad songs are rarely blessed with good spirits. People who are used to slow music are only rarely able to rouse themselves into lively activity. The spirits of people who are used to listening to decadent music can seldom be elevated. People who are accustomed to vulgar, lewd and lascivious music can hardly be expected to be of upstanding moral character and behavioral rectitude. And a people who are accustomed to listening to loose music that lacks a clear and vigorous rhythm will never be able to work together and cooperate. Seen in this light, the malevolent power of music is terrifying indeed! And our whole Chinese nation is at this very

moment besieged by this malevolent power. If our government does not immediately find ways to eliminate it, if they don't take immediate action in order to put the enterprise of musical education in order, there will be absolutely no hope of ever rousing the spirits of our nations' citizens, of fostering cooperation and unity.[88]

The decadent and lascivious sounds in question, of course, are urban folk songs (*xiaodiao*), imported jazz, and the sort of mass-mediated music that represents a hybrid of the two—modern songs. Just why they are so objectionable is a question explored in greater detail in later chapters. In this context, it is enough to note the way in which they are associated with political (and sexual) indiscipline, the way their loose rhythms undercut the monolithic drumbeat of an aggressive cultural nationalism in which collective solidarity, rather than the pleasure of the listening subject, is of paramount importance. Xiao continues by suggesting how the dangers posed by this sort of music might be ameliorated.

And so, my hope is that the government will immediately assign a group of music experts the task of inspecting the nation's popular music. The music which they believe is damaging to public morals or decadent should be banned from either being performed or distributed. At the same time, we need to improve the music curricula in our schools, make sure that music teachers have proper credentials, encourage and promote the creation of new works and new songs, and pay more heed to specialized music education. . . . I would also hope that each and every wireless station will ask an expert to help them choose an inventory of good records suitable for broadcast, so that the souls of everyone in the radio audience will gradually be able to come around to good music.[89]

What is remarkable here is the marked (and obviously elitist) emphasis that Xiao places on "credentials," and "experts"—on the necessity, that is, of identifying those who possess the necessary cultural capital (Western musical training) to distinguish between good music and bad music and those who do not. In turn, his speech is a transparent attempt to leverage the cultural capital of these elite technocrats in order to garner the dividend of increased government support for their project of musical modernization. Apparently, the government was won over by Xiao's logic. In 1934, the KMT contributed sixteen acres of prime Shanghai real estate and an $80,000 subsidy toward the construction of a new campus for Xiao's National Conservatory. Cheng Maoyun and his colleagues at the Jiangxi Committee for the Advancement of Musical Education collaborated with the KMT in a New Life-style campaign dedicated to banning the performance and dissemination of any music that his team of experts might find unacceptable. Soon thereafter, the Nanjing government established its own bureau of music within the Ministry of Education in order to tighten the control of musical curricula and disseminate officially approved school songs and patriotic music among the school-age population.

Xiao concludes his speech with less weighty fare. After admonishing parents to foster the musical talent of their children so that China will in time produce its own "Beethovens and Mozarts," he leaves his audience with a final recommendation. Instead of listening to the vulgar Chinese radio stations that are to be the object of his experts' discipline and surveillance (or, for that matter, attending rallies to hear the nationalist anthems and military marches he praised earlier in the speech), he urges them to tune to the Alliance Française Station Radiophonique. For, despite the regrettable exception of a few jazz records ("a bad kind of Western music," Xiao explains), this station invariably broadcasts European classical music of the highest order.[90]

The irony here is that Xiao's conclusion unwittingly underscores both the coloniality of the musical field in which he participated and the increasing importance of media technologies such as wireless broadcasting and the gramophone to the constitution of that field. Xiao's interest lay in music as a technology for nation-building. But the way in which music participated in these ideological struggles was fundamentally altered in the early twentieth century by new technologies for the mass production and dissemination of music. I now turn to these emergent technologies and the way in which their presence in China is imbricated with the condition of colonial modernity.

CHAPTER TWO

The Gramophone in China

Sometime around the turn of the twentieth century, a young Frenchman named Labansat set up an outdoor stall on Tibet Road in Shanghai and began to play gramophone records for curious Chinese passersby. Labansat, whose career up to that point had consisted of operating a peep show for Shanghai theatergoers, had recently purchased an imported gramophone from a foreign firm, Moutrie & Company. His new business gambit was simple and effective; when a sufficiently large crowd had gathered around the machine, he would ask each listener to pay ten cents to hear a novelty record called "Laughing Foreigners" (Yangren daxiao). Anyone able to resist laughing along with the chuckles, chortles, and guffaws emerging from the horn of the gramophone would get his or her money back.[1]

Labansat himself, it seems, laughed all the way to the bank. By 1908 he had earned enough from this routine that he was able to establish China's first record company as a subsidiary of the multinational Compagnie-Générale Phonographique Pathé-Frères. With the help of a Chinese assistant from Ningbo and a French recording engineer, Labansat's new company, Pathé Orient, began to record Peking opera, sending the masters back to Paris for processing and manufacturing before selling the finished products to local Chinese. By 1914 the necessity for this last step was eliminated when Labansat established China's first recording studio and record-pressing plant in the French concession. By the 1930s, Pathé (which had recently become a subsidiary of another multinational, Electrical and Musical Industries) not only dominated the domestic Chinese record industry, but was the hub of a distribution network that extended throughout Southeast Asia. Pathé had become a central player in the urban media culture of the Republican era, a pioneer in the transnational dissemination of Chinese-language popular culture, and the principal purveyor of an entirely new musical genre: Mandarin popular song.

However important it was as the linchpin of a new industry dedicated to the production and consumption of the "decadent sounds" of jazz-inflected modern song, Pathé is only part of the story of the gramophone in China. Indeed, one of this chapter's central contentions is that the Chinese record industry itself is merely one piece in a global puzzle. Thomas Alva Edison invented his first tin-foil phonograph in 1877, but it was not until the turn of the century that the technology of sound recording yielded a new industry predicated on the industrial reproduction and mass-marketing of music. This new (and immensely profitable) industry was—from its very inception—transnational in character. Almost as soon as they were established, companies like Pathé-Frères (founded in 1897), the Gramophone Company (founded in 1898 in England), the Victor Talking Machine Company (founded in 1901 in New Jersey), the Columbia Graphophone Company (which entered the global market in 1902), and the German Beka-Record (1903) fanned out in search of new markets and new material, profoundly altering the nature of musical life around the globe.

GRAMOPHONE CULTURE

Many of these changes were invariant, regardless of geographical locale. Music was made to conform with the technical constraints of electroacoustic recording and mechanical reproduction, effectively limiting the sort of ensembles and compositions that might be phonographically represented and sold on the open market. The commodification of musical performance in the form of 78-rpm discs also imposed new, market-oriented constraints on production. Perhaps the most important consequence of these dual constraints was the emergence (in the United States and Europe as well as in China, India, and any number of other colonized nations) of a vast range of new urban popular musics. The extended compositional forms of European classical music were not ideally suited to the two and half minutes per side allowed for by the gramophone records of the era; popular songs and operatic arias not only could be recorded with greater fidelity than orchestral pieces, but they could be performed far more profitably within the urban record market.[2]

The gramophone also profoundly altered the nature and context of musical consumption. Indeed, the gramophone was one of the principal agents of the sort of "space-time compression" that David Harvey identifies as characteristic of the condition of modernity.[3] The technology of sound recording and reproduction enabled both the preservation of individual musical performances (and thus previously unrepeatable moments in historical time) and their rapid and seemingly effortless diffusion across vast spaces. The power of the gramophone, as Jacques Attali points out, was that it could "stockpile" time and space in the form of musical representation and thus embody "the internationalization of social relations" already transforming everyday life in the early twentieth century.[4]

In practical terms, this meant that a heretofore unimaginable cornucopia of music, diverse in both historical and geographical provenance, was suddenly made available to the gramophone owner, regardless of whether he or she lived in New York or Shanghai, London or Calcutta. While the easy availability of the Western musical repertoire to non-Western ears certainly spurred the supplanting of indigenous music by European and American forms, the opposite also is true. The gramophone, in freeing a variety of non-Western and folk musics from the tyranny of a European system of musical notation ill-equipped to represent their subtleties, actually resulted in an unprecedented proliferation of a variety of traditional, regional, and hybrid musical forms. This counterintuitive conclusion, of course, contradicts standard accounts of the complicity of modern communications technology with the forces of Western cultural imperialism.[5]

The advent of the gramophone also served to fundamentally alter the political economy and social meaning of musical consumption. The gramophone record "turned the performance of music into a material object, something you could hold in your hand, which could be bought and sold."[6] As such, it not only fundamentally altered the way in which musicians made their living, but it shifted the primary context of musical performance away from its traditional locales (aristocratic salons, concert halls, public festivals) and into the home.

Marketed in China and elsewhere as an indispensable accoutrement of the modern home and a marker of petit bourgeois respectability, the gramophone was both a mechanical emblem of modernity and the principal engine whereby music became an object of private, individualized consumption as opposed to the focus of public gatherings.[7] Indeed, the domesticity of the gramophone is foregrounded in many Chinese print advertisements and calendar posters for gramophones, and is also an important aspect of the discourse on the gramophone and its uses in contemporary magazine articles and consumer guides.[8] The gramophone appears

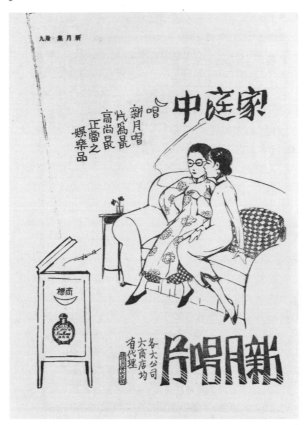

"In the home—New Moon Records are the most
elegant and proper sort of leisure product." From
Xinyue ji 1 (September 1929).

fairly frequently in urban popular literature of the Republican period
as a signifier of middle-class leisure, urban sophistication, and domestic
felicity.[9]

At the same time, the gramophone (and allied technologies like radio
broadcasting and sound films) brought music into a range of new, distinctly modern social spaces. The cinema is one such space. According to
contemporary accounts, many cafés, restaurants, and nightclubs in Shanghai were also fitted with gramophones or wireless radios as a stand-in for
live musicians. Record retailers offered customers the opportunity to pre-
view new records, as did modern department stores like Wing On, Sin-

cere, and Sun Sun. Dance music and the latest screen songs, finally, often poured out into the streets and alleys from corner stores.[10] New listening habits and new musical tastes were one result of this expansion of musical space. New and more heterogeneous (in terms of both class and gender) audiences were another.[11] This unprecedented saturation of quotidian life in the modern metropolis by "gramophone culture" and its radiophonic and cinematic byproducts meant that the financial and ideological stakes of controlling the means of musical production and distribution became extremely high. For that reason, China's nascent "culture industry" became the site of fierce economic competition and intense cultural struggle throughout the Republican period.

These transformations took place in both metropoles and colonial urban centers. And significantly, they occurred almost simultaneously in both places. The history of the record industry in Shanghai belies the assumption of "belated modernity" that all too often governs scholarly approaches to the question of cultural modernization in the Republican period. The arrival of the gramophone in China cannot be understood in isolation from the history of global diffusion of capitalist modernity in the late nineteenth and early twentieth centuries. And precisely because the record industry was global from the very beginning, Labansat's work with Pathé Asia, for example, is not merely another example of the introduction of advanced European technologies into a backward colonial periphery. The record industry grew and thrived only insofar as it invested in international (and domestic minority and immigrant) markets; London and New York were as much participants in the condition of colonial modernity as cities like Shanghai and Calcutta.

I argue in this chapter that studying the historical diffusion of gramophone culture and its imbrication with colonial modernity can help us place recent theoretical debates on the nature of transnational culture on firmer historical ground. Much recent work on global flows of capital and culture in our postmodern and postcolonial era is undergirded by the assumption that these remarkable developments are historically nonpareil. This oversight, I suspect, derives in part from a characteristically postmodern focus in the writings of Arjun Appadurai and other theorists on visuality and the ascendancy of "the image, the imagined, the imaginary . . . in global cultural processes."[12] At the same time, Appadurai's interest in (and perhaps unwitting reduplication of) contemporary culture's "nostalgia for the present" often causes him to lose sight of the historical role of commodities (such as the gramophone and gramophone records) in forging the networks of transnational exchange that constitute his primary analytical object.[13]

In (theoretical) practice, this means that the early history of these networks as almost invariably occluded from contemporary discourse on global cultural flows. While Appadurai's seminal essay, "Disjuncture and Difference in the Global Cultural Economy," begins with a brief consideration of premodern global cultural contacts, he quickly launches himself into the task of constructing a "social theory of [global] postmodernity" without ever examining (or indeed mentioning) the crucial historical trajectory that lies between these two epochs.[14] In a more recent essay on transnational culture titled "Here and Now," Appadurai accounts for this absence by positing a historical rupture between earlier modernities and the modernity we currently inhabit. "This theory of a break—or rupture—with its strong emphasis on electronic mediation and mass migration is necessarily a theory of the recent past (or the extended present) because it is only in the past two decades or so that media and migration have become so massively globalized, that is to say, active across large and irregular transnational terrains."[15] While I agree with Appadurai that the last few decades have brought an unprecedented intensification and massification of these global processes, I also believe it is important to keep the continuities that bind us to earlier "transnationalisms" firmly in mind, if only because they serve to remind us of linkages between colonial power and capital that are by no means irrelevant to our current situation.

Indeed, something of the importance of earlier transnationalisms to our understanding of transnational culture in its contemporary form can be suggested by the following facts. In 1931, the global record market was dominated by six multinational corporations. In the 1990s, six multinational corporations accounted for more than 75 percent of global music production. And despite a tangled hundred-year history of mergers and acquisitions, the origins of the transnational corporations that currently control the market can be traced directly back to corporate ancestors like Pathé-Frères, Victor Talking Machine, and the Gramophone Company.[16]

The operations of these earlier transnational corporations in China and elsewhere cannot be divorced from the colonial contexts in which they took place. In colonial Shanghai, almost all recording and production facilities (with one significant exception discussed later in this chapter) were owned by EMI-Pathé and RCA-Victor and were located in the foreign concession areas. Profits naturally were funneled back to the metropoles. Management and technical expertise was supplied by foreign business-men and technicians, whose knowledge of local music and local markets was supplied by Chinese "musical compradors." Raw musical material, in turn, was often supplied by small-time entrepreneurs and "pocketbook" record companies who signed "native" artists and rented the production facilities of the major labels to serve local markets. Not surprisingly, this patently exploitative situation engendered resistance. Indeed, at the same time that the gramophone became an emblem of modernity for the urban middle classes and an indispensable adjunct to the development of a new mass-mediated culture of consumption, it also became the target of anti-colonial resistance on the part of both the emergent national bourgeoisie and leftist cultural insurgents.

"THE MUSIC GOES ROUND"

There is no better place to begin an examination of the global character of the record industry than with the story of a young American record-ing engineer named F. W. Gaisberg. Gaisberg began his career as an assis-tant to the German-American inventor Emil Berliner, who perfected the gramophone in 1887. Berliner's gramophone differed from Edison's origi-nal phonograph in one essential respect: the wax cylinders that Edison's machine used as a recording medium did not lend themselves to mass re-production and repeatable playback nearly so well as Berliner's flat, shel-lac gramophone discs.[17] Thus, Berliner's gramophone paved the way for the development of a new consumer industry predicated on the mass pro-duction of music.

Berliner's bid to exploit the commercial possibilities of his invention re-sulted in the creation of two international companies. In 1898, Berliner sold the European rights to his patents to a London consortium called the Gramophone Company. In 1901, Berliner's interests (including a por-tion of the Gramophone Company) were taken over by the New Jersey-based Victor Talking Machine Company. In his capacity as a represen-tative of the Gramophone Company, Gaisberg spent the last year of the century traveling across Europe, opening agencies and recording cele-brated classical musicians like Feodor Chaliapin and Enrico Caruso. In September 1902 he was sent still farther afield, to Asia. Gaisberg's jour-ney, undertaken to "open up new markets, establish agencies, and acquire a catalogue of native records," is documented in his autobiography, *The Music Goes Round.*[18] Equipped with a portable recording studio, Gaisberg visited Calcutta, Singapore, Hong Kong, Shanghai, Tokyo, Bangkok, and Rangoon, producing a grand total of 1,700 recordings of local music.

Gaisberg's modus operandi in Shanghai was typical of the journey as a whole. Having selected a sheet music dealer as the company's local sales representative—in this case, Moutrie & Company, the same outfit from whom Pathé's Labansat had purchased his first gramophone—Gaisberg found a musical comprador who would arrange a series of recording sessions with Chinese artists in Gaisberg's hotel room.

> Wednesday, March 18th [1903]: We made our first records. About fifteen Chinamen had come, including the accompanying band. As a Chinaman yells at the top of his power when he sings, he can only sing two songs an evening and then he becomes hoarse. Their idea of music is a tremendous clash and bang: with the assistance of a drum, three pairs of huge gongs, a pair of slappers, a sort of banjo, some reed instruments which sounded like bagpipes, and the yelling of the singer, their so-called music was recorded on the gramophone. On the first day, after making ten records we had to stop. The din had so paralyzed my wits that I could not think.[19]

Despite Gaisberg's discomfort, he made another 325 records in Shanghai before moving on to Hong Kong. In Hong Kong, Gaisberg (for reasons known only to his local comprador) occupied himself by recording 200 songs sung by "teahouse girls," whose voices he likens (in terms remarkably similar to those of Berlioz fifty years before him) to "the sound of a small wailing cat."[20] All of these records were sent back to Europe for manufacturing and then sold to record buyers in the colonial treaty ports as well as to "the Chinese of America, the Malay States, and Australia."[21] This last point is particularly revealing, because it shows the extent to which the defining terms of Appadurai's theory of transnational culture—mediation and migration—were already shaping the development of a global media culture in the first decade of the twentieth century.[22]

If Gaisberg had been the only representative of a record company to visit Asia, his story might merely represent an interesting instance of transcultural contact and colonial miscomprehension of "native" musical forms. But as Pekka Gronow notes, Gaisberg was only the first of many emissaries dispatched to Asia in order to spur on the expansion of the industry.[23] In the next seven years the subsidiaries that Gaisberg had established in India and the Far East recorded more than 10,000 titles. And by the time that a recording engineer for Beka-Record G.m.b.H, Heinrich Bumb, arrived in Hong Kong in 1906 (just three years after Gaisberg's initial trip), a host of U.S., British, and German companies had broken into the business as well. "The Columbia Graphophone Company had just finished its latest recordings—said to be one thousand titles, for which fees of 50,000 dollars had been paid. 'Victor,' 'Grammophon,' as well as 'Zonophon-Records' and 'Odeon' were all represented in the colony."[24]

So rapid was the expansion of the industry into Asia and Latin America that these regions soon came to represent more than one-fifth of worldwide record sales.[25] By 1907, Victor and the Gramophone Company found it necessary to divide their respective spheres of influence, with Victor agreeing to restrict itself to North and South America, China, Japan, and the Philippines, leaving the Gramophone Company free to operate anywhere else in the world.[26] By the middle of the next decade, this remarkable growth had rendered the industry's earlier (and distinctly mercantilist) system of production and distribution obsolete and inefficient. Rather than collecting raw musical materials in the colonies for manufacturing in the metropole and then shipping them back "home" with value added, companies like Pathé-Asia began to import manufacturing equipment for local use. Between 1910 and 1931, most of the companies that had weathered the fierce competition of the early years of the industry by way of consolidation into massive multinational concerns moved quickly to establish local manufacturing facilities and transnational distribution centers throughout Asia, Latin America, and Africa.[27] Shanghai was one such center.[28]

THE RECORD INDUSTRY IN SHANGHAI

The story of how Pathé Asia came to dominate the Shanghai record industry is symptomatic of these global trends. The corporate history is complex and more than a little confusing, but deserves comment. When Pathé opened its factory in Shanghai in 1916, the field was littered with competitors like Beka, Odeon, Columbia, Victor, and others. In 1925, Pathé's parent company merged with a London-based company, Columbia Graphophone. At the same time, Columbia Graphophone annexed its American counterpart, Columbia Phonograph, as well as the German Lindström concern (which included Beka-Record and Odeon). In 1931, finally, Columbia Graphophone and the Gramophone Company merged to form a new conglomerate, Electrical and Musical Industries.

In practice, this meant that Pathé-EMI had effectively swallowed almost all of its competition.[29] Pathé's house label (featuring its famous rooster trademark) specialized in popular music and screen songs recorded by the most famous singers and movie actresses of the era. Popular music was also issued on the former Gramophone Company's flagship label, His Master's Voice (HMV), using the famous dog and gramophone logo for which it had been named. In addition, the company released second-rate popular music and introduced new artists at cut-rate prices on its Regal (Lige) label. Beka (Beikai) and Odeon (Gaoting) continued to issue Chinese operatic music under their own trademarks, but they were owned and operated by Pathé and beholden to its recording and manufacturing facilities.[30] In addition to Chinese records, the plant manufactured music for the overseas Chinese, Vietnamese, Burmese, Laotian, Indonesian, Malayan, and Philippine markets. The entire operation was self-sufficient. The Pathé factory on Xujiahui Road employed more than 300 workers operating twenty-four automated record-pressing machines, maintained a workshop for processing raw materials like shellac, and was equipped with a press for printing record sleeves and labels. All of this added up to a production capacity of 2.7 million records a year.[31]

The merger with EMI left Pathé with only one serious multinational competitor for the gramophone business in China and Southeast Asia: RCA-Victor. Nippon Victor (a Japanese subsidiary of Victor Talking Machine) had established itself in Shanghai in the late 1920s. When Victor merged with the giant Radio Corporation of America in 1932, the new company became the second multinational to establish a factory in China, albeit with only half the production capacity of Pathé-EMI. RCA-Victor issued a mixture of Chinese operatic, folk, and popular songs using the familiar dog and gramophone trademark pioneered by HMV, to which it was entitled by its earlier affiliation with the Gramophone Company. The company was called American Victory (Meiguo shengli) in Chinese, however, to distinguish it from HMV, which was referred to as Victory (Shengli) or transliterated as Victor (Wukeduo).

The vagaries of this tangled corporate history should not obscure the fact that the means of production were almost entirely controlled by transnational capital. Indeed, the sole Chinese-owned company to possess production capacity—a venture called Great China Records (Da Zhonghua changpian), to which I will return shortly—was established only with the aid of Japanese financiers. Pathé-EMI sat atop the heap, followed by RCA-Victor and Great China. The heap itself consisted of a host of locally owned pocketbook record companies (*pibao gongsi*). Equipped with little more than an office (and sometimes not even that), these companies negotiated recording contracts with local and regional musicians and rented studio and manufacturing time from the majors to produce their own records.[32] Many of these companies specialized in traditional genres and catered to niche and regional markets. Some of the more interesting examples of these enterprises were Great Wall Records (Changcheng changpian gongsi), which recorded many of the era's most prominent performers of Peking opera (including Mei Lanfang), and Baige Records, which catered to local fans of Shanghainese (*huju*) and *yue*-style opera (*yueju*).

Provincial pocketbook companies were responsible for the mass-mediated proliferation of a variety of regional musics as well as the creation of new distribution networks in China's hinterlands. The importance of this development should not be underestimated, for much of this music was frowned upon by May 4th era music educators, barred from national music curricula, and effectively excluded from distribution in the form of sheet music and songbooks using European notation. Emei Records recorded Sichuanese opera (*chuanju*), traditional art songs (*qingyin*), and folk music in Shanghai and shipped their products back to Sichuan. Lianxing Records distributed a variety of Fujianese local opera records in Xiamen and Fuzhou. Beihai Records issued recordings of Peking opera and northern Chinese music for audiences in Hebei.[33]

Despite their commitment to a range of traditional musics shunned by the Westernized musical establishment of the treaty ports, none of these companies could extricate themselves from the colonial economy in which they were enmeshed. Without access to production facilities of their own, these companies functioned as "proletarian" subsidiaries of the transnational corporations. It also should be noted that while these pocketbook companies managed to provide consumers with a limited amount of local "software," the "hardware" upon which their business depended (gramophones and accessories such as replacement needles) was manufactured abroad by EMI and RCA and other multinationals and sold in China by their corporate subsidiaries.

Indeed, one might argue that the pocketbook companies' position within the market was structurally analogous to that of the Chinese musical compradors who worked for European general managers within the Pathé-EMI and RCA-Victor organizations. A brief perusal of commercial directories and import and export manuals of the time reveals that all of the transnational record companies were managed by Europeans and Americans. Pathé, for instance, was managed by Labansat (in the capacity of as "Managing Director for the East") until the EMI merger, at which time he was replaced by a management team led by R. Degoy, R. L. Read, and H. L. Wilson. The only Chinese name to appear is Labansat's original Chinese collaborator, Zhang Changfu, who served as "Chinese manager" of Pathé Asia until 1928.[34] While the precise nature of the balance of decision-making power within companies like Pathé remains unclear, it is safe to say that the foreign managers were responsible for all major business decisions and even attended to tasks like approving song lyrics (which were translated into English for their benefit) before recording sessions. Chinese workers were relegated to providing musical expertise and negotiating with performers and local distributors.[35]

The company's internal hierarchy was complicated still further by the presence of other foreigners in nonmanagerial positions. These included French and English recording engineers and technicians responsible for the installation and upkeep of the company's manufacturing plant. More interesting—especially in light of Shanghai's multiple colonization and consequent status as global entrepôt—was the fact that Pathé's in-house studio orchestra throughout the 1930s and 1940s consisted primarily of White Russian émigrés, most of whom were both classically trained and conversant with the idioms of American jazz and Tin Pan Alley popular song.[36] Other record companies hired groups of Filipino musicians as well as local Chinese for popular music (as opposed to Chinese operatic) recording sessions.[37] Racial hierarchies held sway in this arena as well, as Chinese musicians—with the exception of female vocalists—were routinely paid substantially less than their foreign counterparts.[38] The profits accruing from all of these efforts (a substantial portion of which derived from their dealings with the Chinese pocketbook companies) were either funneled back into the business, or remitted to parent companies overseas.

ANTICOLONIAL RESISTANCE AND
THE NATIVE BOURGEOISIE

Pathé-EMI and RCA-Victor, of course, were just two of the actors in a larger drama of imperialist economic exploitation in China. By 1918, more than 7,000 foreign companies had established a presence in China, and throughout the 1920s and 1930s multinational corporations owned controlling stakes in a number of crucial industries (including shipping, coal mining, petroleum, chemicals, tobacco, textiles, and banking). China's balance of trade with the West and Japan was equally lopsided.[39] This dire situation provoked sporadic resistance on the part of both the Nationalist government and the national bourgeoisie. The efforts on the part of native elites to wrest control of the means of phonographic reproduction away from transnational conglomerates like Pathé-EMI are one example of this fight against imperialist economic domination.

Great China Records marked one such effort. This company was brought into being by no less than the "father of the Chinese republic," Sun Yat-sen, and was explicitly conceived of as part of a larger project of national industrialization.[40] While still in exile in 1916, Sun urged a group of Japanese businessmen to help finance the construction of a Chinese record factory in Shanghai's Hongkou district. The company (which Sun himself had christened) was established soon thereafter with a mixture of both Japanese and Chinese capital. In 1924, Sun Yat-sen even recorded two promotional discs of his own speeches, urging the company (and, by extension, domestic goods and the national bourgeoisie who produced them) on to ever greater success. By 1927, Great China was wholly owned by local capitalists. The company's facilities were limited (possessing just eight pressing machines to Pathé's twenty-four) but complete, and it issued records on three separate labels (green for modern songs, red for Peking opera, and blue for regional operas). Even so, the company was hardpressed by its more amply financed foreign competitors, and the factory seldom operated at full capacity. Some of this slack was taken up by renting to pocketbook companies, but the company never represented a serious threat to Pathé-EMI's domination of the record market.

A second example of this sort of nationalist resistance to foreign monopoly was a Hong Kong-based pocketbook company that worked in close collaboration with Great China in the early 1930s. New Moon Rec-

Cover of the first issue (1929) of *New Moon Collection*
(*Xinyue ji*).

ords (Xinyue liusheng ji changpian gongsi), founded in 1927 by a charis-
matic and musically inclined Cantonese businessman named Qian Guangren, is interesting in a number of ways. First, Qian (who was something
of a self-styled intellectual) published his own trade magazine, *New Moon
Collection* (*Xinyue ji*). This publication offers us a rare and fascinating look
into the business operations of a Chinese pocketbook record company as
well as providing insights into the ideological positions and cultural sensibilities that informed those commercial activities.

What emerges most prominently from the magazine (both in Qian's
own writings and the advertisements and promotional materials) is the
explicit foregrounding of the company's nationalistic commitment to pro-

moting the manufacture and consumption of domestic goods. The company recorded only with Great China, and this relationship became a prominent part of both their corporate identity and their marketing strategy. Certifications of the "domesticity" of New Moon's products are exhibited prominently on the inside cover of the magazine, and advertisements for the label (and the larger Great China) feature such slogans as "There isn't a patriot who doesn't support Great China Records." In addition, almost every issue of the magazine features a polemic (usually written by Qian himself) advocating the promotion of native industry and domestic goods.[41] By the early 1930s this commitment also had led the company to pioneer the domestic manufacture of gramophone tonearms, needles, and other accessories.

Secondly, the magazine provides a window onto the mass-mediated emergence of a distinctly regional (and unmistakably hybridized) popular culture in interwar Hong Kong. Despite New Moon's nationalist stance, its market and musical specialization was restricted to Hong Kong and its Cantonese-speaking environs. Many of the Cantonese opera singers brought by Qian Guangren to the Great China recording studio in Shanghai were stars of the nascent Hong Kong film industry.[42] Some of these figures remain household names in Hong Kong today: for example, Xue Juexian (Sit Gok-sin) and the child prodigy Xin Ma Shisheng. Other recording artists for New Moon went on to fame in the Shanghai film industry, the most notable being the celebrated silent film actress Ruan Lingyu.

Perhaps even more significant than New Moon's role in developing a stable of local Cantonese talent was the new genre of music that it produced for phonographic consumption. In addition to traditional operatic arias, Qian Guangren and his friends created a hybrid genre that incorporated Cantonese folk melodies with Western instruments like the saxophone and electric guitar that were new to China. These songs also were wedded to lyrics that fully reflected the polyglot coloniality of Hong Kong's linguistic idiom, rhyming Cantonese street slang and standard Chinese with fractured English and French phrases.[43] Several questions and conclusions can be drawn from this phenomenon. First, it prompts us to rethink the relationship between nationalism and regional identity in the 1930s. Second, it places into serious question the familiar proposition that the mass-mediation of culture necessarily results in cultural homogenization. Finally, it should be noted that this sort of complex colonial transculturation was by no means unique to Hong Kong but was a

```
(1) 有个女子。         瓜子口面。
    佢喺東方。         我喺西便。
    大家分離。         眞是可憐。
    叫佢番嚟。         見吓我面。
(2) SOME LIKES SWEETIE.  SOME LIKES MONEY
    你要蜜糖。         我愛仙士。
    BLOW THE WHISTLE.   吹吓啤啤。
    兩家  TALKEE.       揀个日子。
(3) SHE WILL LOVE ME.   佢好愛我。
    嗎介東西。         叫造 WHAT FOR.
    四月廿四。         APRIL 24TH.
    去渡密月。         眞是冇錯。
(4) GO TO PAREE.        去到巴黎。
    COM, PAN, LI VU,    你好喇嗅。
    BEAUFITUL DOLL.     好靚公仔。
    買个番嚟。         比你一睇。
(5) WHO'S YOUR FATHER.  問我老子。
    我个老豆。         叫造 BILLIE.
    你叫老爺。         我叫爹爹。
    滿面 WHISKER.       好似羊咩。
(6) 佢好孤寒。         STINGY FELLOW.
    POCKET EMPTY.       个袋冇貨。
    THIRTY CENTS.       買的燒鵝。
    同埋食飯。         唔使肚餓。
(7) TOO MUCH CHOW CHOW.  食飯大多。
    胃口太窄。         點能收科。
    佢望天公。         來保祐我。
    賜个 BABY.          當作 KAM SHAW.
(8) GET ONE AMAH.       請个使婆。
    來 臭 BABY.         快的大个。
    洗牛奶樽。         切勿打破。
    順手掩門。         CLOSE THE DOOR.
(9) 若然唱錯。         請你諒我。
    才疏學淺。         見識無多。
    大家聽過。         笑口呵呵。
    HAPPY NEW YEAR.     恭喜多賀。
```

"Shouzai goes dating." A song recorded by New Moon
Records, from *Xinyue ji* 2 (September 1930).

salient characteristic of mass-mediated musical culture in Shanghai (and
the other treaty ports) as well.

GRAMOPHONE CULTURE AND THE LEFT

If Chinese businessmen were largely concerned with taking a piece of
the business associated with this new gramophone culture away from the
multinational companies who controlled it, the concern of leftist cultural

workers was the feudal and colonial nature of gramophone culture itself. This is not to say that leftist critics were mere Luddites. As early as 1928, no less a figure than the prominent writer and critic Guo Moruo had suggested the phonograph as a model for cultural production, urging leftist cultural workers to "be phonographs" that would objectively record the lives of the proletariat and play back what they had found for the benefit of society at large.[44] For leftist musicians, then, the problem was not so much the gramophone itself, but the new urban media culture—born of the commercial interactivity of records, radio, musical cinema, and the popular press—in which it participated. That culture, they believed, was irredeemably tainted by its colonial decadence, political escapism, and its association with both the "vulgar" commercial culture of the urban petit bourgeois and imperialist economic domination. Their agenda was to forge a new mass culture that would serve less as an object of private consumption than a means for the mobilization of collective resistance against Japanese territorial encroachment and Western imperialism.

With the annexation of Manchuria in 1932 by Japan, leftists set about this project with redoubled urgency. In order to succeed, they needed to infiltrate both Chinese film studios and transnational record companies like Pathé-EMI. The leftist composer Ren Guang was a central figure in this effort. Ren—who had spent the 1920s studying music in France and working for a French piano manufacturer in Vietnam—was hired as Pathé's musical director in 1928 to play the musical comprador role of his immediate predecessor, Zhang Changfu.[45] In the early 1930s, Ren Guang began to involve himself in a number of left-wing musical organizations devoted to the proletarianization of Chinese music. It was through study groups like the Soviet Friends Society (Sulian zhi you she) that he became friends with many of the most prominent leftist musicians and filmmakers of the era, including Nie Er (whose career is covered in detail in chapter 4), He Luting, Tian Han, and others. These figures, in turn, secured positions at Shanghai's major studios at the dawn of the Shanghai sound era in 1932.

Ren Guang thus became instrumental to the release of almost fifty leftist screen songs and national salvation anthems from 1932 to 1937.[46] This new music set itself in direct opposition to the modern songs that continued to dominate the market, replacing their Chinese melodies, jazzy harmonies, and melismatic female crooning with march rhythms, orchestral effects, and choral singing drawn from the example of Soviet mass music. Leftist music also reflected Guo Moruo's phonographic aesthetic. Nie Er's songs about dockworkers and newspaper boys were composed only after he had spent time living among the proletarians he sought to musically represent. Many of these songs remain classics even today; some of the more prominent examples include Nie Er's "March of the Volunteers" (Yiyong jun jinxingqu), which became China's national anthem, and Ren Guang's own composition, "Song of the Fishermen" (Yuguang qu). The commercial success of these songs, finally, allowed Ren to bring a number of his leftist colleagues (including Nie Er and, later, Xian Xinghai) into the company as the directors of Pathé's in-house Chinese music ensemble.

Ren's success as a comprador for leftist music rested on a pair of ironies. Although Ren's efforts met with occasional resistance from his English and French managers, the relationship was smoothed by his fluency in the French language and his experience working as a manager of a French colonial enterprise in Vietnam.[47] More importantly, the colonial nature of the Pathé-EMI operation itself functioned as a sort of ideological shield against government censorship.[48] Much of the more overtly anti-Japanese material that Ren was able to push past his foreign superiors could not have been released through pocketbook companies, which lacked the extraterritorial status conferred on Pathé-EMI by Chinese authorities and the foreign-run Shanghai Municipal Council. Ultimately, the managers of Pathé-EMI were only too happy to exploit the limited but nonetheless lucrative market for this sort of music. The flow of leftist music into the mass media market was cut off only after the military occupation of Shanghai in 1937, when Japanese military officials forced Pathé-EMI to fire Ren Guang.[49]

That Pathé-EMI actually profited from the anticolonial critique launched by the leftists is a final irony. Much of the force of this critique is summed up by a promotional image from a 1937 issue of a movie magazine, *New China Pictorial* (*Xinhua huabao*).[50] The magazine was the official organ of the leftist-controlled Xinhua Studio; this image was a photographic still from a new film starring the most popular slapstick comedian of the day, Han Langen. Han, playing a country bumpkin, crouches in front of a gramophone being demonstrated to a Chinese crowd by a foreigner. The rhetorical force of the image is made clear by the appearance in the lower right-hand corner of what is indisputably the single most famous trademark of the transnational gramophone industry, that of the dog listening to His Master's Voice.[51] Thus, Han—and by extension the Chinese people—is likened to a dog in a rhetorical move that subtly alludes to the probably

"His Master's Voice." A promotional still from *New China Pictorial* (February 1937).

apocryphal (but nonetheless pointed) anecdote about the municipal park in colonial Shanghai barred to "dogs and Chinese." And in a masterful play on words (and images), the gramophone itself stands in for the Voice of China's colonial Masters. If that were not enough, Han's disingenuously naive exclamation—"Damn! These foreign devils are cheaters"—steers the viewer of the photo toward a sharp awareness of the technological machination, economic exploitation, and cultural dislocation that characterize gramophone culture and the condition of colonial modernity in which it was embedded.

This scene, of course, is more than slightly reminiscent of the anecdote with which I began the chapter. We might even want to imagine the figure in the center of the photo as Labansat himself, demonstrating his new gramophone to curious Chinese passersby. In the first anecdote, audiences were encouraged to chuckle along with "Laughing Foreigners." In this case, however, Chinese viewers have the last—albeit bitter and even self-deprecating—laugh.

CHAPTER THREE

The Yellow Music of Li Jinhui

If Li Jinhui really is the kind of artist who represents the Chinese national character, then those foreigners who say the Chinese people are the most degenerate on earth are entirely correct. —He Luting, "On Li Jinhui" (1934)[1]

We found that on this new job we were obliged to play Chinese music so we began to learn how. I sketched out some of the most popular Chinese songs at the time and after a few rehearsals we were playing it like we had been doing it a long time. It wasn't too much different from our own music except the Chinese have a different scale tone, but as long as it could be written in on the American scale it could be played. —Buck Clayton[2]

Li Jinhui is a towering presence in the history of modern Chinese popular music. Between 1927 and 1936, Li pioneered a new and hugely influential brand of Sinified jazz music; recorded literally hundreds of "modern songs" for companies like Pathé-EMI, RCA-Victor, and Great China, composed screen songs for fifteen popular entertainment films, and even led the first all-Chinese jazz big band at an upscale Shanghai nightclub.[3] This imposing shadow is lengthened still further by the fact that Li Jinhui was single-handedly responsible for launching the careers of almost every notable singer, popular musician, and movie star of the era. Indeed, the rolls of Li's Bright Moon Song and Dance troupe read something like a litany of the luminaries of Shanghai's entertainment firmament in the 1930s and 1940s; and include figures as diverse as the legendary "golden voice" of modern songs, Zhou Xuan, the film actress Wang Renmei, and the leftist musician Nie Er.

Li's life and career, however, have long been shadowed by calumny and criticism. He endured an unrelenting barrage of attacks throughout the 1930s from critics of every political stripe. He was scorned by the May 4th

Li Jinhui in 1926. From the first edition of Li
Jinhui's *Night of Bright Moonlight* (Shanghai:
Zhonghua shuju, 1926).

era musical establishment for his interest in folk and popular forms. Officials of the KMT attempted to ban his music for its "decadence" and "vulgarity." And in the wake of the Japanese annexation of Manchuria in 1932,
leftist critics labeled his music (and the new media networks and new
stars that it had helped to forge) as a vulgar capitulation to commerce at
the expense of the imperatives of national salvation. In the wake of the
Communist victory of 1949, Li's reputation as a purveyor of "yellow" (or
"pornographic") music solidified into an article of socialist historiographical faith.[4] Li himself paid dearly for his ill fame as the progenitor of yellow
music; he died in 1967 at the height of the Cultural Revolution, a victim of
political persecution.[5]

These clouds of controversy have obscured the complexity of Li's legacy. Only recently have historians in Mainland China and elsewhere begun to acknowledge that Li was not merely—indeed, not even primarily—a popular musician. A product of the social, political, and intellectual ferment of the May 4th era, he was an avid patriot and educator. His efforts to popularize Mandarin Chinese on a national level led to the promulgation and wide distribution of language textbooks throughout China. He was the editor of one of the first (and certainly the most successful) Chinese magazines published exclusively for children, *Little Friend* (*Xiao pengyou*). It was in the pages of *Little Friend* that he published the first of a series of twelve innovative children's operas designed to promote aesthetic education (*meiyu*), good citizenship, and the use of Mandarin as a national language. He was, finally, an advocate of the popularization of folk musical forms as well as a prolific composer of patriotic anthems. Each of these activities bore the imprint of the larger agenda of nation-building that had so galvanized Li's generation of Chinese intellectuals, for all of his efforts promoted national music, a national language, and nationalized educational standards.

How, then, do we reconcile these disparate portraits? Was Li Jinhui an intellectual or a businessman? A nationalist or a sellout? An enlightened advocate of children's music or a shameless huckster selling cheap tunes and decadent spectacles to the benighted masses? Li's biographers in the People's Republic have tended to resort to "stage theory" in order to resolve these sharp contrasts. At a certain point in his trajectory, the "good Li" is driven by financial necessity into the corrupt embrace of the Shanghai culture industry; spiritual pollution and moral decline rapidly ensue, and the "bad Li" is born.[6] The problem with such assessments, of course, is that they make for good morality tales but sloppy history. Li's nationalism and his entrepreneurial efforts usually went hand in hand; the release of the collection of *Family Love Songs* (*Jiating aiqing gequ*, 1930) that most socialist critics identify as the beginning of Li's disastrous downward spiral into commercial depravity was followed by a second collection, *Patriotic Songs* (*Aiguo gequ*, 1932).

In this chapter, I set out to rescue the ambiguity and complexity of Li Jinhui's story from this singularly reductive sort of socialist historiography. Li Jinhui's career is interesting precisely because it straddles the May 4th era nation-building project discussed in relation to music in chapter 1 *and* the emergent world of media technology and mass culture that was the focus of chapter 2.[7] Indeed, I show here that both Li's yellow music and the mass-mediated sing-song girls who performed it were as much a product of nation-building as they were of mass culture.[8] Despite the vehement criticisms leveled at popular music by May 4th musicians like Xiao Youmei, Li's distinctive fusion of jazz and Chinese folk melodies was indirectly inspired by the climate of intellectual and political ferment that the two men experienced on the campus of Beijing University in the early 1920s. Li's musical project, in other words, was as deeply informed by the nationalist agenda of the New Culture Movement as was that of Xiao Youmei. Nor was the often decadent and controversial world of urban popular musical performance and consumption entirely unrelated to May 4th era ideologies of antifeudalism, emancipation for women, and nation-building. The story of Li's pivotal contributions to the development of a new star system in Shanghai originated (and found a potent discourse of legitimation) in these same ideologies.

If these suggestions seem counterintuitive or far-fetched, it is because modern Chinese cultural history has usually been written by way of a neat binary division between elite literary production and the domain of popular media culture. It is my contention here that a careful reconsideration of yellow music—its origins, its development, and the social formations and discourses through which it was articulated and practiced—will prompt us to rethink the ways in which we have come to understand the relationship between "serious" and popular forms of cultural production in the Republican era. Our conceptualization of this problem has heretofore been shaped by an unfortunate tendency to take May 4th commentators on urban popular culture at their word. The writings of canonical literary intellectuals like Lu Xun and Mao Dun position popular cultural forms as the polar opposite of May 4th ideals.[9] If May 4th literature is modern and progressive, popular songs, martial arts movies, and the middlebrow romance fiction of the "Mandarin Ducks and Butterfly" school are necessarily feudal and reactionary. If May 4th-inspired art and literature represent an agenda of humanistic enlightenment and national mobilization, popular culture, at best, signifies little more than capitalistic consumption and, at worst, the political pacification of the masses.

This reductive logic has been reproduced by historians and cultural critics working in modern Chinese studies in the Euro-American context. Part of the problem, of course, is a lack of access to contrary opinions and voices. This quandary is both practical and theoretical. Much of the archival material (be it in the form of texts, films, or other types of ephemera) that might provide a more complex picture has been destroyed by the depredations of time and history, or secreted away by archivists eager to occlude aspects of the record uncongenial to official histories. Even when access to materials has been relatively easy (as in the case of popular literature), however, scholars have relied on May 4th-derived genre categories and narratives of literary history to interpret them.

Perry Link's pioneering and meticulously researched work on the Mandarin Ducks and Butterfly school of popular fiction is a case in point.[10] The Butterfly label is itself a derogatory term assigned to certain strains of urban popular fiction by adherents of critical realism, thus reflecting the efforts of May 4th writers to "appoint themselves as the harbingers of modern literature, and by the same token, relegate their rivals to the traditional camp."[11] Link, in portraying Butterfly fiction as a traditionally styled and ideologically conservative antithesis to the elite "Westernisms" of May 4th fiction, does little to question or dispel the rhetorical and ideological force of the Butterfly label.[12] Instead, his deployment of suspect cultural categories like "old" and "new" literature (if not the literary valuations that accompany such loaded terms) merely echoes the discourse of self-legitimation created by critics like Lu Xun, Mao Dun, and Qu Qiubai in the 1920s and 1930s.

The problem with this approach is that it effectively forecloses other interpretive possibilities. Might Butterfly fiction represent not the expression of a residual (and thus resistant and feudal) traditional consciousness in commodified form, as Link argues, but instead an emergent mode of commercial cultural production characterized by its interactivity with other mass-mediated genres (cinema, picture stories, and the like)? Is the relationship of the "new literature" and the "old" merely antagonistic? Or might there be ways to describe their complicity in the maintenance of a hierarchized literary field?

More recent studies of popular literature, although committed to upsetting the canon and exploring heretofore neglected sectors of the modern Chinese literary field, also have failed to dislodge these binaries. Instead, they have merely inverted them. Despite their disparate critical agendas, for instance, both Rey Chow and Leo Ou-fan Lee have argued that urban popular culture (particularly the popular fiction of women writers like Eileen Chang) represents a space of resistance to the elitist and totalizing narratives of nationhood that permeate the literary discourse of May 4th era intellectuals.[13] In the course of rethinking Link's reading of Butterfly fiction by way of feminist theory and gender studies, Chow pits the "feminized, popular methods of cultural subversion" that she identifies as characteristic of popular fiction and Chang's work against the "official representatives of modern Chinese literature—writers of the May 4th period."[14] For Lee—who is interested in identifying and celebrating writing at the margins of the mainstream—Chang's fiction represents a self-conscious attempt to forge a "decadent" counterdiscourse to May 4th narratives of historical progress and nation-building. Neither critic, however, challenges the boundary that separates discourse from counterdiscourse, margin from center.

This is precisely the boundary that a careful reconsideration of Li's career will productively blur. Li's music and its mode of performance reveal the ways in which discourses of nation-building inform and even enable the explosive growth of popular media culture in the late 1920s and 1930s. Nor is this relationship one-sided. In chapter 4, I discuss the ways in which Li and his sing-song girls become the means through which leftist cultural workers like Li's student and nemesis Nie Er simultaneously critique and appropriate the space of mass-mediated culture (especially popular music and the cinema) for their own ends in the years before 1937.

In pointing out these hidden affinities and discursive complicities, I do not mean to deny the real divergence between these forms of cultural production and the political positions with which they were associated. Indeed, to do so would be to fail to account for the controversies and criticism that dogged Li's work and the complexities of its place within the musical field. There is no doubt that Li's yellow music appealed to different audiences, was consumed and discussed by them in different ways, and evoked different constellations of meaning in its listeners than did either elite efforts to create a national idiom or leftist compositions aimed at popular mobilization. However, it is also important to resist orthodox and reductive readings of popular musical phenomena, to allow for and explore the implications of the curious doubleness of yellow music.

This doubleness (explored in the final section of this chapter) is embedded within the signifier for the music itself. On the surface, the yellowness of the music is a reference to the fleshy, supposedly decadent appeal for which Li's music has so often been condemned. But in its very yellowness, the music is also color-coded, identified as Chinese, and thus subsumed under the racialized hierarchies of colonial modernity. Li's music

—not unlike the fiction of Butterfly authors like Zhang Henshui and Zhou Shoujuan—was consigned by serious musicians to the lowest rung of the evolutionary ladder. The top rungs of the ladder were reserved for European classicism and properly "nationalized" variations thereof; urban folk tunes were seen as reactionary and even lewd in comparison. It was only in the presence of this colonial hierarchy that May 4th musical reformers could criticize Li's music for its "Chinese" lack of Western-style harmony and its affinity with low-class American jazz as opposed to European Romanticism, or that the classically trained leftist musician He Luting would feel compelled to voice his contempt for Li Jinhui in terms of the "degeneracy" of the Chinese people as seen through foreign eyes.

Degeneracy, of course, is in the eye of beholder. What if we were to listen to Li Jinhui's music not through the ears of a representative of the native elite like He Luting, or his strategically imagined and scornful colonizer? For a black American musician like Buck Clayton, Li's brand of Sinified jazz is not "too much different" from American music; despite its use of the pentatonic scale, it still can be transcribed into American-style charts and replayed by American musicians. This very translatability—a chimera in the days when Berlioz in the 1850s or even F. W. Gaisberg at the turn of the twentieth century could hear Chinese music only as incomprehensible noise—is an index of the depth of China's immersion in the global culture of the gramophone as well as the changing status of national music in an age of cultural portability.

LI JINHUI AND THE MAY 4TH ERA

Remembered today primarily for his connection with yellow music, Li Jinhui's youth was typical of many intellectuals in the May 4th era. He was born in 1891 in Hunan province to a wealthy, distinguished, and politically progressive gentry family.[15] Li studied the Confucian classics at home and attended new-style schools in Shaoshan and Xiangtan.[16] As a teenager, he was passionately interested in all forms of regional folk music, as well as Western instruments like the harmonium, and even before he had graduated from the Changsha Normal High School, he was hired as a part-time music instructor. As part of his duties, he led a student choir in singing Japanese-derived school songs that advocated science, national regeneration, and agitation against the Manchu regime. He graduated one year after the Republican revolution in 1911 and moved to Beijing to work as a

secretary in the new National Assembly until its closure in 1914. Return-
ing to Hunan, Li continued to lead school choirs. He also began to compose politically satirical lyrics (based on local folk songs) for the Changsha
newspapers, one of which so incensed a local warlord that Li was physi-
cally assaulted in retribution.

In 1916, Li returned to Beijing just in time for the first salvos of the
New Culture Movement. He taught language and music at four different schools simultaneously, and he also began to immerse himself in the
study of Chinese folk music, spending his nights attending performances
of Peking opera or listening to drum songs at Tianqiao, a traditional entertainment quarter in south Beijing. His studies in traditional and regional
music were further facilitated by a gramophone, referred to at that time
in Beijing as a "talking box" (*hua xiazi*), to which he would listen on rainy
nights. Influenced by his brother, Li Jinxi, a prominent linguist and educator, Li Jinhui also began to write Mandarin language instruction materials
for the classroom. These two interests—folk music and language education—were to inform much of his activity throughout a long and varied
career.

On the eve of the May 4th Movement of 1919, Li (like many of the writers
and intellectuals of his generation) became a faithful reader of new literary journals like *New Youth* (*Xin qingnian*) and the *Weekly Review* (*Meizhou
pinglun*), and he joined the ranks of auditors at the intellectual epicenter
of the movement, Beijing University. He was soon appointed by the university's president, Cai Yuanpei, to head the Hunanese music division of
the school's newly established Institute for the Promotion and Practice of
Music. Li shared with his colleagues at the institute a commitment to "harnessing music as a means to promote the New Culture Movement."[17] He
differed from musicians like Xiao Youmei, however, in his lack of Western
musical training. Li's interests lay primarily in transcribing, playing, and
"improving" the music of the common people (*pingmin yinyue*)—music
that some of his colleagues in the music department (inclined as they were
toward European Romanticism) found vulgar beyond redemption. At one
point, several of his colleagues even refused to print Li's transcriptions of
several Hunanese folk songs in their in-house magazine. A minor dispute,
perhaps, but one that foreshadowed the serious schisms that would develop between Li and the arbiters of proper musical taste at the Shanghai
Conservatory of Music in the 1930s.[18]

These differences notwithstanding, Li Jinhui was very much within the intellectual and political compass of the New Culture Movement of the 1920s. His iconoclastic interest in nonelite music was analogous to Zhou Zuoren's calls for a new vernacular "literature of the common people" (*pingmin wenxue*).[19] His efforts to collect and adapt folk music, moreover, echoed those of Liu Fu's folk song collection movement. This interest led Li to compile several collections of folk songs, children's songs, and nursery rhymes.[20] His willingness to improve the specimens of drum song and opera that he collected along lines suggested by the West finally set him apart from the conservative literati who studied *kunqu* opera and other traditional musical forms as a means of preserving the "national essence." Rather, Li was an adherent of Cai Yuanpei's celebrated dictum advocating "combining what is compatible from both China and West and accommodating every sort of influence."[21]

The name Li chose for the Bright Moon ensemble that he established in 1920 (eventually to become his vehicle for the creation of a new kind of urban popular music) reflected the rhetoric of the New Culture Movement as well. "We raise the banner of a 'music for the common people,' like the bright moon in the sky, shining across the land for all the people to enjoy." To reach the sort of common people whom he had in mind, Li became editor of a newspaper, *Common People's Weekly* (*Pingmin zhoubao*), in 1920, which proselytized the movement by way of new hortatory lyrics set to traditional drum songs.

In 1921 the Ministry of Education acceded to the insistent demands of May 4th intellectuals like Hu Shi and Li's eldest brother, Jinxi, by mandating the use of vernacular (as opposed to classical Chinese) in public schools. Virtually overnight, this change created a huge market for new textbooks. The two giants of commercial publishing in China—Shanghai's Commercial Press (Shangwu yinshuguan) and the China Book Bureau (Zhonghua shuju)—were sympathetic to the agenda of the New Culture Movement and eager to meet this new demand (and cash in on the opportunity that it represented). Li, who had begun to develop his own Mandarin language curricula at Jinxi's behest, was quickly hired as an editor by the China Book Bureau. His language textbook was soon approved by the Ministry of Education and quickly became standard fare for primary school students across the nation.[22]

On the strength of this success, Li was appointed as the principal of the ministry's National Language Institute in Shanghai (Guoyu zhuanxiu xuexiao) in 1922. About the same time, China Books handed him the

Cover art from the first issue of *Little Friend* (*Xiao pengyou*),
April 1922.

editorship of a new weekly children's magazine, *Little Friend*. In his spare
time, Li organized a Bright Moon ensemble in Shanghai to play his own
musical compositions. Unlike its earlier incarnation in Beijing, however,
this group included Western instruments like violin and piano, reflecting
both Li's increasing exposure to Western music in the context of the multiply colonized treaty port of Shanghai and the influence of Cai Yuanpei's
doctrine of cultural cosmopolitanism.

   The convergence of all these activities set the stage for the introduction of yellow music onto China's urban scene. Searching for innovative ways to teach Mandarin and instill children with a healthy dose of antifeudalistic and patriotic feeling, Li started to write songs and short musical dramas for his students to learn and perform.[23] These creations, in turn, were printed in *Little Friend*—which had rapidly become the single bestselling periodical in the country—and distributed nationwide. So overwhelming was reader response that in 1923 one of Li's first children's operas, *The Grape Fairy* (*Putao xianzi*), was published as a mass-market paperback. Within three years the play went through no fewer than twenty-one printings. That same year, Li's Bright Moon Ensemble entered the gramophone record market for the first time, recording five discs to accompany *The Grape Fairy*, along with two other "children's performance songs" (*ertong biaoyan qu*). Li's teenage daughter, Li Minghui, provided the vocals for these records.

The Grape Fairy was just the first of a cascade of children's music—eleven other musical dramas as well as some twenty performance songs—that Li produced in the ensuing years. All of these works were published by China Books Bureau (most went through many print runs), and the majority were accompanied by records sung by Minghui and released by Great China. These records were promoted in the final pages of each play script as a handy reference to how the music ought to sound in performance, but presumably they also served to entertain and edify listeners in schools, homes, and other places where people had gramophones.[24] Significantly, all but two play scripts were published in simplified musical notation (using only numbers to designate the pitch value of each note and thus rendering the transcription of harmony impossible) in order to further broaden their appeal and facilitate performance in schools and homes.

Taken as a whole, Li's children's dramas are imbued with the May 4th spirit of humanist enlightenment, antifeudalism, and nationalism. *The Little Painter* (*Xiao xiao huajia*, 1926), for example, relates the story of a young boy who is forced to study the *Analects* of Confucius rather than develop his talents as a painter. According to Li, the play was inspired by his disgust at the Ministry of Education's insistence that children continue the mandatory study of the Confucian classics, and it was intended as a blow against feudalism in education.[25] While works such as *Three Butterflies* (*San hudie*, 1924), *The Happiness of Spring* (*Chuntian de kuaile*, 1924) and *A Little Lamb Saves His Mother* (*Xiaoyang jiumu*, 1927) strove to inculcate school-

Li Minghui in 1926. From the first edition of Li Jinhui's *Night of Bright Moonlight* (Shanghai: Zhonghua shuju, 1926).

children with a love of beauty and the natural world, they also endorsed moral values such as filial piety, a spirit of cooperation, and a positive work ethic.

The pedagogical agenda of Li's children's music, as Sun Ji'nan notes, was deeply informed by the humanist ideologies of progressive May 4th era educators and was characterized by a concern for providing students with an "education in love" (*ai de jiaoyu*) in all of its multivariate forms: between parents and child, children and animals, or simply between friends.[26] Several of Li's dramas transpose these abstract notions of uni-

（左）紅蝴蝶 登慧珍 女士　　（右）黄蝴蝶 李麗貞 女士
（中）白蝴蝶 林籠珠 女士

Shanghai schoolchildren performing Li's "Three Butterflies" (San hudie), 1926. From Li Jinhui, *Three Butterflies* (Shanghai: Zhonghua shuju, 1926).

versal love onto the contemporary political scene in order to criticize prevailing trends and spur along the implementation of a humanistic political regime in China. *The Final Victory* (*Zuihou de shengli*, 1926) was inspired by the KMT's Northern Expedition and uses martial music and marches to convey a message of "anti-imperialism, the elimination of warlordism, and the implementation of democracy."[27] *Fairy Sister* (*Shenxian meimei*, 1925) was a dramatic representation of Sun Yat-sen's "Three People's Principles," in which a young girl leads three little children ("the masses") to victory against enemies on land (a tiger), at sea (a crocodile), and in the air (a hawk).

Li's lyrics to these dramas mated standard Mandarin with rhythmic prosody to create an effect reminiscent of nursery rhymes. And appropriately enough for a man whose work was grounded in the collection of folk songs and children's rhymes, some of Li's songs survive as folklore today. One example from "Fairy Sister," still known by children throughout China, is a rhyme from a song called "A Tiger at the Door" (Laohu jiaomen, 1920): "Child, be good, good / Open the door like you should, should / Open up quick / I want to come in."[28] The musical accompaniment to tunes like these was similarly stripped down to basics. Because Li's plays were published in simplified notation in order to reach the broadest possible audience (not just the tiny minority of instructors and students conversant with European notation), they necessarily stressed melodic content as opposed to complex harmonies. Stylistically, these songs mirrored the experiments of the Bright Moon Ensemble, fusing pianos, violins, and guitars with Chinese (and, on occasion, European) melodic material.[29] Vocal accompaniment—at least on Li Minghui's recorded renditions of the songs for Great China Records and Pathé—was typically high-pitched and childish in tone.

GENDER AND PERFORMANCE

This brief description of the thematic and musical content of these children's dramas, however, does little to account for the passions they aroused in the late 1920s and 1930s. Those passions were often volcanic. Indeed, the vehemence with which some of Li's contemporaries savaged his work seems excessive, even inexplicable, to today's sensibilities. "Li Jinhui's style of music has filled our primary schools, besmirching and corrupting the purity of our students' souls and planting evil seeds among the people. Although [his songs] are not music at all, and lack any of the value inherent in music, they have still managed to monopolize the masses, just as if the people are unaware that there is such a thing as great music, and know only these salacious and decadent sounds. . . ."[30]

What is at stake here? To what do we attribute both the tone of the polemic and the ability of this new musical form to "monopolize the masses"? One would be hard-pressed to find either decadence or sexually suggestive content in Li Jinhui's dramas, and it is difficult to see how a story about a little lamb rescuing its mother (for instance) might corrupt a child's soul. Nor is there anything inherently salacious about the melodic profiles of his songs.[31] For this reason, it is essential that we examine not the play scripts and music per se, but the manner in which they were performed.

While it would be difficult, if not impossible, to reconstruct exactly what these performances looked, sounded, and felt like to their audiences, we can piece together a fragmentary notion from existing photographic and textual evidence.[32] Perhaps most striking, these dramas were performed almost entirely by schoolgirls ranging in age from seven to seventeen. In existing photographs of Li's own dramatic troupe as well as troupes from other schools, the performers are often arrayed in rows, clad in whimsical costumes that leave their arms and legs unencumbered.[33] This focus on female performers—and indeed Li's emphasis on "song and dance drama" (*gewuju*) itself—reflects the direct influence of Japan's famous Takarazuka Song and Dance Troupe. Takarazuka was founded in 1914 as a commercial venture in Tokyo that overturned the traditional gender arrangements of Kabuki theater, replacing its all-male casts with young female performers.[34] Li attended a Takarazuka performance in Shanghai as early as 1920, and he acknowledged that the experience "inspired" the creation of his first children's dramas and his emphasis on the beauty and grace of young females.[35] Takarazuka was not the only kind of commercial performance culture that left its mark on Li's new form; the chorus lines and leg kicks he integrated into his choreography as the 1920s wore on are clearly reminiscent of vaudeville revues, Broadway musicals, and the Hollywood films through which they were seen and disseminated in China's urban centers and colonial treaty ports.

These innovations alone account for much of the critical ire directed against Li's work in the 1920s and 1930s. It is difficult from our historical vantage point to understand the shock value that these sorts of performance possessed for audiences in Li Jinhui's time. Katharine Hui-ling Chou, in a brilliant article on performance and gender in the May 4th period, relates a fascinating anecdote that serves as a potent reminder of the political and cultural context in which Li's dramatic experiments unfolded.[36] In 1919, the eminent scholar and May 4th activist Hu Shi published a play called *Till Death Do Us Part* (*Zhongshen dashi*, 1919) in *New Youth*. A loose adaptation of Ibsen's *A Doll's House*, the drama (like many others of its era) told the story of a "new woman" who revolts against an outmoded system of patriarchal oppression (represented by traditional familial structures and arranged marriages) in pursuit of liberty and love. As Chou points out, however, when the play was first performed on stage, this courageous "new woman" was played not by a woman, but a cross-dressed man! This sort of casting was typical of traditional operatic forms and the New Drama of the early twentieth century alike. It was not until 1923 that May 4th era dramatists like Hong Shen, Tian Han, and others overcame traditional restrictions against the appearance of women on stage and thus instituted a new representational regime predicated on realist aesthetics.[37]

Viewed in this light, Li Jinhui's appropriation of the Takarazuka aesthetic begins to seem positively avant-garde. This forgotten affinity between Li's children's operas and the more celebrated and "serious" proponents of the spoken drama movement was grounded in collaborative activity. Li's first dramatic efforts were staged with the help of an organization called the Shanghai Experimental Theater Group (Shanghai shiyan jushe).[38] As an organization dedicated to the promotion of socially conscious spoken drama, the group pioneered the use of female actresses taking on female roles on stage. And as Li Jinhui relates in his memoirs, it was in fact his own daughter, Li Minghui, who was the first to break the taboo as the female lead of a Shanghai Experimental Theater production staged in Hangzhou in 1923. The production—an exposé of unethical business practices in the pharmaceutical industry called *Conscience* (*Liangxin*)—was quickly banned by local police because "the troupe's males and females perform together, thus corrupting public morality."[39] This sort of resistance to women appearing on stage was the rule rather than the exception throughout the 1920s. Tian Han's celebrated dramatic troupe, the South China Society (Nanguo she), with whom Li Jinhui briefly collaborated during the mid-twenties, also met with frequent criticism and interdiction for the same reason during its tour of southeast China as late as 1927.[40]

Unlike such contemporaries as Tian Han, Li was unable to justify his controversial use of female performers in terms of heightened realism (because his plays were essentially fairy tales) or the emancipation of the "new woman" (since his performers were still children and young girls). Instead, Li's rhetoric emphasizes the pedagogical utility of the plays, while at the same time echoing some of the grander humanist themes of the New Culture Movement, stressing the emancipation of the body beautiful from the shackles of feudal discipline. Wang Renmei, one of the many film actresses and singers of the 1930s whose career in the culture industry began under Li's tutelage, sheds interesting light on this agenda (and the resistance it engendered).

> In the Shanghai of the time, feudal power was deeply entrenched, and young girls wore braids and long gowns and stockings. In the eyes of these conservatives, it was shocking enough that women should appear on

screen. When Minghui [Li Jinhui's daughter and a member of the troupe] appeared on stage with a bob and bare feet, dancing and singing like a free and unfettered little bird, they must have thought the end of the world had come.[41]

For others, of course, this sort of performance signaled the advent of a new world of modernity and liberty. Writing in 1930, the liberal writer and art critic Zhu Yingpeng praises Li's dramas for the unprecedented way in which they "give free expression to the vigor, health, and beauty of the human form." [42] In some of Li's own writings, this emancipation of the body becomes at the same time a contribution to China's nation-building effort. This argument is clearest in Li's introduction to the drama *Three Butterflies*. In the course of defending his use of the Takarazuka aesthetic, Li proposes that "just as butterflies represent the glory of insectdom, beautiful people represent the cream of humanity." [43] By the same logic:

China's most beautiful people represent the glory of the Chinese race . . . but our custom is to look down on "pretty boys and girls," which is a "great shame for the Chinese nation"! [This distrust of beauty] could even lead Chinese culture and the Chinese essence into degeneracy, so I ask you all to take care. Think about it . . . if we look at the press and all kinds of performances in the West, we can see how very much the citizens of the civilized nations of Europe respect, protect, and actively appreciate beautiful people . . . which is why these brave, honest peoples are so full of vitality and life and never despair; because they love the beautiful and the good, they strive to make their surroundings beautiful and good, and are never simply content to let their days slide by apathetically. This is why they grow smarter, more capable, and more powerful day by day! [44]

As outlandish as Li's rhetoric may seem, it was by no means unusual in an intellectual climate in which China's national weakness vis-à-vis Japan and the West was often attributed in part to the perceived "physical weakness" and "poor hygiene" of its citizens, and vocal advocates of eugenics extolled their "science" as a viable means of national self-strengthening.[45] This sort of eugenicist argument—which shares with much May 4th cultural criticism a fervent belief in Social Darwinism—is echoed in a 1930 article in Li's support by one Bi Fen. Arguing that thousands of years of misguided aesthetic ideals have resulted in the "emaciation" of the figures of Chinese women, Bi Fen praises song-and-dance troupes as a means to buck the evolutionary trend and thus foster development of full, vigorous bodies that can approximate "the ideal type for modern young females" in China.[46] The display of feminine youth and physicality that was so much a part of Li's dramatic idiom, then, dovetailed with May 4th era discourses of national regeneration. Writing in 1931, the progressive film director Sun Yu praises the girls of Li's troupe for embodying just such an ideal. He proclaims, after having seen one of their performances: "Let us rise together and loudly proclaim the rejuvenation (*qingchun hua*) of the Chinese people!"[47]

LI JINHUI AND URBAN MEDIA CULTURE

It was, in turn, precisely this sort of antifeudal and nationalist rhetoric which authorized the emergence of a new media culture predicated on the circulation and consumption of the voices, images, and personal lives of mass-mediated female performers. As Chou argues in discussing spoken drama in the May 4th era: modernity and voyeurism came hand in hand.[48] For at the very moment in which female performers began to appear onstage (thus enacting a form of cultural modernity), they entered the public realm as objects on display. The curiosity and controversy surrounding their appearances, moreover, fueled their transformation by the popular press into objects of desire, speculation, and passionate ideological debate.

Li Jinhui and his daughter, Li Minghui, played a crucial role in this process of mediatization and commercialization. The series of training institutes and song and dance troupes that Li established in the late 1920s produced a talented group of stars who would go on to dominate Shanghai's recording and film industries for more than two decades. More important, Li's pioneering work—coupled with the advent and explosive growth of new technologies like sound film and wireless broadcasting—helped to establish this star system in the first place. Sadly, the circulation of Li's music within these new media circuits would destroy both his reputation and his career.

Li unwittingly set this process of professionalization in motion by providing an institutional funnel through which talented youngsters would graduate from his children's dramas into the wider world of the musical cinema. Financially and otherwise buoyed by the nationwide popularity of his work, Li decided in 1927 to found the China Song and Dance Institute (Zhonghua gewu zhuanmen xuexiao) in Shanghai to promote his new art form and train (primarily female) talent in music, dance, and drama. The school, funded with proceeds from Li's book royalties, was a non-profit organization. Li charged no tuition. Many of his recruits were either orphans, whom Li had essentially adopted as his own, or poor children enrolled by parents drawn by the free tuition, or artistically inclined youths fleeing from restrictive family backgrounds. The makeup of the student body was unsurprising in this respect. Musicians and actresses had traditionally been stigmatized, and the entertainment industry was usually seen as tawdry and shameful business in which children of well-heeled families by no means could be allowed to participate. This was especially true of daughters, for in the popular discourse of the day, there was only a very fine line between "selling songs" (*maichang*) and selling sexual services. The teachers were drawn from the ranks of the Shanghai Experimental Theater Group and included several members of Li's own family, the most notable of whom was Li Jinguang (who would go on to serve as the musical director for Pathé Records throughout the late 1930s and 1940s). Aside from classroom instruction, the school organized a number of benefit performances for other schools and civic organizations. The philanthropic agenda and progressive pedigree of the school's staff, in short, were beyond question.

Li Minghui's growing reputation as an actress, recording artist, and child movie star increasingly brought this venture into the public eye.[49] Minghui's fame, as Wang Renmei notes, directly resulted from her position at the "front lines of the New Culture Movement: . . . the more they [conservative critics] loudly and cruelly cursed her [public appearances], the more youth who had been influenced by the New Culture Movement supported her. . . ."[50] Her pioneering debut with the Experimental Theater in 1923 resulted in an invitation to appear in a silent film in 1924. One year later, at age sixteen, she won her first title role in a silent picture, *The Little Factory Boss* (*Xiao changzhu*, 1925). By 1927, she had starred in as many as nine silent films. Her fame was further enhanced by the many recordings of Li's compositions that she made for Great China and Pathé Records throughout the 1920s. Li parlayed Minghui's fame into greater exposure for the school's brand of musical drama—his students often performed before screenings of Minghui's films, and the association meant that the school was invited to perform for audiences in cities as far afield as Nanjing and Nantong.

The high profile of the school soon led to its undoing. Faced with financial difficulties and political pressure from both the newly victorious KMT and the colonial authorities, Li was forced to shut down after just one year.[51] Unfazed, he established a second training institute (funded by a friend in the business world) in 1928 called the Beauty School for Girls (Meimei nüxiao). This new venture was not, of course, a cosmetic institute—its name presumably reflected both Li's emphasis on "aesthetic education" and the beauty of the female form—but rather a means of retaining fifty students from the original school as well as the chrysalis through which Li hoped to carry out a new and ambitious project—a tour of Southeast Asia.

This plan was realized in just three months, when the staff and students of the school, reconstituted as the China Song and Dance Troupe (Zhonghua gewutuan), sailed for Hong Kong in May 1928. Funded by overseas Chinese capital, the tour was undertaken for both patriotic and commercial purposes. Li hoped to make enough money to reestablish his school on a firm financial footing. At the same time, he saw this series of performances in colonial Southeast Asia as a further opportunity to promote a national language and national consciousness among overseas Chinese audiences.[52] By all accounts, this work of patriotic propaganda was achieved despite the interference of colonial authorities in Hong Kong, Singapore, Malaysia, Siam (Thailand), and the Dutch East Indies (Indonesia). Indeed (as several participants have noted in their memoirs), one of the tour's proudest moments came when British members of the audience in Hong Kong were compelled to stand up along with the rest of the Chinese spectators as the troupe performed "In Memory of the Prime Minister" (Zongli jinian ge), a musical tribute to the great nationalist and Chinese republican Sun Yat-sen.[53]

Perhaps more significant was the way in which the year-long tour opened new transnational networks for the distribution of pan-Chinese popular culture. Li's itinerary overlapped with, and undoubtedly helped to spur development of, the regional distribution channels in the process of being established by Pathé Records and its competitors in Shanghai. Li's comments regarding a recording session that he undertook just months before he embarked for Southeast Asia are instructive in this regard. This particular set of more than ten discs for Great China Records included children's songs, selections from his operas, and two new love songs, all performed by Li Minghui and a group known as the Eight Sages of the

Recording Studio (guanyin baxian). These selections "sold extremely well indeed, and even reached Southeast Asia, which gave us as much free promotion for our upcoming tour as we could ever have wanted, even before we actually left the country."[54]

The path Li's records (and subsequently Li himself) blazed across Southeast Asia, of course, was circumscribed by older colonial trade routes and punctuated by the commercial and administrative centers (Hong Kong, Singapore, Batavia, and Bangkok) where overseas Chinese immigrants tended to cluster. But the opening of these paths for the circulation of commercial culture was a boon not only for colonial operations like Pathé-EMI, but also for the domestically owned culture industry. Li's promotion of Mandarin-speaking popular cultural forms helped clear the way for the success of talking pictures produced in Shanghai in these overseas markets. That these films featured singers and actresses who had first become known to audiences through their participation in Li's troupe surely was a factor in their success.

Despite all of these elements, the tour was not a financial success. The troupe disbanded in 1929, and Li found himself stranded in Singapore with Minghui and his new wife, Xu Lai (herself a performer from the troupe). Buoyed by news from Shanghai of the success of several love songs he had written, including the classic tune "Drizzle" (Maomao yu), for the urban sheet music market, Li turned in earnest to the composition of love songs. He soon sold a collection of twenty-five *Family Love Songs* to a Shanghai publisher to fund his return to Shanghai and the reconstitution of the troupe.[55]

These songs represented a new creative direction for Li Jinhui. Inspired by American jazz records, the music of George Gershwin, and Chinese folk melodies, they included classics of yellow music like "Express Train" (Tebie kuaiche) and "Darling, I Love You" (Meimei wo ai ni). The lyrics were cobbled together from a variety of different sources, including Tang dynasty love poems, Chinese and European folk songs, and the romantic clichés of Tin Pan Alley. Many of the songs reflected the humanist agenda of "sentimental education" discussed in the context of his children's songs; others strike notes of urbane satire. "Express Train," for example, is a deft parody of love at first sight in which a couple marries just minutes after having met, while another immensely popular tune, "Peach Blossom River" (Taohua jiang), tells the story of a man who stays true to his love despite temptation. The book was a runaway bestseller, and the dissemination of the sheet music in simplified notation further facilitated the growing popularity of Li's compositions throughout urban China.

For mainland Chinese historians, Li's headlong tumble down the slippery slope of commercial degradation began at precisely this point in his trajectory. This sort of historiography, of course, presents us with a narrative of one man's fall from socialist grace; the originary purity and innocence of Li's children's music is besmirched by his involvement with the tawdry world of capitalist commodity culture. The problem with such a narrative, of course, is that it radically impoverishes our understanding of Li Jinhui's activities both before and after his "fall," thus eliding the ways in which Li's music (and Minghui's recordings) were implicated with the growth of commercial media culture. Li's children's songs, in other words, were just as much commodities competing in the record market as his later compositions for adults. Nor does the lyrical content of these love songs suggest a qualitative break with his earlier thematic preoccupations and ideological positions. Finally, it should be noted that Li continued to work actively to promote patriotic music and education for the common people well after producing this batch of love songs in 1930.

What did change at this point was the context in which these songs were performed. Li's music no longer was exclusively for children. Instead, because of the commercial availability of sheet music and gramophone records, it was increasingly performed in nightclubs, cabarets, and cafés, as well as in the domestic parlors of the urban petit bourgeois. One effect of the music entering wider commercial and social circulation was a proliferation of the meanings that audiences and commentators might attach to Li's texts. Popular musical meaning is contextual; the same text (be it a children's song, a patriotic anthem, or a love song) said dramatically different things when performed by a child in a school auditorium or by a young woman to a group of paying customers in a theater. As these performative contexts multiplied, and the students who performed his music began to transform themselves into teenage media stars, Li's work was increasingly characterized (and dogged) by just this sort of ambiguity, as indicated by this hostile commentary, printed in 1936, on the entrance of Li's idiom into wider commercial circulation:

Musical drama began six or seven years ago with the advent of Li Jinhui's plays "The Grape Fairy," "Night of Bright Moonlight" [Yueming zhi ye], and "The Magpie and the Child" [Maque yu xiaohai]. These little plays were originally intended for small children and primary school students. They were fairy tales, easy to act out and easy to sing, and thus suitable for performance by children. But as time went on, when every school began to arrange shows and use "big girls" of seventeen or eighteen to perform these children's plays, what resulted was forced, unnaturally flirtatious, and unbearably maudlin. Not a shred of the original innocence was left. What replaced it was a frighteningly lewd sort of vulgarity. Still later, once the girls who had appeared in these dramas got out of school, other people began to organize "song-and-dance troupes" for them to perform in front of the public, singing songs full of salacious and decadent lyrics and exposing their thighs just to attract paying customers. These people claim that they are promoting art, but all they really do is seduce young people for profit.[56]

The first of these song-and-dance troupes was established by Li upon his return to Shanghai in 1930 and represented an effort to continue (and fund) his educational mission. To recruit new Mandarin-speaking talent, he soon moved his reconstituted Bright Moon Song and Dance Troupe (Mingyue gewutuan) to Beijing (which was then known as Beiping). After a period of training and consolidation, the troupe embarked on a tour of North China and the Northeast, performing for receptive audiences at theaters and universities in Tianjin, Beijing, Shenyang, and elsewhere.[57] The eclectic format of these performances reflected the diversity of settings where the troupe performed. Each show was divided into three sections: children's music performed by the youngest members of the troupe preceded love songs performed solo by each of the four oldest girls: Wang Renmei, Li Lili, Xue Lingxian, and Hu Qie. The show culminated in choral renditions of Li's hortatory school songs and patriotic anthems. The tour was covered extensively in local newspapers and national publications.[58] This media exposure, coupled with three successful new recordings of Li's love songs released by RCA-Victor, catapulted the troupe to fame.[59] And perhaps unsurprisingly, the four young women who sang these songs increasingly became the focus of both audience attention and the media, who anointed them as the "four sky kings" (*sida tian wang*).[60]

This exposure brought further opportunities in the burgeoning urban media culture industry—opportunities that Li Jinhui, responsible for the livelihood of nearly fifty troupe members and eager to establish a new school, was only too happy to exploit. In 1931, Great China Records signed an exclusive contact with the troupe to record no less than a hundred new records over the course of six months. When news of the deal leaked out, representatives of the two multinationals (cognizant of the success of the three love songs recently released by RCA-Victor) approached Li in an effort to outbid Great China. This bidding war resulted in a flood of records (encompassing all aspects of Li's oeuvre) from Great China, Pathé's subsidiary label Odeon, and RCA-Victor. The popularity of these records inspired a raft of imitators, and Li's brand of Sinified jazz quickly became a staple in dance halls, nightclubs, and cabarets in Shanghai and other urban centers throughout Southeast Asia.

SING-SONG GIRLS AND "MASS ORNAMENTS"

Li Jinhui's growing popularity coincided with a period of explosive growth for Shanghai's wireless broadcasting industry. In 1931 and 1932 alone, some thirty new radio stations were established in the metropolitan Shanghai area.[61] A number of song-and-dance troupes, loosely modeled on Li's Bright Moon Song and Dance Troupe and made up of young female crooners backed by male musicians, quickly began to cater to this new market. The most popular groups, such as the Plum Blossom Song and Dance Troupe (Meihua gewutuan), the Hibiscus Troupe (Furong tuan), and the Shanghai Society (Shanghai she), often performed live on as many as six different stations each day, helping to attract listeners and fill airtime between advertisements.[62] By 1935, according to an item printed in a Shanghai entertainment weekly, *Variety* (*Yule zhoubao*), no fewer than twenty-six such spin-off troupes were singing over the airwaves.[63] Many musicians and singers filling the ranks of these troupes had graduated from Li's troupe. Others were inspired by the example of stars like Li Minghui and the "four sky kings" to try their luck in the broadcasting field.

The Bright Moon troupe itself was soon eclipsed by a second new media technology: talking pictures.[64] With the introduction of sound technology, music and the motion pictures were linked in a productive symbiotic relationship. Obligatory screen songs helped to promote the pictures, while the films themselves helped to sell records of the songs. The trend was augmented by a wave of new musicals produced by Hollywood's dream factories and shown on Chinese screens, as testified to by a contemporary journalistic account.

It was [Maurice Chevalier and Jeanette MacDonald's 1929 hit] *The Love Parade* that made Chinese film producers realize the magnetic power of theme songs. For every film they now insert a theme song, although the picture itself may be a silent one. . . . Secondary school and college students throng to theatres where "musical extravaganzas" are billed. They like Bing Crosby, Dick Powell, and George Raft. They like tuneful songs and snappy dance steps. Chinese who cannot speak English can nevertheless enjoy a musical comedy, even though the plot may be more vague, if possible, than it is to those who understand the language. . . .[65]

In 1931, the Lianhua Film Studio (United Photoplay) annexed the Bright Moon Song and Dance Troupe as a means of competing with this tide and securing an in-house supplier of Chinese language screen songs and dance numbers for its talking pictures. The troupe soon embarked on a new program of recruitment and training. These efforts yielded two young people who would figure prominently in the unfolding of Chinese popular music history: a neophyte musician from Yunnan province, Nie Shouxin and a talented orphan, Zhou Xiaohong. Nie Shouxin would lead a musical and filmic insurrection against Li Jinhui's brand of popular music following Japan's 1932 attack on Shanghai's Zhabei District in his incarnation as Nie Er. Zhou Xiaohong—renamed Zhou Xuan (a play on a set phrase meaning "skirmish with the enemy") by none other than Li Jinhui as a gesture of resistance to the Japanese—would go on to stardom as a modern sing-song girl.

With these new members and in its new incarnation as the Lianhua Song and Dance Team (Lianhua gewuban), the troupe starred in a musical production called *Twin Stars of the Silver Screen* (*Yinhan shuangxing*), performing a title song written by Li Jinhui called "Twin Star Theme" (Shuangxing qu), as well as one of his children's performance pieces, "Work Hard" (Nuli). The film remained well within the domain of nationalist and May 4th humanist ideals and was promoted as such in Lianhua's house journal, *Film Magazine* (*Yingxi zazhi*): "Starring the Lianhua Team's musical star Li Lili and ten other dancers in military outfits and jackboots complemented with shiny swords, the film inspires us to work hard and make progress, spurring on our will to struggle into the future. This is truly a musical that suits the needs of our times."[66] Even more interestingly, the film (largely ignored by music historians like Wang Yuhe, whose work de-

"All kinds of performances": The Lianhua Song and Dance
Team in 1931. From *Film Magazine* (*Yingxi zazhi*), July 1931.

pends on drawing a rigid line between serious, May 4th-derived music
and degraded commercial music) featured nondiegetic music composed
by none other than the president of the Shanghai Conservatory, Xiao Youmei. Even within the film itself, this line is repeatedly blurred. The Lianhua Team's dance routine is followed by a rather provocative "Egyptian
dance" performed by the female lead, Violet Wong, on a set that mixes

faux-Egyptian and art deco decorative motifs in an obvious nod to the fascination with Egypt that suffused the cinematic production and popular imagination of the United States and Europe in the wake of the discovery of the tomb of Tutankhamen in 1923. This promiscuous dialogue with globally circulating trends in popular culture is further reflected by a scene in which the protagonists, both stars in the stable of the same socially responsible film studio, flirt their way across a miniature golf course landscaped to resemble a pastiche of famous Chinese scenic spots, including a pagoda, serpentine bridges, and what appears to be a tiny replica of Hangzhou's West Lake.

The success of this production was followed by a botched attempt to film color shorts of Li's performance pieces.[67] A brief collaboration with another film studio, Tianyi (Unique Photoplay), produced a second box-office flop, the color musical *Poems on a Plantain Leaf* (*Bajiao ye shang shi*). Despite these setbacks, Li would continue to compose music for this new medium throughout the rest of his career. Indeed, Li wrote three screen songs for one of China's first musical talkies, *Romance at the Dancehall* (*Wuchang chunse*, 1931).[68] In a sense, this film represented the creation of a new media loop—the sort of urban milieu in which Li's yellow music had first gained popularity became the object of filmic representation in movies about the lives of sing-song girls who performed it. The screen songs from the movie, in turn, were published in collections of sheet music and film magazines, made into gramophone records, broadcast, and ultimately emulated by sing-song girls in the dance halls.

This media loop, in turn, was fundamental to the emergence of a star system in Shanghai's commercial media culture. The growth of the broadcasting industry, the availability of gramophone records, and the popularity of sound films all ensured that Li's music could move out of schools and theaters and into public and private social spaces: cinemas, stores, street corners, and homes. These new spaces, of course, allowed for the creation of larger and more heterogeneous audiences. To keep these new consumers informed, a host of movie magazines, celebrity pictorials, and daily gossip tabloids known as "mosquito papers" began to be published as guides to this new consumer culture.[69] And just as in Hollywood, part of the business of these publications was to manufacture, organize, and channel consumer desires through the creation of stars. This resulted, of course, in institutionalizing just the sort of voyeurism that Chou identifies as the underside of a May 4th representational regime which required (for the sake of modernity and emancipation) that women display themselves on stage.

Just how these publications tend to channel desire toward fetishized (usually female) star images is a question I cannot answer here in anything more than a piecemeal way. One particularly illuminating example of such fetishized images was a monthly magazine called *Pop Star Pictorial* (*Gexing huabao*), first published in March 1935. Each of the three issues that I have been able to locate follows a similar format. The face of an established star (Zhou Xuan, Bai Hong, and Xu Lai, respectively, all graduates of Li's Bright Moon Song and Dance Troupe) adorns the front cover. Sandwiched between pages of gossip, brief star profiles, information on radio programming, and dance hall advertisements, are photographs of members of Shanghai's various song-and-dance troupes in poses typical of the day: lounging in bathing suits at the municipal pool or modeling stylish outfits in the park.[70] As the editor makes clear in the premier issue, these photos are meant to serve a specific purpose. All too often, he laments, listeners to wireless broadcasts "can't tell the different stars apart."[71]

The magazine, then, exists to fill in this gap, to offer these (heretofore invisible) women up to the gaze of the consumer.[72] This process of individualized consumption is furthered by articles in which each singer's voice is characterized in terms of tastes (sweet, sour, salty, etc.) or rated in terms of her looks.[73] Readers also are invited to identify uncaptioned photographs of faces to test their knowledge of the stars. This sort of fetishization was pervasive at the time. Even in *Art Sound* (*Yisheng*), a serious monthly devoted to film and music and edited by leftist musicians Ren Guang and his wife An E, a spread shows readers cropped pictures of various body parts (feet, legs, hands, and eyes), and they are asked to identify the star to whom they belong.[74] A final and highly significant aspect of this process took the form of popularity contests in which readers of periodicals like *Pop Star Pictorial* and *Nightly News Magazine* (*Da wanbao fukan*) were asked to send in ballots ranking their favorite sing-song girls.[75] The popularity of these sing-song girls can be gauged by reader response to the first of these contests (sponsored by the *Nightly News*), which resulted in a flood of more than 70,000 ballots!

These individual performers shared the stage and screen in the 1930s with a phenomenon that the Weimar era film critic Siegfried Kracauer dubbed "mass ornament": formations of dancing chorus girls and female athletes arranged in precise geometrical arrays.[76] Best exemplified by the kaleidoscopic choreographic wizardry of Busby Berkeley's depression era musicals for Warner Bros., this form made its way to China by means of Hollywood films screened in Shanghai and other Chinese cities and was quickly taken up by local studios.[77] The first months of 1934 alone brought several musicals featuring elaborate, Berkeleyesque production numbers, including *A Fairy on Earth* (*Renjian xianzi*, with music composed by Li Jinhui), and *The Health and Beauty Movement* (*Jianmei yundong*).[78] Unsurprisingly, the personnel for these films was drawn largely from the Bright Moon and other song-and-dance troupes. The association between these individual and collective displays of female bodies became a principal ground on which critics of all ideological persuasions attacked Li's music. But at the same time that leftist musicians battled the new culture of consumption with which Li had increasingly become associated, they also appropriated many of its techniques. Mass ornaments gave way to mobilized masses, while sing-song stars like Zhou Xuan became mass-mediated emblems for the plight of an embattled nation.

THE DOUBLENESS OF YELLOW MUSIC

By 1934, Li Jinhui's own star had been eclipsed by the extraordinary growth of the star system he had helped to create. Although he continued to compose and record a staggering number of jazz tunes and screen songs, his efforts to put a new, reconstituted Bright Moon Society on firm financial footing fell victim to the exodus of his brightest pupils to more lucrative positions in the broadcasting and motion picture industries.[79] Li's children had grown up, and he turned increasingly toward composing film music, writing music textbooks for primary school students, and experimenting with the fusion of Chinese folk music and big band jazz.

This last activity perhaps best evinces the ideological (and semantic) doubleness of yellow music, its capacity to signify both pornography and racial identity. In 1935, Li was asked to organize a band for the dance hall at the Yangtze River Hotel by the notorious gangster (and erstwhile civic leader) Du Yuesheng. Du requested, and Li agreed, that the band be composed entirely of Chinese musicians—an unprecedented move when most bands were either imported from the United States (as with Buck Clayton's Harlem Gentlemen), or the Philippines, or were made up of White Russian émigrés. Indeed, in order to underscore the Chineseness of the band, Li went so far as to hire only "tall, Northern Chinese [musicians] so they wouldn't be mistaken for Filipinos."[80] The group, which Li called the Clear Wind Dance Band (Qingfeng wuyue dui), had a repertoire consisting of jazzy versions of Chinese folk songs combined with the latest dance tunes and screen songs from the United States.[81]

This patriotic gesture, of course, unfolded in the flashy and fleshy world of urban nightlife in the colonial metropolis, a world replete with taxi dancers, hostesses, and sing-song girls. And it is this off-color milieu—as well as the mass-mediated consumption of sing-song girls and mass ornaments—that allowed Li's critics (regardless of their particular political orientation) to label his music pornographic. What I want to argue in this final section, however, is that the yellowness to which critics objected was as much racial as sexual. In other words, the problem was not so much the pornographic quality of this music, but its Chineseness (and perhaps its blackness as well).

In chapter 1, it was argued that many elite May 4th era musicians (and particularly those affiliated with Xiao Youmei's Shanghai Conservatory) shared an agonistic relationship to Chinese and popular forms. This antagonism, of course, derived in part from their ideological and symbolic investment in European classical idioms, an investment legitimated by the sort of cultural Darwinism so characteristic of the May 4th era. In the works of Xiao Youmei and others, Chinese music was relegated to the bottom of an evolutionary ladder presided over by the legendary composers of European (and particularly German) Romanticism: Beethoven, Berlioz, Brahms, Schubert, Wagner. These convictions were further informed by a commitment to the creation of a new national idiom, one that would ideally be brought about by retooling carefully selected elements of indigenous musical tradition along European lines.

That Li's music—a fusion of Chinese folk, Tin Pan Alley pop, and African American jazz—raised the hackles of this elite is hardly a surprise. The rhetoric with which they expressed their outrage, however, deserves our attention. An acrimonious 1929 polemic, "After Writing 'On Lewd Music,'" by one Chang Ping (a pen name) is a good place to start, precisely because it conflates the putative "obscenity" of Li's music with its ethnic identity—its Chineseness.[82] For Chang Ping, the "lewdness" of Li's music has nothing to do with the lyrics of his songs or the context in which they were performed. Instead, he argues that, "even if you set some revolutionary words to a lewd pentatonic melody, you will never be able to completely hide its basic obscenity."[83] Chang Ping's attack on the educational value of Li's children's music continues in a similar vein: "Because urban folk tunes [*xiaodiao*] are off-color, they are not suitable for molding the character of young children, and since folk music is 'primitive music' composed with the pentatonic scale, all they are really good for is amusing the silk spinning ladies who absently hum them on the factory floor, certainly not as educational materials! But Li Jinhui's children's operas are mostly made up of these same tunes. . . ."[84]

This evolutionary assumption—European music is advanced and Chinese music primitive—is played out over and over again in this and other criticisms castigating Li for his lack of Western training and his failure to grasp or incorporate European classical harmonies into his music. Thus, Chang Ping criticizes Li for publishing his operas in simplified notation because of the way in which the system precludes the representation of harmonic changes. A similar controversy raged over Li's rough-and-ready instructional techniques in the various institutes and song-and-dance troupes that he presided over throughout the 1920s and early 1930s. As Wang Renmei relates:

> You ask what the Li-style instrumental technique was all about? Simply put, Teacher Li used simplified notation instead of European notation, playing the melody with his right hand, and the harmonic support with his left. This obviously wasn't the right way to play piano, and you could never get very good playing like that. I heard that one female piano teacher saw him play and fled the room laughing and crying at the same time. A lot of other musicians thought Li was "a heretic" and a "charlatan."[85]

The name-calling is attributable in part to sheer snobbery. Chang Ping, for instance, is openly scornful of Li's lack of advanced musical training and his "vulgar" emphasis on plebeianizing his music.[86]

Chang Ping's distaste for the music of the common folk, of course, is in keeping with colonial hierarchies that privilege elite European forms of musical knowledge and practice over all others, including gramophonic imports from the United States, like jazz (which was, in Xiao Youmei's estimation, "a bad form of Western music").[87] In the popular discourse of the Republican era, jazz was racialized (and thus assigned to the lowest level of an evolutionary hierarchy dominated by European cultural forms) in much the same manner as were Chinese folk tunes. The following characterization of the form, printed in the influential monthly journal *Eastern Miscellany* (*Dongfang zazhi*), is a good example of this process.

"Jazz! Jazz! A freak of modern times. Even in our Chinese cities you hear its lascivious but infectious sound everywhere you go. 'Jazz music' was originally the music black people in America played as they danced in the forest. And yet now it has become a fashionable commodity circulating among civilized people." [88] The mistake this commentator makes, of course, is to counterpose a primeval jazz against civilized modernity. It need hardly be mentioned that jazz music was an eminently urban phenomenon, a creature of modern recording technology, global commercial networks, and the modish consumption of music that they enabled. The same is true, of course, of Li's children's music and modern songs, which had entered the urban record market as early as 1923 and played an important role in the creation of transnational routes for the distribution of Mandarin Chinese media culture.

The irony here, of course, is that Li's music was far more "modern" than the elite but already outdated nineteenth-century European forms that Xiao and others hoped to reproduce (with Chinese inflections) on their native soil. Symphonic music represented the heyday of musical nationalism in Europe, but the gramophone and its culture heralded the advent of a new transnational economy of musical production and consumption. And it was Li's participation in this new global culture—and his renegotiation of jazz music in national terms—that allowed his music to stand in a relation of, if not equality, then commensurability with that of American counterparts like Buck Clayton: "[Chinese popular music] wasn't too much different from our own music except the Chinese have a different scale tone, but as long as it could be written in on the American scale it could be played." [89] This sort of translatability—unheard of in the nineteenth century and for better or worse a fact of the twentieth because of the portability of musical culture brought about by the gramophone—was achieved without entirely dispensing with pentatonic markers of Chinese "national character." And it is in this specific sense that Li's yellow music represents an ironic and unacknowledged realization of one of the most cherished dreams of the May 4th era: the creation of a new musical idiom both modern and distinctly Chinese.

CHAPTER FOUR

Mass Music and the Politics
of Phonographic Realism

Mist envelops the cold water, moonlight envelops the sand

By night I moor on the Qin-Huai canal, close to the wine shops

The sing-song girl knows not the grief of fallen dynasties

From across the river comes the sound of "Flowers in the Courtyard"

—Du Mu, "Mooring on the Qin-Huai Canal"[1]

The new woman is the productive mass of working women

The new woman is the labor force of society

The new woman is the vanguard in the construction of a new country

The new woman wants to be the same as a man . . .

—Nie Er and Sun Shiyi, theme for *New Woman* (1935)[2]

In February 1932, Nie Er, a talented young man from Yunnan province studying music under the auspices of Li Jinhui's Bright Moon Song and Dance Troupe, witnessed the Japanese military attack that left much of Shanghai's Zhabei district in ruins. His experience of war (which included a daring foray into contested territory to photograph Japanese destroyers on the Huangpu River and American soldiers standing behind sandbagged gun emplacements) was a formative moment in his decision to dedicate himself to an entirely new sort of music-making.[3] On his twentieth birthday, with the sound of artillery fire ringing out in the distance, he wrote the following remarkably prescient entry in his diary.

> The whole world has already begun to convulse. The clash with imperialism, the advent of the Second World War, these are already realities which cannot be concealed. And the question of my own prospects seems to have been shaken up along with everything else. There isn't much future

in my so-called studies of art, because social conditions don't allow for it, what with the constant obstacles and distractions. And what's more, the *classic music* which I've been taking so seriously seems so counterrevolutionary to me now![4]

He continues this train of thought a few days later.

"How to create revolutionary music?" That's the question I've been thinking about all day, but I haven't come up with any concrete plans yet. Isn't so-called *classic* music just a plaything of the leisure class? I spend a few hours every day slaving over my basic exercises. After a few years, even a decade, I become a *violinist*. So what? Can you excite the laboring masses by playing a Beethoven *Sonata*? Will that really be an inspiration to them? No! This is a dead end. Wake up before it's too late![5]

Nie Er's turn away from the European classical tradition marked the advent of a new style of mass music that was to have profound effects on Chinese musical culture and political aesthetics for decades to come. Arising from the exigencies of Japanese territorial encroachment, mass music became an increasingly popular form of political expression throughout the eight years of war with Japan. And in the wake of the Communist victory of 1949, Nie Er's musical aesthetic (as well as that of contemporaries such as Xian Xinghai) was enshrined as an article of state orthodoxy and came to saturate musical life on the Mainland until the late 1970s.

Nie Er's first ideological target in the wake of his battle-triggered revelation was not so much Western classical music, but yellow music, the popular hybrid of jazz and Chinese folk melody pioneered by his own teacher and patron, Li Jinhui. Indeed, just six months after the Japanese attack on Shanghai, Nie Er, using the pseudonym Black Angel (Hei tianshi), published a series of scathing critiques of the "decadence" and "political passivity" of Li's music, which led to his expulsion from the Bright Moon Song and Dance Troupe and the beginning of his startlingly prolific career at the forefront of China's burgeoning leftist music movement, a career cut short by his accidental drowning on a beach near Tokyo in 1935 at the age of twenty-three.[6]

Nie Er's response to the urgent question of how to create a new and explicitly revolutionary music emerged from the confluence of modern warfare, the rise of a mass-mediated culture industry, and the radicalization of Chinese literary theory and cultural practice in this particular histori-

故名作曲家聶耳先生

Late Mr. George Njal, well Known Chinese Music Composer

Commemorative cover of *Denton Gazette* 7 (1935).

cal moment. Mass music, I argue here, partook of an aesthetic of phonographic realism formed of precisely this confluence. I derive the term not from Nie Er's own writings, but from the literary critic Guo Moruo's 1928 injunction that leftist writers must serve as phonographs, "recording" the struggles and aspirations of the proletariat and subsequently playing them back to the society at large as a means of political mobilization.[7] Guo's formulation of this artistic program arose out of a sharp exchange with Li Chuli—a colleague in the radical literary clique called the Creation Society (Chuangzao she), of which Guo was the principal spokesperson—

in which the two authors debated the means by which they would create, seemingly ex nihilo, a new revolutionary literature in China.[8] This
dialogue, in turn, was nestled within an acrimonious debate between the
ideologues of the Creation Society, pragmatic leftists like Lu Xun, and liberal advocates of "art for art's sake," concerning the prerogatives and pitfalls of just such an explicitly Marxist, willfully proletarianized literature
and art.[9]

Read in the light and heat of this debate, which is commonly viewed as
a watershed in modern Chinese literary history, Guo's essay, "The Echo of
the Phonograph" (with which a young leftist intellectual like Nie Er would
surely have been familiar) represents an early and immensely influential
deployment of the language of Marxist cultural criticism. More significantly for this study, Guo's invocation of the phonograph signals the re-
fraction of literary realism through a newfound lens: that of the emergent
media technologies that were rapidly transforming quotidian life along
with the means of cultural production in urban China.

"Be a phonograph: this is the best article of faith for literary and artistic
youth."

I still believe today that this admonition is absolutely correct. "The
phonograph" represents needless to say an admonition whose significance lies in "dialectical materialism."

The sound emitted by a phonograph comes from the objective world.
If such a sound exists in the objective world, the phonograph stands by it,
and then emits the same sound. It can only react in this manner because
of its objectivity.

Put in terms of people, this reaction is ideology, because the objective
world determines ideology, but ideology does not determine the objective
world.

We are now in a world in which class difference is consolidating and
intensifying. You either belong to one class or the other. There is no longer
any middle ground to be found.

But what of China's literary and artistic youth? To tell the truth, nary
a one of them is from a proletarian background. They are all products
of bourgeois ideology. Just what is this ideology? An idealistic tendency
toward subjectivism and individualism.

If we do not overcome this ideology, China's literary and artistic youth
can never take the road of revolutionary literature and art.

This is why I say: "Don't just blow your broken trumpets (bourgeois ideology). Become phonographs for a while!" [10]

This is precisely what Nie Er sets out to do in the wake of the destruction of Zhabei in 1932. Indeed, the series of leftist anthems and screen songs that Nie composed between 1932 and his untimely death three years later represent a nearly systematic application of just such an aesthetic. With his forceful, Soviet-inspired musical representations of the lives of newspaper sellers, dockworkers, female factory laborers, sing-song girls, and other subalterns—lives he had made serious efforts to observe and "record" firsthand—Nie Er sought to create a new form of popular music that would, in his own words, "cry out *on behalf* of the masses" (*daitizhe qunzhong zai nahan*).[11]

What Guo's theoretical formulation and Nie Er's musico-political praxis share, of course, is their reliance on recording technology (as metaphor as much as medium) to bypass one of the most vexing problems facing leftist cultural workers in the interwar period: could elite Chinese intellectuals effectively represent the lives of the oppressed and unlettered? And, if so, what would be the ethical implications of such a representational regime? In a brilliant article, "The Morality of Form: Lu Xun and the Modern Chinese Short Story," Marston Anderson points out that Republican era fictional depictions of the subaltern (be they peasants, women, or children) are continually haunted by the way in which critical realism as a literary form reproduces the very relations of power (between the lettered and the illiterate, the voiced and the voiceless, the narrating subject and the narrated object) that its practitioners seek to upset.[12] Recording, then, may well have seemed a conveniently neutral medium for those same intellectuals, a mechanical process from which the "taint" of the cultural producer's bourgeois subjectivity is magically removed.

As Nie Er's telling phrase transparently indicates, however, even this newly technologized form of representation inevitably involves a process of mediation—and thus substitution. In the process of speaking for and mobilizing the proletariat, in other words, Nie Er and contemporaries like Xian Xinghai and Ren Guang still ran the risk of standing in for (and thus silencing) the objects of their phonographic representation. Indeed, the political ventriloquism involved in the production of these songs becomes clearest when we consider the language in which they were sung. In place of the rich variety of (sometimes mutually unintelligible) regional dialect and class-based sociolect that Nie Er and his colleagues would have encountered in the streets and workshops of Shanghai, mass music is set in the ringing tones of standard Mandarin.[13] This process of linguistic mediation had immediate practical benefits, for the use of the national language allowed the music to reach a mass, as opposed to any one regional, audience.

Even more significant was its ideological value. Just as Li Jinhui's music derived from a commitment to the propagation of Mandarin as a national language, Nie Er's mass-mediated music leverages Mandarin as the unitary voice of a unified national body. Recording, thus, eliminates the traces not only of bourgeois subjectivity, but of unassimilable regional and class identities. According to Walter Benjamin's crucial (and roughly contemporaneous) observation as to the complicity of media technologies with modern forms of political mobilization, the masses themselves may well be an aftereffect of the technological processes of mass mediation. Writing against a backdrop of the rise of fascism in Europe, and with reference to the propagandistic use of newsreels and radio broadcasts in Hitler's Germany, Benjamin offers a caution in the final footnote of his seminal 1935 essay, "The Work of Art in the Age of Mechanical Reproduction."

> Mass reproduction is aided especially by the reproduction of the masses. In big parades and monster rallies, in sports events, and in war, all of which nowadays are captured by camera and sound recording, the masses are brought face to face with themselves. This process, whose significance need not be stressed, is intimately connected with the development of the techniques of reproduction and photography. Mass movements are usually discerned more clearly by a camera than by the naked eye. A bird's-eye view best captures gatherings of hundreds of thousands. And even though such a view may be as accessible to the human eye as it is to a camera, the image received by the eye cannot be enlarged the way a negative is enlarged. This means that mass movements, including war, constitute a form of human behavior which particularly favors mechanical equipment.[14]

Benjamin's insight may well allow us to assess Nie Er's contributions to modern Chinese cultural history from a new vantage point. For in examining Nie Er's role as the progenitor of a new sort of musical praxis (one which eventually swept yellow music into its post-1949 exile in Hong Kong and Taiwan and came to monopolize the musical life of the People's

Republic of China), we should not neglect the sense in which Nie Er's mass music (as much as visual media such as newsreels and newsprint) also helped to engender as well as nationalize the very masses that his soundscapes purport to describe.

In a second and more material sense, Chinese mass music can be referred to as phonographic realism. From the very start, the production and consumption of Nie's music was deeply implicated in the technology of sound recording and the culture industries that had grown up around it. The bulk of his songwriting career was spent as an employee of the dominant player in the Chinese record industry, Pathé Records and a Chinese film studio, Lianhua (United Photoplay), and most of his compositions were written either for the musical screen or gramophonic reproduction. Indeed, Nie Er's "The March of the Volunteers"—the national anthem of the People's Republic of China and the composition for which he is most renowned—began its life as a screen song cowritten with Tian Han for a 1934 Denton Film Company (Diantong yingye gongsi) production called *Children of the Storm* (*Fengyun ernü*).[15] Nie Er and other leftist musicians attempted to represent the masses in their music and to market these representations to them by way of the mass media. This engagement with the urban media culture of the colonial treaty ports and the star system through which it was structured (as I detail through an examination of the sing-song girl in Nie Er's music and her cinematic representations) inevitably left its gendered and technologized traces on leftist musical production.

Nie Er, of course, was not the only cultural worker transformed by the Japanese bombing of Zhabei. The annexation of Manchuria by the Japanese Imperial Army, coupled with the looming threat of further territorial encroachment, catalyzed a fundamental reconfiguration of China's cultural field in the 1930s. In the leftist camp (which had consolidated itself to some extent with the formation, of the League of Left-Wing Writers spearheaded by Lu Xun, and its various subsidiaries in 1930), urgent calls for the creation of an anti-imperialist national culture began to intensify at the same time that the iconoclastic and antifeudalist agenda of earlier May 4th era intellectuals came to be viewed as insufficiently proletarian. As the decade wore on and the Japanese threat loomed ever larger, this overt politicization of literature and the arts was further heightened by insistent calls for the creation of a literature of "national defense" (*guofang wenxue*).[16] These developments were paralleled by stepped-up efforts on the part of the Nationalist center to suppress leftist cultural production and to mobilize support for the regime and its two-pronged policy of anti-Communist warfare on the domestic front, coupled with the diplomatic appeasement of Japanese militarism.

Guo Moruo's *The Echo of the Phonograph* was one among a chorus of polemics on the literary front that unfolded in this volatile cultural climate.[17] Leftist efforts to infiltrate Shanghai's film studios, and the suppression that filmmakers faced at the hands of KMT authorities and anticommunist thugs, have also been thoroughly documented (often to the point of exclusion of other aspects of Chinese film history) in Mainland Chinese scholarship.[18] What is usually neglected, however, is the centrality of music in the articulation of these cultural struggles. Efforts of the KMT (in the words of Chiang Kai-shek) to "militarize the life of the people of the entire nation," an agenda that culminated in the New Life Movement of 1934, began in part with efforts to ban popular music and sponsor mass rallies in which citizens might learn "a habit and an instinct for unified behavior" by way of singing patriotic anthems.[19]

Music, precisely because of its capacity to straddle different media (gramophone records, wireless broadcasting, sound cinema) and places of performance (concert halls, dance halls, and stadium rallies), was also central to the efforts of leftist intellectuals to transform media culture in China and, in doing so, mobilize the citizenry to resist the twin specters of Western imperialism and Japanese territorial encroachment. Indeed, in leftist films of the era like *New Woman* (*Xin nüxing*, 1935) and *New Year's Coin* (*Yasuiqian*, 1937), the music on the soundtrack and representations of music-making within the diegesis serve as one of the primary sites through which critiques of the social order are launched and rituals of collective resistance enacted for the benefit of Chinese film audiences.[20] At the same time that images of workers singing in unison for national salvation lit up Shanghai's silver screens, leftist musicians successfully promoted and organized patriotic mass singing rallies in public spaces removed from the world of the cinema in an effort to disrupt the circuit of capitalist production and passive consumption that they felt characterized the Shanghai culture industry.

The opening salvos of both the KMT and the leftists in their respective battles to dominate the musical field were aimed squarely at Li Jinhui and his yellow music. The New Life Movement in music began with an effort—led by Cheng Maoyun's Jiangxi Committee for the Advancement of Musical Education and its journalistic mouthpiece, *Music Education*—to criticize and ban the performance of Li Jinhui's music. Nie Er's own *prise de position* (and by extension that of the leftist music movement as a whole) was similarly predicated on a critique of Li's work.[21] Li's music also became a discursive linchpin of the leftist musical cinema in which Nie Er was an active participant, serving as one of the primary means through which struggles between a culture of mass-mediated consumption and one of national mobilization are staged for the benefit of film viewers. In classic examples of the genre such as *New Woman* and *New Year's Coin*, for example, Li's songs for the dance hall are recycled and rewritten as anthems of national salvation by characters within the film.

Given Li's dominant role in the development of mass-mediated modern songs, it is less than surprising that he should become a target for critics of all persuasions unhappy with the ideological tenor of the new media culture. What is more interesting, though, is the extent to which these critiques shared a similar set of discursive strategies—strategies that deployed traditional gender biases as a means of discrediting and delegitimating Li Jinhui's music and the culture of mass-mediated consumption that it had spawned. The most prevalent of these tropes was the rhetorical equation of mass-mediated sing-song girls with courtesans and prostitutes. In a discursive climate in which the nation was consistently figured as a woman, and prostitution deployed as a figure for national humiliation at the hands of Japan and the West, these accusations inevitably painted yellow music as a betrayal of nationalistic ideals.[22]

But it is also in the realm of gender politics in which the difference between the two camps becomes clearest. The KMT's New Life campaign was ideologically underwritten by an appeal for the restitution of Confucian social mores. For this reason, a major aim of the campaign was the regulation of the public profile of women, even to the extent of counseling against female participation in public gatherings and promulgating "proper" hemlines for skirts.[23] This sort of legislation—which should be read as a backlash against precisely the sort of public display exemplified by the controversial career of Li Jinhui's daughter, Li Minghui, who had been among the first women to break the Qing dynasty taboo against public performances by women in the mid-1920s—spilled over into the realm of public media culture in the form of rules restricting the "erotic" content of musical films and songs broadcast over the radio.[24]

If the policy of the Nationalist center (as represented by figures like

Cheng Maoyun and the president of the Shanghai Conservatory of Music, Xiao Youmei) toward this new form of urban musical culture was primarily repressive, that of their leftist and progressive counterparts was characterized by altogether different tactics: appropriation and assimilation. Rather than endeavoring to eliminate the sing-song girl and her (in Nie Er's words) "fragrant and fleshy appeal" (*xiangyan rougan*) from the airwaves and motion picture screens, leftist filmmakers enlisted her as a potent (as well as commercially expedient) means of figuring China's humiliation and the prospect of national salvation.[25] This strategy was fundamentally of a piece with both leftist gender politics and the aesthetic imperatives of phonographic realism. Just as the modern "new woman" (in the 1935 Nie Er composition of the same title) would be assimilated to the leftist mobilization effort as a "vanguard" who "wants to be the same as a man," the sing-song girl was represented in leftist films not as frivolous courtesan ignorant of "the grief of fallen dynasties" (as in Du Mu's famous Tang dynasty quatrain), but rather as an oppressed subaltern eager to add her voice to the chorus of enlightened citizens crying out for national salvation.

DECADENT SOUNDS

The initiatives launched by both the left and the KMT center in the early 1930s to take the high ground of the musical field (and the media culture through which it was increasingly constituted) were conducted in and through a process of naming, and thus delegitimating Li Jinhui's music. In polemics written by critics of every persuasion, the music of Li and the song-and-dance troupes that he had spawned were labeled as producers and purveyors of "decadent sounds" (*mimi zhi yin*). Indeed, the term decadent sounds appears so frequently and insistently in these attacks (and has proved so durable as a derogatory term for popular music on both sides of the Taiwan straits) that its provenance in traditional Chinese historiography and the semantic field that it evokes merit further exploration.

The phrase first appears in the chapter "Basic Annals of the Yin Dynasty" in Sima Qian's Han dynasty text, *The Records of the Historian* (*Shiji*). The pertinent section tells the story of how the enormously cruel and extravagant emperor Zhou allowed the dynasty to fall to pieces as he caroused with courtesans and threw absurdly decadent parties. His licentious activities are, of course, set to music: "Zhou ordered Juan the music master to write new lewd tunes (*xin yinge*), northern district dances (*beili zhi wu*) and decadent sounds (*mimi zhi yin*)." The character *mi* has several connotations, including "waste," "extravagance," and "vulgar commerce" (*shangsu mimi*).[26] The "northern lanes" were red-light districts where prostitutes plied their trade. Given these connotations—and the link between music, sing-song girls, and national dissolution provided by the surrounding cautionary narrative—it is no surprise that the phrase was enthusiastically taken up by patriots of all stripes in order to assert that Li's yellow music was a portent of social dissolution that needed to be eliminated for the sake of national reconstruction.

This complex of traditional associations is evoked over and over in Nationalist efforts (spearheaded by Cheng Maoyun and his Jiangxi Committee for the Advancement of Musical Education) to suppress popular music. In a manifesto published just months before the beginning of the New Life campaign—which was, significantly, initiated by Chiang Kai-shek from his headquarters in Nanchang, Jiangxi Province—Cheng sets out his agenda for the elimination of Li Jinhui's music. The manifesto is divided into four sections, each of which invokes nationalist imperatives— "To Improve the Quality of the Nation's Citizens," "To Protect Our Children," "To Allow for the Elevation of Our National Culture," "To Raise the Artistic Standards of Our Citizens"—and ends with the refrain, "We Must Eliminate Popular Music."[27] From the start of the essay, the music itself is linked with prostitution and moral degradation.

As far as the popular tunes and vulgar ditties that are popular in our nation's cities, although there are a handful of good songs among them, the majority describe the amorous relationships between petty merchants and whores. Their sentiments are not as sincere and pure as peasant songs, nor do they reflect the real conditions of folk life, and in this sense they are not worthy of "National Airs" [Guo feng] in the *Book of Odes* [*Shijing*], which create something beautiful out of their observation of the common. These songs are thoroughly obscene [*yindang*], in intention and in sentiment, in terms of their music and lyrics. Li Jinhui and others like him often take their inspiration from and even imitate these sorts of ditties. Although the original lyrics have been replaced with decorative words, the tunes themselves still lead the hearts of their listeners into degeneracy and cause unhealthy imaginings. These songs first became popular in schools, and later spread broadly among the folk. Of late, records and movies are full of this kind of song, and those who listen are intoxicated by them and deluded into falling into a cheap sort of enjoyment, without any capacity for reflection. This is certainly not the sort of sound that can arouse the nation [*shu fei xingguo zhi yin*].[28]

The persistence of this sort of rhetoric is evidenced in a 1936 essay by the leftist songwriter He Luting. While the Confucian revivalist rhetoric with which propaganda for the New Life Movement was usually interlarded is missing here (replaced by a critique of capitalist culture), the metaphorical invocation of prostitution and the emphasis on the corrupt power of the mass media remains the same.

There are two other types of people to whom we should pay serious attention: the first are those who write obscene songs and who broadcast sexually obscene songs over the wireless. They are prostitutes in disguise, whose only talent is for poisoning society. The second are these shameless music merchants, who talk a good line about promoting music for the masses, but who actually take advantage of their special position to sell as much vulgar and salacious music as they can in order to poison the Chinese people. We must rise up together to overthrow these kinds of people.[29]

Even when prostitution per se does not enter the discursive arena, the politics of gender difference are central to these efforts to clear the musical field of Li Jinhui's ostensibly pernicious influence. Nie Er's revolt against his teacher represents just such a deployment of a significatory scheme in which the feminine is linked to frivolity, decadence, and degradation, and the masculine to probity, righteous struggle, and the nation. In a strident broadside, "A Brief Essay on Chinese Musical Drama," published in the leftist journal *Film Art* (*Dianying yishu*) just months after the Japanese attack on Zhabei, Nie Er foreshadows the preoccupation with gender that would come to play such a crucial role in the phonographic realism of the new leftist music movement.

Whenever one speaks of Chinese musical drama, credit is due to the man who came up with this stuff, Li Jinhui, who dauntlessly led a troupe of pretty young boys and girls from east to west and back again, inside the country and out, showing off their soft-core skills for more than ten years. So very admirable!

But fragrant and fleshy appeals to the audience and the expression of passion are about the only achievements our so-called musical drama have managed to muster in these ten years.

They claim that this stuff is art, that it has educational value. But the young performers themselves are experiencing the unspeakable bitterness of missing out on their own opportunity for education, so what of the education of society as a whole? The education of children? Oh! Countless children! countless young people, all drugged by this so-called art!

Not everything Li Jinhui has written is completely bad. There are among his works elements of anti-feudalism as well as depictions of the division in society between rich and poor. But what we need now is not soft tofu, but the hardness of real swords and real guns! Think about it! The capitalists are sitting in their skyscrapers enjoying their wealth while the sweat-drenched workers silently cry out under their machines. What sort of means should we adopt to save the oppressed, laboring masses? [30]

The gendered distinction that Nie Er draws between the display of "soft" female flesh, and the "hardness" of a revolutionary art needs no further elaboration. More interesting perhaps is the conspicuous silence of the cries emitted by the workers, a silence that presumably would be filled by Nie Er's own compositions. Ironically, though, the discursive and performative economy of his own work as a songwriter came to hinge not on the mobilization of "sweat-drenched workers," but of sing-song girls and female proletarians as mediated by the machinery of the culture industry. Through this same process, Nie Er also attempted to legislate a new (and harder-edged) kind of Chinese femininity.

NEW LIFE

The KMT's efforts to legislate public listening habits proved less successful. In May 1934, just weeks after the opening salvos of the New Life Movement—which in Shanghai included public processions and candlelit vigils attended by thousands of students and workers singing party anthems (some written by Cheng Maoyun himself)—the Ministry of Education, following the lead of the Jiangxi Committee, promulgated regulations banning the live performance and wireless broadcast of several of Li Jinhui's compositions, including "Peach Blossom River" and "Little Sister, I Love You." Similar bans on the production of these records were precluded by the fact that the editorial policies of the two major transnational record companies operating in Shanghai, Pathé Asia and RCA-Victor, did not come under the jurisdiction of Chinese authorities. A contemporary report on the ban in the film magazine *Movietone* (*Diansheng*) half-heartedly regurgitates the New Life rhetoric undergirding the ban, rhetoric that underscores the political importance accorded by the KMT to the control of the electronic media.

> Some have expressed approval of the ban on the broadcast of "Peach Blossom River" and other songs, and others are against it. Although the lyrics of "Peach Blossom River" aren't really very licentious at all, it is true that "decadent sounds" really do guide people down the road of debauchery and passivity. So one really can't put the improvement of public morality on the back burner just for the sake of a few songwriters who only care about getting rich writing licentious music. This is especially true when it comes to broadcasting and recording records, in which case the poison spreads much faster and much further than otherwise, because when all is said and done the education of the people is the vanguard of the New Life movement and also the duty of the patriarch of each and every family.[31]

By 1936, these (largely ineffective) measures were strengthened by way of strict new controls on broadcasting imposed by the KMT's Ministry of Transport and Communications (Jiaotong bu). The criteria for radio programming imposed by the ministry evinces an interesting melange of May 4th era iconoclasm, nationalism, authoritarianism, and Confucian revivalism.

> This bureau's standards for programming are as follows—
> 1. Programs must have a clear and righteous purpose
> 2. Must not be injurious to public security
> 3. Must conform to the principles of the Party
> 4. Must not be obscene
> 5. Must not contain superstitions, spirits, and ghosts
> 6. Must not defy scientific principles
> 7. Must not defy the ethical spirit
> 8. No low-class vulgarity
> 9. No promotion of feudal thinking[32]

This repressive agenda was coupled with an "active" policy intended to replace censored programming with party propaganda. "In order to elevate the consciousness of the Chinese people, we have also purchased recordings of Party songs and famous lecturers in great quantity, which we will lend out to be broadcast by each and every radio station free of charge. . . ."[33] These party songs would have presumably taken the form of didactic choral pieces originally published in *Music Education,* such as the KMT party anthem written by Cheng Maoyun, as well as propaganda pieces like "The Song of the New Life Movement."[34] This offer, of course, was a belated and ineffectual attempt to address fundamental flaws in the KMT's approach to the regulation of the culture industry, flaws nicely skewered in the same 1934 article on the ban of Li Jinhui's music, which had begun by parroting the rhetoric of the campaign.

> But the [songs provided by the Party] better not be too dull or too proper, because nowadays most people in shops and homes see the wireless as a form of entertainment, so it wouldn't hurt if the songs are a little soft, even a little fragrant and fleshy. As long as they add a few inspiring patriotic slogans to these soft, fragrant and fleshy tunes, we'll soon have what we might call "entertainment that doesn't neglect national salvation"![35]

The article concludes by noting that although the ban had been in effect for two weeks, Shanghai's dance halls were still reverberating to the decadent sounds of Li Jinhui's music, if for no other reason than that "no other Chinese dance music" was available to replace it.[36]

NEW SOUNDS

When Ren Guang and Nie Er (who had secured employment at Pathé Asia as a musical consultant) invited the public to a "Pathé New Sounds Seminar" (Baidai xinsheng hui) a few months after the ban was put into effect, their intention was precisely to promote an alternative to Li Jinhui-style modern songs. The format of the seminar, held on October 13, 1934, in the auditorium of the (British colonial) Royal Asiatic Society in Shanghai, was unusual. Rather than featuring a band, the concert consisted of thirty new Pathé records played on a gramophone.

While the records included traditional music, regional opera, and several screen songs written by Li Jinhui, the event focused on the unveiling of several revolutionary (in terms of both style and content) film songs composed by Nie Er.[37] This new music—an amalgam of the choral style of Republican school songs, Soviet mass music, and military marches—was an unlikely candidate for the hit parade. Even so, in the wake of the seminar and, more importantly, the success of the films in which Nie Er's compositions were featured, these leftist anthems began to share the airwaves, record store racks, and mass-produced songbooks with their jazzier "yellow" counterparts, which still flourished despite intermittent KMT suppression.

By the 1930s, revolutionary anthems per se were nothing new; the lineage of Nie Er's self-consciously innovative genre can be traced back to the Protestant hymns and nationalist school songs that were such a fundamental part of Chinese musical life in the first two decades of the twentieth-century. The advent of explicitly Marxist music in China dates from 1921, when the "Internationale" (Guoji ge) was first published in a special issue of *Short Story Monthly* (*Xiaoshuo yuebao*) devoted to Soviet arts and literature.[38] The song was retranslated into Chinese and printed in the May 4th journal *New Youth* by the influential theorist of Chinese Marxism, Qu Qiubai.[39] By 1926, this and other revolutionary anthems had undeniably become part of the repertoire of Chinese political culture, as evidenced by the publication of a songbook titled *Songs of Revolution* on the eve of Chiang Kai-shek's Northern Expedition.[40] The collection, edited by one of the founders of the Chinese Communist Party, Li Weisen, included the "Internationale," the "Marseillaise," and other anti-imperialist and nationalist anthems.

The foundational moment of the particular form of mass music subsequently celebrated by socialist historians as the Leftist New Music Movement (Zuoyi xin yinyue yundong), however, did not arrive until the creation of the Soviet Friends Society in early 1933. Composed of a small group of like-minded musicians and songwriters—including Nie Er, Ren Guang, An E, and Zhang Shu (a political activist who had dropped out of the Shanghai Conservatory) and the leftist writer and cultural impresario Tian Han—the society was devoted to the study of Soviet music and the composition of a new proletarian music for the Chinese masses. In this endeavor, they were assisted on a theoretical level by the Communist literary critic Zhou Yang's translation of an American treatise on Russian revolutionary music as well as a series of Japanese articles on proletarian music translated into Chinese and printed by a group of left-wing musicians in Beijing in a magazine called *Music Weekly* (*Yinyue zhoukan*).[41]

As these affiliations and interests suggest, the group maintained covert links with the Chinese Communist Party through underground Communist cultural workers like Yu Ling. The Soviet Friends Society was only the first of a series of similar organizations for the promotion of leftist music; these groups continued to operate throughout the 1930s, each of them composed of the same tight-knit group of friends and colleagues. They ranged from the New Chinese Music Research Group (Zhongguo xinxing yinyue yanjiu hui), founded in the spring of 1933 by Tian Han; the Music Cell of the Chinese Federation of Leftist Dramatists (Zhongguo zuoyi xiju jia lianmeng hui yinyue xiaozu), initiated in early 1934; the Songwriters Association (Ciqu zuozhe lianyi hui), started in 1936; and the Song Research Association (Ciqu yanjiu hui), founded in 1936 by Lu Ji.

The musical activities of these groups were considerably less drab than this litany of organizational names might suggest. Their activities were divided into two primary spheres of action: the mass media and mass choral singing. The first project is most aptly represented by the collaborative efforts of Nie Er and Ren Guang to "promote and create a real mass music" by way of their affiliation with Pathé. This route, in which leftists sought to inject new sounds and new ideologies into what they saw as an urban media culture market hopelessly tainted by the coloniality and vulgarity of the urban petit bourgeoisie, inevitably involved a degree of compromise with the vagaries of the urban record market and experimentation with the aesthetic and commercial possibilities of the cinema through which those records were most effectively promoted.

For this reason as well, the phonographic realism of leftist musicians hinged on (to borrow a phrase from Lu Xun) "grabism" (*nalai zhuyi*), or the pragmatic appropriation of materials and methods from multiple sources. To an extent still unacknowledged by critics and historians in the People's Republic of China, leftist film musicians drew their expressive palette from Hollywood and Tin Pan Alley as well as the Soviet Union.[42] Part of the reason for this borrowing is that they were compelled to compete with American products for a slice of the urban culture market; an estimated 80 to 90 percent of all films shown in Shanghai in the 1930s were of foreign origin.[43]

A second reason was that their creative activities unfolded in a colonial contact zone characterized by its disjunctive cultural hybridity. This hybridity is evident not only in the cultural products of the era, but also in its "material unconscious," in the life-styles and quotidian material culture of the figures involved in the leftist music movement.[44] Ren Guang, for instance, was an employee of a British multinational corporation who lived in a French apartment house and drove an American car. In the glossy film and music magazine he helped to edit with his songwriter wife An E, *Art Sound*, Betty Boop cartoons and photographs of Hollywood bathing beauties rubbed shoulders with the notation for Nie Er's "March of the Volunteers." Nie Er himself—his fierce nationalism notwithstanding—was a stylish young man who wore suits, frequented Shanghai's many first-run cinemas, and styled himself as "George Njal" after having read the Norse folk epic, *Njal's Saga*.[45]

The humiliating cognizance by leftist composers of the unequal political terms of this sort of cultural cosmopolitanism (or perhaps more accurately, colonial bricolage) led to their deployment of both crowd-pleasing cinematic and musical techniques borrowed from Hollywood *and* Soviet agitprop and mass music with its rhetoric of anti-imperialist and anticapitalist struggle. On the level of content, moreover, the dance halls and sing-song girls that had become so much a part of Shanghai's entertainment cinema in the late 1920s and early 1930s also proved irresistible to leftist cultural workers; they provided both a means to please film patrons and a way to depict the process whereby decadent sounds and the alluring women who sang them might be transformed and mobilized for national salvation.

Indeed, as will be discussed in more detail, leftist films habitually portrayed the assimilation of the mediatized (and fetishized) figure of the sing-song girl into a larger group of mobilized (and desexed) citizens singing nationalist anthems. These films also figured (and endeavored to promote) the popularity of a second realm in which leftist musicians were active: mass-singing rallies. These rallies, organized as a means of stirring up patriotic fervor in support of resistance against Japanese territorial encroachment, represented a direct attack on the culture of consumption in which the leftists were themselves implicated. Was popular music about the individualized consumption of the mediatized body of the sing-song girl? Or would it involve the mobilization of the masses into a collective body singing in unison for national salvation? Beginning in 1935, leftists organized mass choral groups like the People's Anthem Society (Minzhong geyong hui), groups that shifted the context of popular music consumption away from cinemas, nightclubs, and petit bourgeois homes and into the streets, stadiums, and factories of Shanghai, and in so doing, attempted to disrupt the semiotic circuitry of the mass media machine.

POLITICAL VENTRILOQUISM

Nie Er's new mass music, not unlike the self-consciously proletarian literature being produced in leftist literary circles in the same period, set
out to give voice to the voiceless, to represent the struggles of China's
subalterns. Leafing through Nie Er's collected works, a consistent pattern
emerges: almost every song speaks for a different oppressed group, and
each oppressed group speaks in turn for the predicament of the nation
as a whole. This sort of political ventriloquism is accomplished, in part,
through a simple but profoundly productive alteration of the standard
rhetoric of popular song. Terms of address (i.e., pronouns) are essential to
decoding the contextual and ideological meaning of most popular song
lyrics. Love songs, of course, typically speak in terms of "you" and "I."
One of the innovations of Nie Er and his lyric-writing collaborators (who
include figures like Tian Han, Sun Yu, and Sun Shiyi) is that they almost invariably chose to write of the struggles of workers, oppressed
women, and exploited children in terms of a collective "we." A partial
list of the occupations represented in this manner includes mineworkers
("The Miners' Song"), newspaper boys ("Song of the Newspaper Sellers"
and "The Voice of the Newsboys"), bricklayers ("Bricklayers' Song"), construction workers ("Piledriving Song"), longshoremen ("Song of the Longshoremen"), coolies ("Song of the Coolies"), road builders ("Song of the
Great Road," "The Road-building Pioneers"), soldiers on the anti-Japanese
front ("Song of Survival," "March of the Volunteers"), female factory workers ("New Woman"), female farmworkers ("The Lotus Pickers' Song,"
"Tea Gatherers' Song," "Song of the Shepherd Girl"), and child laborers
("Little Worker").[46] Several of these categories, particularly road builders
and soldiers, lent themselves particularly well to the sort of process of
allegorization toward which this political ventriloquism aimed.

Most of these songs were based on Nie Er's firsthand investigation of
the lives of the objects of his phonographic representations. The two songs
composed for the rag-clad urchins who sold newspapers on the street, for
instance, were written (and eventually recorded for Pathé by Gong Qiuxia)
only after he had befriended and spent several days with a newsgirl on the
Avenue Joffre in the French Concession known as "the Kid" (Xiao mao-
tou).[47] His portraits of longshoremen and female factory workers were
produced only after visiting their quays and workshops. Nie's modus

China's national anthem in its earliest incarnation as a
screen song. From *Denton Gazette* 2 (1935).

operandi is strongly reminiscent of Guo Moruo's advice that leftist practitioners of phonographic realism "stand by" the proletariat in order to
accurately record its struggles.[48]

Some of Nie Er's most successful sonic representations of subalterns,
however, did not require him to go so far afield. Both as a student of Li
Jinhui and an employee of Pathé Records, he was surrounded almost daily
by representatives of another oppressed occupational group: the mod-

ern sing-song girl. Nie Er's representations of this group are of special interest because of their implicit critique of Li Jinhui's musical idiom and because they help us understand the ways in which gender and nationalism were inflected by and through leftist political ventriloquism during the Republican period. Indeed, no better example of how the left harnessed the pathos of the sing-song girl as a figure of oppression, national humiliation, and national resistance exists than in Nie Er's song for the 1935 film *Children of the Storm*, "The Sing-Song Girl Under the Iron Hoof" (Tieti xia de genü).[49] The film's scenario, written by Nie's colleague in the Soviet Friends Society, Tian Han, tells the story of a group of young people in Shanghai, who, driven by social disorder and external threat, either sink into lives of dissipation or resolve to devote themselves to the anti-Japanese war effort in the north of China. The film climaxes with a stirring rendition of the song that was to become China's national anthem, Nie Er's "March of the Volunteers," set to a sequence in which a group of peasants pledge themselves to militant resistance.[50]

The clear-cut attempt to mythologize (and thus mobilize) nationalist sentiment is leavened by a subplot portraying the life of Ah Feng (played by Li Jinhui's student, Wang Renmei), an orphaned child compelled by poverty into a career as a sing-song girl who eventually redeems herself in the struggle against military encroachment. The film follows Ah Feng on a tour with her song-and-dance troupe to the seaport of Qingdao. After the troupe regales theatergoers (including the prominent actor and director Yuan Muzhi, playing a dissipated poet and dandy) with a Spanish-inspired dance routine (performed by two more graduates of Li Jinhui's troupe, the rising star Zhou Xuan and Bai Hong), Ah Feng's song inserts a note of patriotic urgency into a scene that otherwise would have been indistinguishable from a host of others in the "soft" Chinese musicals of the era. Indeed, the juxtaposition of sing-song girl and nation in Xu Xingzhi's lyrics (and their saturation by the discourse of prostitution-as-national humiliation) is transparent to the point of clumsiness.

Everywhere we sell our songs
We perform our dances all around
Who doesn't know that the nation's on the brink of disaster?
So why have we been taken for courtesans?
Because of hunger and cold
We sing our sad songs everywhere

We've tasted all of life's cares
Dancing girls are condemned always to drift
Who's willing to be someone's slave?
Who wants to let our homeland fall into enemy hands?
The sing-song girl under the iron hoof is pitiful,
Whipped until her whole body is torn and bleeding[51]

Obviously, the lyric signifies a refusal of consumer culture, a disruption of the circuit of pleasure in which the sing-song girl serves as a medium for commercial exchange, as one who "sells songs" (or, by means of her mass-mediated voice, radio advertising and cinema tickets), and, by extension, her own body. Implicit here as well is the notion of recuperation, the implication that the oppressed sing-song girl is ready and willing to be enlisted to the cause of national salvation. This recuperation, though, is equivocal at best. In an industry that functioned by way of a gendered division of labor in which men wrote lyrics and women sang them, Xu Xingzhi's lyrics represent as much a ventriloquistic appropriation (and in a sense, a silencing) of the sing-song girl as a modern song in which the words put in her mouth are nothing more than a titillating salve to male fantasies or an invitation to commercial exchange.[52]

POLITICS AND PERFORMANCE

Just as significant as these lyrics is Nie Er's musical language and the ways in which it was enunciated in performance. In describing music in any other terms than the strictly musicological, as Roland Barthes has pointed out, we condemn ourselves to the realm of the "poorest of linguistic categories," that of the merely adjectival.[53] But these adjectives—and the musical facts to which they refer—are, in a very real sense, gendered. Wong Kee-chee has noted a distinct transformation wrought on the singing styles of the day by the introduction of leftist "mass music" into the urban media market.[54] Essentially, Nie Er and his compatriots in the left-wing music movement replaced the high-pitched, nasal, and melismatic style characteristic of Li Jinhui's more popular tunes—sometimes mocked in contemporary writings as the "little sister style" (*meimei qiang*)—with a deeper, more open-throated approach to vocal production imported from dominant European bel canto and martial models. This shift in vocal production was accompanied by analogous changes to the melodic and rhythmic profiles of the form appropriated from Soviet mass music and European martial music.

The ideological implications of this change cannot be overestimated. To contemporary critics, the former style implied tradition (and specifically the tradition of the courtesan-cum-sing-song girl ensconced in her urban demimonde), vulgarity, sexuality, vulnerability, and exaggerated femininity—in short, the complex of meanings evoked by contemporary critics with the phrase decadent sounds. The contrasting style was imbued (as Nie Er wrote under an assumed name in a self-congratulatory article on his own contribution to the creation of the new music) with qualities of "strength, originality, masculinity and solemn grandeur" (*xionglie beizhuang*).[55]

In this light, it is not surprising that many of the film songs produced by Nie Er, He Luting, Ren Guang and Xian Xinghai throughout the 1930s were written not for female vocalists, as was overwhelmingly the case in the commercial pop music of the period, but for men.[56] Nor is their experimentation with rousing martial choral effects—as in "The March of the Volunteers" and Nie Er's adaptation of the mock Soviet/Hollywood screen song "Song of the Volga Boatman" (from Cecil B. DeMille's 1926 film *The Volga Boatman*) in Sun Yu's *The Great Road* (*Dalu*)—insignificant in terms of gender and ideology.[57] Instead, choral arrangements represented a musical figure for collectivity and nationhood, a figure in which the voice of the sing-song girl was submerged and assimilated into the larger group.

Another crucial determinant of musical meaning is its performative context and the "metamusical aspects" of performance (or its representation in cinematic terms).[58] This strikes me as one of the most important aspects of leftist efforts in the mid-1930s to shift the locale of music-making away from nightclubs and into stadiums and parks in which mass "national salvation song-meets" were sporadically held. In nightclubs and cabarets (and the musical cinema that often took such locales as settings) the very setup of the performance space was redolent of the notion of music-as-consumption. The sing-song girl stands isolated on stage behind a microphone, exposed to the gaze of the audience. The orchestra was hidden toward the back of the stage, or in an orchestral pit in front of her. As Richard Middleton points out, this sort of spatial relationship—in which the mechanics of musical performance are elided to focus attention on the singer—is one of the best indicators that we are in the presence of "the star syndrome."[59] A filmic equivalent of this syndrome is evoked in many of the Mandarin musicals of the late 1930s and 1940s when, as Sam Ho notes, the star bursts into song out in the open air—to the accompaniment of an invisible, off-screen orchestra![60]

The semiotics of performance in the mass-singing meetings with which leftist musicians sought to stir up patriotic fervor in the years from 1934 to 1937 could not have been more different. Here, the most appropriate metaphor is martial. In one such meeting held in Shanghai Stadium in 1936, a thousand singers of the People's Anthem Society were serried into ranks, surrounding an elevated platform on which a male conductor led them in singing anthemic examples of what had come to be known as National Defense music.[61] The fetishized female star is subsumed by the collective; commercial exchange is replaced by ideological solidarity and voluntarism; the (gendered) consumer becomes a desexed citizen participating in a ritual enactment of national solidarity.

LEFTIST FILM AND POPULAR MUSIC

In many leftist films of the period, a similar process of political mobilization is explicitly staged in musical terms. Cai Chusheng's 1935 film, *New Woman,* for which Nie Er contributed a suite of five screen songs, is one example of how music (and the gendered discourse through which it was understood) comes to serve as a linchpin of leftist political critique. The movie tells the story of a beautiful woman writer-musician named Wei Ming (played by the legendary actress Ruan Lingyu) who is driven to suicide by a heartlessly patriarchal and capitalistic society.[62] Wei Ming's character is counterposed with a different sort of "new woman" who lives next door: a strong and distinctly masculine proletarian named Li Aying, who is actively engaged in the political education of women factory workers. Early in the film, Wei Ming—in a moment of what the already radicalized Li Aying might characterize as petit bourgeois weakness—allows herself to be taken out for a night on the town by a sexually predatory, foreign-educated comprador named Dr. Wang. The sequence that follows represents in many ways a distillation of leftist discourses on music and gender as well as an illuminating example of the selective appropriation of foreign models that characterized the leftist artistic approach.

Dr. Wang and Wei Ming's evening unfolds at a large, well-appointed ballroom whose associations with the politically compromised pleasures of a specifically colonial modernity are strategically foregrounded by an establishing shot of a large sign next to the club's entrance: "International Dance Hall" (Guoji wuchang). A moment later, inside the hall, the orchestra conductor holds up the sheet music, the cover prominently displaying "Peach Blossom River" superimposed over a stylized art deco illustration of a nude woman. The band begins to play this representative example of Li Jinhui's yellow music (the implications of which would have been familiar to the vast majority of viewers) as couples (men in Western suits and women in the close-fitting *qipao* characteristic of Chinese women's fashion in the 1930s) sway across the dance floor to the orchestra's jazzy sounds. Suddenly, the film cuts to an entirely different sort of conductor. Li Aying in a meeting hall filled with women workers dressed in plain cotton tunics leads them in a strident chorus of a song—directly adapted from the preceding Li Jinhui piece—called "Huangpu River" (Huangpu jiang) after the body of water abutting Shanghai's waterfront. A split-screen montage juxtaposes the steely determination of the singing workers with a series of images of colonial Shanghai (foreign banks and gunships along the Huangpu River, streetcars, modern industrial installations, a church, and the clock tower of the customs house administered by the municipal council). A subsequent montage sequence, set to jaunty jazz music, is framed by this clock tower and its tolling bells. The camera places the dancing shoes of the revelers in the dance hall and the tramping, swollen, poorly clad feet of Shanghai's oppressed workers, both of which are projected onto the clock face itself, within the same (implicitly capitalist and colonial) time frame.

This deployment of Eisensteinian intellectual montage (in which Marxist dialectics commingle with the language of film, graphically representing class struggle through the juxtaposition of carefully selected images) is accomplished by means of an interesting (and, in light of official historiography, ironic) sort of appropriation.[63] Just as Nie Er's "Song of the Great Road" was an adaptation of a Hollywood version of a Russian folk song in *The Volga Boatman,* these ground-level images of Chinese workers—spliced into the sequence in a manner typical of Soviet agitprop—are lifted almost frame-by-frame from Cecil B. DeMille's 1926 vision of those same boatmen tramping along the banks of the river.[64] The leftist use of Soviet techniques, in other words, is mediated through the prism of Hollywood motion pictures, just as their promotion of mass music can be articulated only by way of a simultaneous appropriation and critique of Li Jinhui and the spaces with which he is associated. This process of bricolage, finally, is self-referentially foregrounded by the filmmakers. When Li Aying entrusts Wei Ming with the task of setting the lyrics for "New Woman" to music, she explains, "I've added new lyrics for classroom use to some popular songs which aren't any good for us workers at all, but this is just a stop-gap measure until we can create some songs of our own."

A similar dynamic is at work in the gender politics of the film. As the film's theme song suggests, the new woman who has been mobilized for (and subsequently subsumed by) the nation-building effort is a woman (like Li Aying and emphatically unlike Wei Ming, who remains an object of self-consciously scopophilic representation throughout the film) who is not really a woman at all.

> The new woman is the productive mass of working women
> The new woman is the labor force of society
> The new woman is the vanguard in the construction of a new country
> The new woman wants to be the same as a man. . . .[65]

This message is delivered most forcefully when Li Aying, in an interesting twist on Hollywood genre films, rolls up her sleeves and delivers a stunning knockout punch to Dr. Wang, thus delivering the helpless Wei Ming from his unwanted sexual advances.

The gala premiere of the film on February 2, 1935, provided leftist cultural workers with another opportunity to enact the ideological premises of these lyrics. Before and after the show, Nie Er himself led a choral group composed of the Lianhua Studio's brightest female stars in a rendition of the *New Woman* theme song. In accordance with the film's theme (and what might be identified as a sort of "radical chic" sweeping Shanghai's film world at the time), this particular assembly of mass-mediated sing-song girls was clad not in the usual tailored silk finery, but in the shapeless blue cotton robes of the female factory workers that the song was meant to phonographically represent.

MEDIATED SPACE

New Woman was not the only film in which the products of commercial media culture were rewritten as narratives of national salvation. Indeed, popular songs and the women who sang them became perhaps the primary vehicle for the articulation of a discourse of national salvation in the

Nie Er leading a chorus of movie starlets in proletarian garb at the 1935 premiere of *New Woman*. From *Denton Gazette* 7 (1935).

leftist cinema of the 1930s. Just such a rewriting lies at the heart of the 1937 film *New Year's Coin*. The film's scenario, written by Xia Yan, relies on a clever gimmick to deliver to the viewer a roughly synchronic slice of Shanghai life in all of its class-stratified diversity: the camera follows a silver coin for one year as it circulates throughout the city. To this narrative baton, a second device is added to knit the story together; a single melody (written by He Luting) is performed in a number of different contexts and styles throughout the film by two different sing-song girls and a schoolteacher.

The first occurrence of this melody comes early in the film. The coin has found its way into a petit bourgeois household where a party is being held. The camera focuses on a wireless radio set, from which a tune called "The Song of the Dance Hall" (Wuxie zhige) is heard. One guest at the party, a sing-song girl named Miss Yang (played, ironically enough, by Li Minghui), is prevailed on by the party's host to perform the song (which we are told is so popular that "even the children on the street know how to sing it"). In a melismatic warble typical of yellow music, Miss Yang obliges, accompanied by a rudimentary melody on the piano.

Here dusk is when we wake and morning when we sleep
Here you'll find cloud dark coiffures and bright red lips
Here the red lamps smile and the music leaps
Here is paper money and hearts led astray
Here are sleepwalking souls and extinguished love
Here there are soft words and tender sentiments
Here there are sweet emotions and intimate entanglements
Here is your happiness and joy
Here is my pain and sorrow
Here there is everything except dawn
Here there is everything except dawn

In the second occurrence of the melody, Miss Yang sings the song accompanied by a large jazz orchestra in the sort of decadent and "dusky" milieu portrayed by the lyrics—an elegant nightclub. She is then joined on the nightclub stage by a second sing-song girl, Jiang Xiuxia (played by Gong Qiuxia), who performs along with her tap-dancing six-year-old daughter, billed as the "Chinese Shirley Temple" (played by Gong's daughter and child star, Hu Rongrong). From this point onward, the paths of these two performers diverge in significant ways. Gong Qiuxia, after an unhappy stint as a taxi dancer in a low-class dance hall, gives up her career in the entertainment business to seek out a new life assisting a female friend who runs a primary school. In the meantime, Miss Yang is dumped by the corrupt businessman by whom she has been kept after his spectacular financial demise and relegated to walking the streets of Shanghai in search of new "clients."

The final scene is a striking dramatization of the film's deployment of music and media in service of its leftist political agenda. We see Jiang Qiuxia's teacher friend (clad in a plain cotton dress not unlike that of Li Aying in *New Woman* and standing at a podium in front of the national flag and a portrait of the nationalist leader Sun Yat-sen), leading her students in a rousing anthem. The choral singing is accompanied this time by off-screen military brass music. The song, as a subtitle emphasizes for the audience's benefit before scrolling the lyrics across the bottom of the screen, is a "Song of National Salvation" (Jiugo zhige), based on the melody of the former "Song of the Dance Hall":

Here there is new life and fiery enthusiasm
Here there is a will to live and the spirit to do battle

Here there is the sharpness of swords and the clangor of iron
Here there is a free people and a secure Great Wall
Here there is one voice united, the masses of one heart
Here are your unlimited prospects
Here is my guiding light
Here is progress and no passivity
Here is progress and no passivity

The overt message of the sequence needs little explanation. Songwriter He Luting has erected a straw dog precisely to tear it down, and the transition from yellow music to mass music becomes a means to figure the very process of nationalist mobilization.[66] Even more interesting, however, is the sequence that follows this initial scene. Instead of remaining in the classroom as the song continues, a series of shots are shown of various individuals and families clustered around their radios at home, listening to a broadcast of this new song of national salvation. What we see here is both a dramatization of the power of the mass media to penetrate into domestic space and its ability to knit people together by way of its mastery over time (that is, the synchronicity of its reception by the listening audience).[67] Finally, a degree of self-referential sentience is embodied in this sequence, for it is only in the mass-mediated enactment of this moment of synchronicity that the leftist collectivity is created. But the creation of this collective voice and "the channeling of its violence and hopes" (to invoke Attali's dictum vis-à-vis the power inherent in technologies of sound reproduction and broadcasting) requires an individual contrast, a moment of silencing. Thus, midway through the radio sequence, the military brass drops from the soundtrack, and we see the solitary sing-song girl, Miss Yang, walking wordlessly down a snowy street in a thin dress, accompanied only by an off-screen chorus.

THE SING-SONG GIRL AND THE NATION

Despite the power and pathos of this sort of image (or perhaps because of it), leftist cinema on the eve of the Japanese invasion could not altogether dispense with the sing-song girl. Part of the reason for retaining the image, of course, was box-office appeal. Filmmaking is capital-intensive; stars like Zhou Xuan and Wang Renmei brought patrons into the theaters. There is a telling moment during the rendition of Nie Er's "March of the Volunteers" that concludes *Children of the Storm:* Wang Renmei regales her cinematic audience with a knowing smile that, in its winning incongruity, breaks free of the diegetic space of the film, forcing an awareness of the fictionality of the story and of the star system through which the cinematic experience is mediated. In other words, Wang's smile is a direct appeal, a reminder not only that her character Ah Feng, but also the actress herself, has been enlisted to the cause of national salvation.

This strategy proved effective. Much of the appeal to contemporary audiences of a now classic film such as *Street Angel* (directed by Yuan Muzhi in 1937), for instance, lay in its skillful deployment of a sing-song girl singing tunes that were more than a little reminiscent of Li Jinhui's "Drizzle" in terms of musical style and melodic contours, if not lyrical content.[68] Indeed, Zhou Xuan's two musical sequences in the film, "Song of the Seasons" (Siji ge) and "Sing-Song Girl at the Ends of the Earth" (Tianya genü) by He Luting and Tian Han, are still celebrated today as classics in the evolution of Mandarin modern song; they are distinctive for the manner in which they invoke not the turgid strains of Western (and specifically Soviet) martial music, as in Nie Er's work, but the mellifluous (and to leftist and more conservative highbrow critics alike, "decadent") melodic material of traditional urban folk song forms (often referred to as *xiaodiao*).

I want to briefly focus on one particularly revealing musical sequence from this justly famous film. Zhou Xuan, playing a sing-song girl modeled so closely on her own life that she shares her real (as opposed to stage) name Xiao Hong, is called by the proprietor of the teahouse where she works to sing a song for a gangster to whom he is trying to sell her as a concubine. The performative context duplicates in almost every particular the classic situation of the sing-song girl. The singer faces the client; the client gazes back appraisingly at her. The sing-song girl is on display. She is the fetishized object of a commercial transaction that is to take place between the gangster and the proprietor, and the song itself is supposed to be the sales pitch that closes the deal.

As in other commercial films of the era, the camera lingers lovingly over Zhou Xuan's body (clad in a cotton *qipao*) and facial expressions, emphasizing her star quality. At the same time, however, her vulnerability and reluctance to be forced into the role to which she had been assigned are clearly marked by her refusal to meet the gaze of the gangster and the fidgety way in which she tugs at her braided hair as she sings. Suddenly, the context of the performance is disrupted (and, more important, enlarged);

rather than dwelling exclusively on the trio in the teahouse, we are shown a montage sequence, keyed to Tian Han's song lyrics, which scroll across the bottom of the screen, pursued by a bouncing white ball:

Spring comes, and the window fills with green
A maiden by the window embroiders a pair of mandarin ducks
Suddenly, a heartless blow
Splits the ducks in two

Summer comes and the willow fronds grow long
The maiden has been blown south of the Yangzi River
The scenery's lovely all over the land
But how can it compare to the green sorghum fields at home?

Autumn comes and the lotus flowers are sweet
The maiden dreams of home night after night
When she wakes up she doesn't see the faces of mom and dad
Just the moonlight shining at the foot of the bed

Winter comes and snow flurries down
When winter clothes are ready I'll send them to my man
The great wall built of blood and flesh is long
Would that I could be the ancient Meng Jiang[69]

The "heartless blow" that separates Xiao Hong from her lover (mandarin ducks being a traditional symbol of conjugal bliss) is cinematically visualized as a barrage of Japanese artillery fire. Xiao Hong's difficulties, we realize, are a consequence of Japanese territorial encroachment; the war in Japanese-occupied Manchuria has made her a refugee from northern China, forced into thralldom as a sing-song girl in Shanghai.

Almost inevitably, the sequence ends with an image that deftly conveys both the ancient glory of the Chinese nation, and the necessity for national defense: the Great Wall. And Xiao Hong, in invoking the legend of Meng Jiang (a legendary heroine who died following the construction of the wall), offers herself as a martyr to the nationalist cause. Through montage, then, the pathos of the sing-song girl becomes an analogue for China's national crisis. Xiao Hong's oppression at the hands of the patriarchy is welded to—and ultimately displaced by—a larger narrative of national salvation. Thus, the filmmakers have had their cake and eaten it too; the fetishized star appeal of Zhou Xuan as sing-song girl is exploited at the same time that it is defused and rewritten by the presence of a larger discourse.

This process of rewriting lends a curious doubleness to this and many other examples of leftist cinematic and musical production, precisely because they cannot erase the physical traces of earlier inscriptions—those of the star system and the female bodies around which its political and discursive economies pivot. We have examined how in musical sequences from *Children of the Storm* as much as from *Street Angel*, voyeurism and nationalism come hand in hand.[70] The pathos of the fallen sing-song girl is appropriated by the discourse of nationalism; her humiliation (and salvation) figures that of the nation. Foregrounding the gendered traces of commercial media culture in these songs and films (and thus deepening our understanding of the history and mechanisms of nationalist discourse) is one of the goals of this study.

A second, and perhaps less immediately apparent agenda, has to do with the work of Li Jinhui. Just as Nie Er appropriates and rewrites Li's music in *New Woman* as a constitutive gesture in the creation of a new realist aesthetic and a new genre of mass music, leftist critics of the 1930s (as well as historians in the post-1949 period) rewrite (and in my view, radically impoverish) our understanding of the career of this pivotal figure in order to enforce nation-centered readings of Chinese cultural history. Strangely enough, conventional accounts of Li's trajectory read something like tales of fallen sing-song girls. The original innocence of his early nationalistic efforts to promote children's education is besmirched by his later descent into the tawdry world of commercial media culture. These accounts, of course, obscure the fact that Li's contributions to Chinese media culture are just as complex and ambivalent as those of his leftist counterparts. The sing-song girl was as much a product of May 4th era discourses of nation-building as of anything else. The brand of mass-mediated voyeurism that Li helped to forge, in other words, is informed by nationalism as much as leftist cinema is informed by voyeurism. And both—as evinced by their common appropriations of elements from the culture of Hollywood and Tin Pan Alley—were entangled in the pleasures and perils of colonial modernity. The task of the cultural historian, then, is to uncover the traces of each in the other, and in doing so, complicate our understanding of both.

Ah Feng	阿鳳
ai de jiaoyu	愛的教育
Aiguo gequ	愛國歌曲
An E	安娥
Bai Hong	白虹
Baidai xinsheng hui	百代新聲會
Baige changpian	百歌唱片
Bailemen	百樂門
Bajiao ye shang shi	芭蕉葉上詩
Beihai changpian	北海唱片
Beijing daxue yinyue chuanxi suo	北京大學音樂傳習所
Beijing daxue yinyue yanjiu hui	北京大學音樂會
Beikai	倍開
beili zhi wu	北里之舞
Bi Fen	碧芬
"Biye ge"	畢業歌
Cai Chusheng	蔡楚生
Cai Yuanpei	蔡元培
Chang Ping	昌平
Changcheng changpian gongsi	長城唱片公司
changge ji	唱歌集
Chiang Kai-shek	蔣介石
Chen Duxiu	陳獨秀
Cheng Bugao	程步高
Cheng Maoyun	程懋筠
Chongbian xuexiao changge ji	重編學校唱歌集
Chuangzao she	創造社
chuanju	川劇
"Chuntian de kuaile"	春天的快樂
Ciqu zuozhe lianyi hui	詞曲作者聯誼會
Ciqu yanjiu hui	詞曲研究會
Cui Wanqiu	崔萬秋

Dalu	大路
Datong she	大同社
Da wanbao fukan	大晚報副刊
Da Zhonghua changpian	大中華唱片
daitizhe qunzhong zai nahan	代替著群眾在吶喊
Deguoren zhi yinyue shenghuo	德國人之音樂生活
Deng Lijun	鄧麗君
Diansheng	電聲
Diantong yingye gongsi	電通影業公司
"Dianying de minzhonghua"	電影的民眾化
Dianying yishu	電影藝術
"Disan guoji dang de songge"	第三國際党的頌歌
Dongfang baidai changpian gongsi	東方百代唱片公司
Dongfang zazhi	東方雜誌
Dongxi yuezhi zhi yanjiu	東西樂制之研究
Du Mu	杜牧
Du Yuesheng	杜月笙
Emei changpian gongsi	峨嵋唱片公司
erhu	二胡
ertong biaoyan qu	兒童表演曲
"Fengjian de xiao shimin de wenyi"	封建的小市民的文藝
Feng Zikai	豐子愷
Fengyun ernü	風雲兒女
Furong tuan	芙蓉團
fuxing guoyue	復興國樂
Fu Ye	茯野
Gaoting	高亭
"Geming de wenxue jia dao minjian qu"	革命的文學家到民間去
genü	歌女
Genü Hong mudan	歌女紅牧丹
gewu ju	歌舞劇
Gexing huabao	歌星畫報
Gengyi ji	更衣記
gongche pu	工尺譜
Gong Qiuxia	龔秋霞

Gu Menghe	顧夢鶴
Guangzhou yinyue yuan	廣州音樂院
guanyin baxian	灌音八仙
guo feng	國風
Guo Moruo	郭沫若
guofang wenxue	國防文學
"Guoji ge"	國際歌
Guoji wuchang	國際舞場
Guoli yinyue yuan	國立音樂院
guomin xing	國民性
Guoyu zhuanxiu xuexiao	國語傳修學校
guoyue	國樂
Guoyue changpian	國樂唱片
Guoyue gaijin she	國樂改進社
Guoyue yanjiu she	國樂研究社
Han Langen	韓蘭根
He Luting	賀綠汀
Hei tianshi	黑天使
Hen dao	恨島
"Heri jun zai lai"	何日君再來
Hesheng changpian	和聲唱片
Hongkew (Hongqiao)	虹橋
Hong Xiuquan	洪秀全
Hu Qie	胡茄
Hu Rongrong	胡蓉蓉
Hu Shi	胡適
"Hua diao"	花凋
hua xiazi	話匣子
"Huangpu jiang"	黃浦江
huangse yinyue	黃色音樂
Huang Shounian	黃壽年
Huang Zi	黃自
huju	滬劇
Jianmei yundong	健美運動
Jiating aiqing gequ	家庭愛情歌曲
Jiangxi tuixing yinyue jiaoyu weiyuan hui	江西推行音樂教育委員會

Jiang Xiuxia	江秀霞
jiaohua	教化
Jiaotong bu	交通部
"Jiao wo ruhe bu xiang ta"	教我如何不想他
"Jiuguo zhi ge"	救國之歌
Kai ge	凱歌
Kaiming	開明
kaipian	開篇
Kunlun changpian	崑崙唱片
kunqu	崑曲
Lan Ping	藍萍
"Laohu jiaomen"	老虎叫門
Li Aying	李阿英
Li Chuli	李初梨
Li Dazhao	李大釗
Lige	麗歌
Li Jinhui	黎錦暉
Li Jinming	黎錦明
Li Jinxi	黎錦熙
Li Jinyang	黎錦揚
Li Jinyao	黎錦耀
Li Junquan	黎均荃
Li Lili	黎莉莉
Li Minghui	黎明暉
Li Shutong	李叔同
Li Weisen	李偉森
Li Xianglan	李香蘭
Lianhua gewuban	聯華歌舞班
Lianhua jiaoxiang qu	聯華交響曲
Lianxing changpian	聯星唱片
Liang Qichao	梁啟超
"Liangxin"	良心
Liangyou	良友
Liu Fu	劉復
Liu Tianhua	劉天華
"Liusheng ji pian"	留聲機片
"Liusheng jiqi de huiyin"	留聲機器的迴音

Liusheng ji	留聲機
Lu Xun	魯迅
Lülü zhengyi	律呂正義
Malu tianshi	馬路天使
"Maque yu xiaohai"	麻雀與小孩
Maxu Weibang	馬徐維邦
Mao Dun	茅盾
"Maomao yu"	毛毛雨
Mei Lanfang	梅蘭芳
Meiguo shengli	美國勝利
Meihua gewutuan	梅花歌舞團
Meimei nüxiao	美美女校
meimei qiang	妹妹腔
"Meimei wo ai ni"	妹妹我愛你
meiyu	美育
Meizhou pinglun	每週評論
mimi zhi yin	靡靡之音
Minguo changge ji	民國唱歌集
Minzu zhi guang	民族之光
Minzhong geyong hui	民眾歌詠會
Mingyue geju she	明月歌劇社
Mingyue gewutuan	明月歌舞團
Mingxing	明星
nalai zhuyi	拿來主義
Nanguo she	南國社
Nie Er	聶耳
Nie Shouxin	聶守信
"Nuli"	努力
Nüsheng	女聲
Ouzhou yinyue jinhua lun	歐洲音樂進化論
Pan Guangdan	潘光旦
pibao gongsi	皮包公司
pingju	評劇
pingmin jiaoyu	平民教育
Pingmin qianzi keben	平民千字課本
Pingmin shitang	平民食堂

pingmin wenxue	平民文學
pingmin yinyue	平民音樂
Pingmin zhoubao	平民周報
"Putao xianzi"	葡萄仙子
qipao	旗袍
Qian Guangren	錢廣仁
qin	琴
Qingfeng wuyue dui	清風舞樂隊
qingyin	清音
Qingzhu	青主
Qiu Jin	秋瑾
Qu Qiubai	瞿秋白
qingchun hua	青春化
qunzhong yinyue	群眾音樂
Ren Guang	任光
Renjian xianzi	人間仙子
Ruan Lingyu	阮玲玉
"San hudie"	三蝴蝶
Sanyou shi	三友式
Sasa Kōka	佐佐紅華
Shanghai she	上海社
"Shanghai wenyi zhi yipie"	上海文藝之一瞥
Shanghai shiyan jushe	上海實驗劇社
shangsu mimi	商俗靡靡
Shangwu yinshuguan	商務印書館
Shaonian Zhongguo	少年中國
Shen Fengxi	沈鳳喜
Shengli	勝利
shenqu	申曲
"Shenxian meimei"	神仙妹妹
Shen Xingong	沈心工
Sheng zhi aige	生之哀歌
shidai qu	時代曲
Shiji	史記
Shijing	詩經
Shizi jietou	十字街頭

shōka (changge)	唱歌
"Shouzai paituo"	壽仔拍拖
shu fei xingguo zhi yin	殊非興國之音
"Shuangxing qu"	雙星曲
sida tianwang	四大天王
"Siji ge"	四季歌
Sima Qian	司馬遷
Sitson Ma (Ma Sicong)	馬思聰
Songzhu shige	頌主詩歌
Sulian zhi you she	蘇聯之友社
Sun Shiyi	孫師毅
Sun Yu	孫瑜
suyue	俗樂
Taiping changpian	太平唱片
tanci	彈辭
"Taohua jiang"	桃花江
Taoli jie	桃李劫
"Tebie kuaiche"	特別快車
Tian Han	田漢
"Tianya genü"	天涯歌女
Tianyi	天一
Tianyun she	天韻社
"Tieti xia de genü"	鐵蹄下的歌女
Wang Daping	王達平
Wang Guangqi	王光祈
Wang Manjie	汪曼杰
Wang Renmei	王人美
Wei Ming	偉明
wenren	文人
"Wuban zhi ge"	舞伴之歌
"Wu ti"	無題
Wuchang chunse	舞場春色
Wukeduo	物克多
"Wuxie zhi ge"	舞榭之歌
xiansheng	先生
Xian Xinghai	冼星海

Xiang Gu	香谷
xiangyan rougan	香艷肉感
Xiao changzhu	小廠主
xiao diao	小調
Xiao maotou	小毛頭
Xiao pengyou	小朋友
xiao shimin	小市民
"Xiao xiao huajia"	小小畫家
Xiaoshuo yuebao	小說月報
"Xiaoyang jiumu"	小羊救母
Xiao Youmei	蕭友梅
Xin Ma Shisheng	新馬師生
Xin nüxing	新女性
Xin qingnian	新青年
xin yinge	新淫歌
Xingqi huabao	興起畫報
Xingshi changpian	醒獅唱片
Xinhua huabao	新華畫報
Xinyue ji	新月集
Xinyue liusheng ji changpian gongsi	新月留聲機唱片公司
xionglie beizhuang	雄烈悲壯
Xu Lai	徐來
Xu Teli	徐特立
Xu Xingzhi	許幸之
Xue Juexian (Sit Gok-sin)	薛覺先
Xue Lingxian	薛玲仙
xuetang yuege	學堂樂歌
Xuexiao changge ji	學校唱歌集
Xuyuan	徐園
Yan Gongshang	嚴工上
Yang Jiuhuan	楊九還
"Yangren daxiao"	洋人大笑
Yangxin shenshi	養心神詩
Yao Li	姚莉
Yasuiqian	壓歲錢
yayue	雅樂
Yazhou changpian	亞洲唱片

Yeban gesheng	夜半歌聲
Yihua yingye gongsi	藝華影業公司
yindang	淫蕩
Yinhan shuangxing	銀漢雙星
Ying Shangneng	應尚能
yingxi	影戲
Yingxi zazhi	影戲雜誌
"Yingxiong shu"	英雄樹
"Yinyue de shili"	音樂的勢力
Yinyue jiangxi hui	音樂講習會
Yinyue rumen	音樂入門
Yinyue yu shenghuo	音樂與生活
Yinyue zazhi	音樂雜誌
Yinyue zhoukan	音樂週刊
Yisheng	藝聲
"Yiyongjun jinxingqu"	義勇軍進行曲
"Youxi"	游戲
Yu Ling	余伶
Yuan Muzhi	袁牧之
Yuan Shikai	袁世凱
yuanyang hudie pai	鴛鴦蝴蝶派
Yueji	樂記
yueju	越劇
"Yueming zhi ye"	月明之夜
"Yuguang qu"	漁光曲
Yule zhoubao	娛樂週報
Zeng Zhimin	曾志忞
"Zenyang jianshe geming wenxue"	怎樣健設革命文學
Zhabei	閘北
Zhang Ailing (Eileen Chang)	張愛玲
Zhang Changfu	張長福
Zhang Henshui	張恨水
Zhang Shu	張曙
Zhang Zhidong	張之洞
Zhao Enrong	趙恩榮
Zhao Meibo (Chao Mei-pa)	趙梅伯
Zhao Yuanren	趙元任

Zheng Junli	鄭君里
Zheng Zhenduo	鄭振鐸
"Zhongguo gewu duanlun"	中國歌舞短論
Zhongguo xinxing yinyue yanjiu hui	中國新興音樂研究會
Zhongguo zuoyi xiju jia lianmeng hui yinyue xiaozu	中國左翼戲劇家聯盟會音樂小組
Zhonghua gewutuan	中華歌舞團
Zhonghua gewu zhuanmen xuexiao	中華歌舞傳門學校
Zhonghua pingmin jiaoyu cujin hui	中華平民教育促進會
Zhonghua shuju	中華書局
Zhongshen dashi	終身大事
zhongxi hebi	中西合璧
Zhongyang yingxi gongsi	中央影戲公司
Zhou	紂
Zhou Shoujuan	周瘦鵑
Zhou Xiaohong	周小紅
Zhou Xuan	周璇
Zhou Yang	周揚
Zhu Yingpeng	朱應鵬
"Zongli jinian ge"	總理紀念歌
"Zuihou de shengli"	最後的勝利
Zuoyi xin yinyue yundong	左翼新音樂運動
Zuoyi zuojia lianmeng hui	左翼作家聯盟會

INTRODUCTION: LISTENING TO THE CHINESE JAZZ AGE

1 Buck Clayton's account of his Shanghai sojourn is included in Buck Clayton, with Nancy Miller Elliot, *Buck Clayton's Jazz World* (New York: Oxford University Press, 1987), 70. Clayton's is not the only account of interwar Shanghai left by an African American traveler. The author and activist W. E. B. Du Bois visited in 1936 and was so disgusted by the open discrimination practiced against local Chinese by white colonials that he likened the city to "Mississippi." See Du Bois, "Shanghai," *Pittsburgh Courier*, February 27, 1937. The testimony of the celebrated poet Langston Hughes, who spent time in Shanghai in 1933 and met with Chinese cultural and political figures such as Lu Xun and Madame Sun Yat Sen, as well as many key participants in the local African American jazz scene, is similarly scalding: ". . . cruelty and violence, corruption and graft were written all over the face of Shanghai the summer I was there. . . . none of the leading hotels in the International Settlement accepted Asiatic or Negro guests. The British and French clubs, of course, excluded Orientals. I was constantly amazed in Shanghai at the impudence of white foreigners in drawing a color line against the Chinese *in China itself*." His impressions of the areas outside the International Settlement, however, were quite different. "On the whole, I found the Chinese in Shanghai a very jolly people, much like colored folks at home. To tell the truth, I was more afraid of going into the world-famous Cathay Hotel than I was of going into any public place in the Chinese quarters. Colored people were not welcomed at the Cathay. But beyond the gates of the International Settlement, color was no barrier." See Hughes, *I Wonder as I Wander: An Autobiographical Journey* (New York: Rinehart, 1956), 248–49, 250–51.

2 Clayton, 60. For a fascinating article on the opportunities available for American jazz bands in the 1930s in Shanghai and elsewhere throughout Asia, see Claude Lapham's "China Needs American Bands," *Metronome* (July 1936), 13. Lapham was an American songwriter and sometime jazz musician who spent a year working for Columbia Records in Japan and touring Asia, subsequently writing a series of articles on jazz in Asia for *Metronome*. Lapham's optimistic assessment of the opportunities available for American in Shanghai is refuted in another article by a musician already working in the city, S. James Staley, who asks "Is It True What They Say About China?," *Metronome* (December 1936).

3 See Lapham, "China Needs American Bands," 13.

4 See E. Taylor Atkins's fascinating study, "The Jazz Frontier: The Japanese Jazz Community in Interwar Shanghai." Unpublished typescript, 1996. Langston Hughes describes Weatherford's role in the Shanghai jazz community thus:

> Shanghai was an enormous city of almost four million people, so I never saw the whole of it. But I did see a great deal of it, from the Bund to Bubbling Well Road and the race tracks and outlying districts, the theaters, amusement parks, and the Canidrome Gardens, where the best American jazz band in the Orient was playing. Headed by the pianist, Teddy Weatherford, this group of Negro musicians at the Canidrome were known from Calcutta and Bombay through the Malay States to Manila, Hong Kong, and Port Arthur. They were very popular in Shanghai, which seemed to have a weakness for American Negro performers. The sparkling Nora Hold had just completed a long engagement at the Little Club shortly before I arrived, singing and playing at the piano her intriguing versions of French and American songs. The young radio singer, Midge Williams, and her dancing brothers had been in China that spring, too. Other performers that Shanghai loved were Valaida Snow, a kind of Josephine Bakeresque artist of stunning gowns and varied songs. Bob Hill's band, Jack Carter's band and Buck Clayton's trumpet thrilled the International Settlements. But these people came, performed, and departed. Teddy Weatherford, however, had become a sort of permanent institution in the Orient."

5 Clayton, 68.
6 Clayton, 70.
7 Clayton, 68.
8 The Canidrome is advertised in a 1935 guidebook to Shanghai as "the Rendezvous of Shanghai's Elite." Buck Clayton and Teddy Weatherford are also mentioned as the featured acts at the cabaret. See *All About Shanghai and Environs: A Standard Guide Book* (Shanghai: University Press, 1934–35), 42.
9 Clayton, 68.
10 Clayton, 71.
11 The hierarchy of Shanghai cabarets in the 1930s is also addressed in *All About Shanghai*: "The cabarets . . . are in three classifications; high class, low class, and no class. You take your choice. The Number One places will be thickly dotted with dinner jackets and Paris frocks and you bring your own girl or engage in a little social piracy; the Number Two's supply the 'dancing hostesses' at a moderate fee if one is stagging it, and the Number Three's—but why bring that up?" See *All About Shanghai*, 75. The Casa Nova, which trumpets its "beautiful dance hostesses" in an advertisement on p. 136 of the same guide, clearly belonged to the low-class echelon of cabarets.
12 Clayton, 76. Interestingly, Clayton speaks of his own growing certainty

that Japan would launch a military assault on China, a certainty fueled by a number of ugly incidents he witnessed in 1936 and 1937 involving mistreatment of Chinese citizens by Japanese military personnel. This apprehension prompted his timely departure from the city in 1937. See Clayton, 77–78.

13 See Wong Kee-chee's definition of the term in "Two or Three Things About Mandarin Pop," in Law Kar, ed., *Mandarin Films and Popular Songs, 40s–60s: Program of the 17th Hong Kong International Film Festival* (Hong Kong: Urban Council, 1993), 18.

14 See Tani Barlow, "Introduction: On Colonial Modernity," in Tani Barlow, ed., *Formations of Colonial Modernity in East Asia* (Durham, N.C.: Duke University Press, 1997), 1. The term "treaty ports" refers to the string of Chinese coastal cities forced open to European and American diplomatic and commercial interests beginning in 1842, with the British empire's resounding military defeat of the Qing dynasty in the Opium Wars of 1839–42.

15 An (as yet unwritten) history of the intense, sustained, and productive engagement of American jazz musicians with the Orient, both real and fantasmatic, might stretch from Fletcher Henderson's 1934 recording of his "Shanghai Shuffle," to the self-consciously exotic stylings of Sun Ra in the 1950s, through Duke Ellington's masterful "Far East Suite," and the "Eastern" philosophical and musical modalities attributed to such leading players as Miles Davis and John Coltrane, with many stops in between.

16 Significantly, scholarly interest in "modern songs" has been relatively strong in (ex-British colonial) Hong Kong, whence two useful volumes focusing on this genre have emerged. The first is a textbook by Wong Kee-chee, *Shidai qu zonglun* (A comprehensive study of modern songs) (Hong Kong: Chinese University of Hong Kong Extension School and RTHK, 1978). The second is Law Kar, ed. *Mandarin Films and Popular Songs, 40s–60s.*

17 See, for instance, Liang Maochun. "Dui woguo liuxing yinyue lishi de sikao" (Thoughts on the history of Chinese popular music), *Renmin yinyue* 7 (1988): 33.

18 Sue Tuohy cites three such instances. See Tuohy, "Metropolitan Sounds: Music in Chinese Films of the 1930s," in Yingjin Zhang, ed., *Cinema and Urban Culture in Shanghai, 1922–1943* (Stanford, Calif.: Stanford University Press, 1999), 201.

19 European and American studies of Chinese popular music (including my own work on Chinese popular music in the post-Mao period), for example, have focused almost entirely on developments in the 1980s and 1990s. See Andrew F. Jones, *Like a Knife: Ideology and Genre in Contemporary Chinese Popular Music* (Ithaca, N.Y.: Cornell East Asia Series, 1992). Journalistic accounts of contemporary popular culture include Jianying Zha, *China Pop: How Soap Operas, Tabloids, and Bestsellers Are Transforming a Culture* (New York: New Press, 1995).

20 See Tani Barlow, "Colonialism's Career in Postwar China Studies," in Barlow, ed., 375.

21 See John Baxendale's study of the relation between sexuality, racial discourse, and the globalization of popular music in Great Britain in the first few decades of the twentieth century, " 'Into Another Kind of Life in Which Anything Might Happen . . .': Popular Music and Late Modernity, 1910–1930," *Popular Music* 14, no. 2 (1995): 251.

22 See Johannes Fabian, *Time and the Other: How Anthropology Makes Its Object* (New York: Columbia University Press, 1983), 31.

23 See Michael Taussig, *Mimesis and Alterity: A Particular History of the Senses* (New York: Routledge, 1993), 199. Taussig by no means exhausts the range of materials that could be subsumed under this particular category of colonial discourse; such tropes suffuse both scholarly and popular culture throughout the first few decades of the twentieth century and beyond. Examples stretch from the Belgian comic book artist Hergé's 1930 *Tintin au Congo* (in which Tintin uses a gramophone and a camera to unmask the chicanery of a tribal chief), to Jane Campion's celebrated 1994 film, *The Piano,* in which a group of hapless Maoris are depicted as being too naive to understand that a frightening murder performed by their nineteeth-century colonizers as part of a shadow play is merely a performance and not the real thing. See Hergé, *Tintin au Congo* (Brussels: Casterman, 1946), 25–27.

24 Taussig, 208.

25 Indeed, Clark's book opens with a sentence that seems intent on casting China and the film medium at opposite epistemological and temporal poles in a manner typical of imperialist historiography: "China is one of the oldest continuous civilizations; film is the most modern of the arts." See Paul Clark, *Chinese Cinema: Culture and Politics Since 1949* (New York: Cambridge University Press, 1987), 1. Other references to film as a foreign medium crop up as well; see Clark, 68, 69, and 101.

26 See Yingjin Zhang, "Introduction: Cinema and Urban Culture in Shanghai," in Zhang, ed., 14. Zhang is summarizing the content of an article by Leo Lee, but I think it is fair to say that the statement captures something of the force of a number of other articles in the book as well as a spate of studies by Chinese scholars on the question of how the traditional shadow play (*yingxi*) mediated the reception of cinema in China. See also Zhen Zhang, "Teahouse, Shadowplay, Bricolage: 'Laborer's Love' and the Question of Early Chinese Cinema," in Zhang, ed., 33.

27 For a brief account of the arrival of cinema in China, see Lee Daw-ming, "How Cinema Came to China: Some Theories and Doubts," in Law Kar, ed., *Early Images of Hong Kong and China: The 19th Hong Kong International Film Festival* (Hong Kong, Urban Council, 1995), 33–36.

28 Wang Dingjiu, *Shanghai menjing* (Guide to Shanghai) (Shanghai: Zhong-

yang shuju, 1932), 20. As cited in Leo Ou-fan Lee, *Shanghai Modern: The Flowering of a New Urban Culture in China, 1930–1945* (Cambridge, Mass.: Harvard University Press, 1999), 89.

29 See Zheng Junli, "Xiandai Zhongguo dianying shilüe" (A brief history of modern Chinese cinema), in Zhongguo dianying ziliao guan, ed., *Zhongguo wusheng dianying* (Chinese silent cinema) (Beijing: Zhongguo dianying chubanshe, 1996).

30 Zheng Junli, 1412.

31 The colonial (even racist) assumptions of such a culturalist logic are immediately exposed by a simple question: Is there any culturally specific reason that Chinese people would have had more trouble assimilating cinematic technology than, say, the French? Why, for that matter, don't we speak of Gutenberg's struggle to adapt to a Chinese medium? Or of French, English, or American efforts to Westernize gunpowder?

32 See Friedrich Kittler, *Gramophone, Cinema, Typewriter,* trans. Geoffrey Winthrop Young and Michael Wutz (Stanford, Calif.: Stanford University Press, 1999), xl.

33 Rey Chow's fascinating rereading of Lu Xun's famous transformative encounter with the "technologized visuality" of a Japanese lantern slide of an execution as a moment of modernist shock and postcolonial subject formation is a striking case in point. See Chow, *Primitive Passions: Visuality, Sexuality, Ethnography, and Contemporary Chinese Cinema* (New York: Columbia University Press, 1995), 4–16.

34 The most notable of these theories of globalization in the realm of culture—one addressed in more detail in chapter 2—is Arjun Appadurai's *Modernity at Large: Cultural Dimensions of Globalization* (Minneapolis: University of Minnesota Press, 1996).

35 See "Zai tingbudao Zhou Xuan de yuanyin gesheng le" (We'll never hear Zhou Xuan's original recordings again), *Yangcheng wanbao,* April 8, 1999.

36 This useful term derives from the work of the British scholar of popular music, Richard Middleton, who deploys a "topographical" mode of analysis (loosely drawn from Pierre Bourdieu's sociology of culture) to sidestep the ever-problematic issue of defining—in an essentializing and ahistorical manner—the precise nature, position, and function of "popular" music in opposition to "folk," "serious," or other such classifications.

37 See, for instance, Stephen Teo, "The Shanghai Hangover: The Early Years of Mandarin Cinema in Hong Kong," in Law Kar, ed., *Mandarin Films and Popular Songs, 40s–60s,* 17–25.

38 Teng's repertoire included many of the most immediately recognizable songs of the pre-1949 era of modern song, including Zhou Xuan's controversial 1938 piece, "When Will You Return?" (Heri jun zai lai). The complex history of the song is worth recounting. Originally recorded for a forgettable (and no longer extant) 1938 entertainment film, *Three Stars*

and the Moon (*Sanxing ban yue*), the song has come to represent the ostensible "decadence," escapism, and sensuality of what authorities in Mainland China and Taiwan alike usually denigrate as "yellow music." Part of the reason for this notoriety is the lyrical content. A Shanghai singsong girl/prostitute drinks with her lover/client, at the same time espousing a philosophy of sensual pleasure and living for the moment that was seen as highly inimical to the nationalist cause. Despite the seemingly apolitical nature of the lyrics, however, the song was inexorably drawn into the labyrinth of wartime politics in Shanghai in a manner that reveals both the intertwining of culture and politics in modern China and the mercurial nature of popular musical meaning. First released during the "orphan island" period in Shanghai (when all of Greater Shanghai was occupied by the Japanese, except for the International Settlement, which remained under the control of U.S., British, Japanese, and French authorities until the outbreak of the Pacific war in December 1941), the song was attacked for its above mentioned escapist celebration of sensuality by Chinese nationalists in Shanghai, and banned by the Nationalist government from its wartime capital in Chongqing. In 1939, it also was recorded in Japanese by a pop singer named Watanabe Hamako and subsequently banned by Japanese military authorities, who feared its "foreign decadence" would sap the military morale of invading forces. A final irony: in the closing stages of the war, the song began to be interpreted as a political allegory—rather than a mere love song; it was alleged that the "you" of the song actually referred to the Nationalist Party, and that the singer in effect was entreating the Nationalists to return to Shanghai from Chongqing and rescue its downtrodden people from Japanese occupation. In 1944, Li Xianglan (a controversial wartime star who was Japanese-born and raised in China and who concealed her real identity from Chinese audiences to more effectively serve the propaganda needs of the Japanese occupying forces) was even interrogated by Chinese collaborators in the Shanghai police force, who accused her of singing the song in concert as a gesture of anti-Japanese protest! Seen in this context, Teng's reintroduction of the song to Mainland audiences in the early 1980s takes on a complex, ironic cast.

39 This question is informed in part by the theoretical concerns voiced in the preface to Lydia Liu's *Translingual Practice: Literature, National Culture, and Translated Modernity* (Stanford, Calif.: Stanford University Press, 1995), xv. Liu, in asserting the necessity of attending to the problem of translation and translingual practice in "cross-cultural interpretation," asks what it means "to translate one culture into the language of another on the basis of commonly perceived equivalences?" The transposition of this question into musical terms is one of the many analytical threads that runs through the present study.

1. THE ORCHESTRATION OF CHINESE MUSICAL LIFE

1   Hector Berlioz, *Evenings with the Orchestra* (New York: Alfred A. Knopf, 1956), 247–48.

2   Zhang Ailing, *Liuyan* (Written on water) (Hong Kong: Huangguan, 1994), 213.

3   My understanding of the "musical field" is loosely adapted from Pierre Bourdieu's sociological understanding of a cultural field, "structured by the distribution of available positions (e.g., consecrated artist vs. striving artist, novel vs. poetry, art for art's sake vs. social art) . . . [and] the struggles between these positions, a struggle often expressed in the conflict between the orthodoxy of established traditions and the heretical challenge of new modes of cultural practice, manifested as *prises de position* or position-takings." See Randal Johnson, "Editor's Introduction," in Pierre Bourdieu, *The Field of Cultural Production: Essays on Art and Literature* (New York: Columbia University Press, 1993), 16–17.

4   An enormous amount of literature exists on the question of the relationship of music to language. Michael Chanan provides a cogent summary of some of the major positions in his *Musica Practica: The Social Practice of Western Music from Gregorian Chant to Postmodernism* (London: Verso, 1994), 81–89.

5   Richard Kraus, *Pianos and Politics in China: Middle-Class Ambitions and the Struggle Over Western Music* (New York: Oxford University Press, 1989), 197. Kraus devotes pages 30–32 to debunking this myth.

6   See Jacques Attali, trans. Brian Massumi, *Noise: The Political Economy of Music* (Minneapolis: University of Minnesota Press, 1985), 7.

7   The phrase belongs to Attali, 6.

8   For a detailed account of the relation between Protestant hymns and the Taiping rebellion, see Isabel K. F. Wong, "*Geming gequ:* Songs for the Education of the Masses," in Bonnie Macdougal, ed., *Popular Chinese Culture and Performing Arts in the People's Republic of China, 1949–1979* (Berkeley: University of California Press, 1984), 113–14.

9   See Borthwick, *Education and Social Change in China: The Beginnings of the Modern Era* (Stanford, Calif.: Stanford University Press, 1983), 137. As Isabel Wong and others have noted, these appropriations of Western musical forms exercised a profound influence on subsequent efforts on the part of both leftist musicians in the 1930s and Communist Party officials after 1949 to mobilize the masses by way of revolutionary songs.

10   The first phrase derives from Xiao Youmei, "Yinyue de shili" (The power of music), *Yinyue jiaoyu* 3 (March 1934): 9. The second phrase is from Chao Mei-pa, "The Trend of Modern Chinese Music," *T'ien Hsia Monthly* 3 (March 1937): 271. For a rich account of the status of the piano as a privi-

liged signifier of Western musical culture, see Kraus, *Pianos and Politics in China.*

11   See Chao Mei-pa, 280. The discourse of nationalism remained very much a part of European musical criticism throughout the 1920s and 1930s. One fascinating example is an essay by Adolf Weissman, a prominent German critic, titled "Race and Modernity" and published in the February 1924 issue of *Modern Music,* an influential American journal. In this article, Weissman attacks the tendency of the modern musical avant-garde to strive for a "world-vernacular" and reminds readers that "it is race which colors modernity . . . in music, blood and not mind is the ultimate determinant." See Harry Haskell, ed., *The Attentive Listener: Three Centuries of Music Criticism* (Princeton, N.J.: Princeton University Press, 1996), 260–63.

12   This tendency, of course, was shared by literary counterparts like Mao Dun and Lu Xun in the form of artistic and political disdain for urban popular cultural forms as diverse as "Mandarin Ducks and Butterfly" (yuanyang hudie pai) fiction and commercial cinema.

13   It is important to note that by the 1890s, this gap had begun to be bridged, not only by Chinese reformers, but by European musical modernists such as Claude Debussy, whose work invoked "Oriental" notions of modal harmony and tonal color precisely in order to topple the edifice of Romantic music erected by composers like Beethoven and Berlioz. Significantly, Debussy's turn toward the East was inspired by a performance of Javanese music he witnessed at the Exposition Universelle held in Paris in 1889. That Debussy's revelatory experiments were in part facilitated by the imperialistic project of the world exposition is, of course, a fascinating illustration of the (all too often submerged) colonial character of European modernity. See Chanan, *Musica Practica,* 226–29.

14   The earliest system of notation in China, as described in Sima Qian's *Records of the Historian* (*Shi ji*), dates back to the 6th century B.C. The earliest surviving system dates to the Tang dynasty. A standardized format for pitch notation, called *gongche pu,* derives from the tenth century. In addition, there are various systems of tablature for the *qin* and other musical instruments. For a detailed account of these systems, see Joseph Needham, *Science and Civilization in China,* vol. 4 (Cambridge: Cambridge University Press, 1962), 161.

15   Kraus, 19.

16   See Max Weber, *The Rational and Social Foundations of Music* (London: Feffer and Sims, 1977). As cited in Chanan, *Musica Practica,* 59.

17   Chanan, *Musica Practica,* 77–78.

18   Chanan, *Musica Practica,* 78.

19   Once again, an interesting parallel can be seen here with developments in the literary field. Leo Ou-fan Lee in his work on Chinese literature in the late Qing and early Republican era discusses the emergence of the professional writer (*wenren*) as a distinctly modern occupational category, a de-

velopment he sees as emblematic of the advent of Chinese modernity. See Leo Ou-fan Lee, *The Romantic Generation of Modern Chinese Writers* (Cambridge, Mass.: Harvard University Press, 1973).

20 Attali, 47.

21 Scattered throughout Jacques Gernet's study of quotidian life in thirteenth-century Hangzhou, for instance, are a number of illuminating details about the ways in which music was enjoyed in premodern China. See Gernet, *Daily Life in China on the Eve of the Mongol Invasion, 1250–1276* (Stanford, Calif.: Stanford University Press, 1962).

22 Kraus, 4. See also Jonathan Spence, *The Memory Palace of Matteo Ricci* (New York: Viking Penguin, 1984), 194–95, 197–200.

23 See Wang Yuhe, *Zhongguo jinxiandai yinyue shi* (A history of modern Chinese music) (Beijing: Renmin yinyue chubanshe, 1994), 16.

24 See Ma Hiao-Ts'iun, *La Musique Chinoise de Style Européen* (Paris: Jouve, 1941), 14.

25 Wang Yuhe, 17.

26 Bruno Nettl's *The Western Impact on World Music* (New York: Schirmer Books, 1985) is an authoritative study of the acculturation of European music in the colonized world.

27 For an account of the diffusion of Western music in Meiji Japan, see Elizabeth May, *The Influence of the Meiji Period on Japanese Children's Music* (Berkeley: University of California Press, 1963), 39–56.

28 Morrison's collection was titled *Yangxin shenshi* (Hymns for spiritual cultivation). See Wang Yuhe,17.

29 For information on various editions, see Wang Yuhe, 17–18.

30 See Isabel K. F. Wong, "*Geming gequ*," 113–14.

31 According to Wang Yuhe, a 1989 fact-finding expedition from the Central Conservatory of Music in Beijing found that many of these hymns were still extant among the Lisu and Bulang peoples in Yunnan province. See Wang Yuhe, 18.

32 See Kenneth S. Latourette, *A History of Christian Missions in China* (New York: Macmillan, 1929), 416–34, 495—641. As cited in Isabel K. F. Wong, "*Geming gequ*," 115.

33 Isabel K. F. Wong, "*Geming gequ*," 114.

34 Kraus, 4.

35 The Shanghai Public Band was established in 1879 by the Shanghai Municipal Council. In Beijing, Robert Hart (an Irishman who was acting head of the Chinese customs service as a result of unequal treaties imposed on the Qing by the Great Powers) maintained a similar military band.

36 An instance of this practice is captured on film in the opening sequence of Yuan Muzhi's 1937 masterpiece for the Star (Mingxing) film studio, *Street Angel (Malu tianshi)*.

37 For a general treatment of the relationship, see Akira Iriye, ed., *The Chinese and the Japanese: Essays in Political and Cultural Interactions* (Prince-

ton, N.J.: Princeton University Press, 1980). The influence of Japan on Chinese educational reform is covered in Yue-him Tam, "Meiji Japan and the Educational and Language Reforms in Late Ch'ing China," in James W. White, Michio Umegaki, and Thomas R. H. Havens, eds., *The Ambivalence of Nationalism: Modern Japan Between East and West* (Lanham, Md.: University Press of America, 1990), 61–78.

38   Liang believed that music was an essential tool in the "spiritual education" of the Chinese citizenry. See his *Yinbingshi shihua* (Poetry talk from the ice drinker's studio) (Beijing: Renmin wenxue chubanshe, 1982), 58.

39   Among the group's members were three of the most prolific composers of school songs: Shen Xingong, Zeng Zhimin, and Li Shutong. The late Qing reformer Zhang Zhidong also was a noted composer of school songs.

40   See May, 42.

41   See Cai Yuanpei, "Wenhua jiaoyu buyao wangliao meiyu" (The education of culture must not forget aesthetic education), in Gao Pingshu, ed., *Cai Yuanpei meiyu lunji* (A collection of Cai Yuanpei's essays on aesthetic education) (Changsha: Hunan jiaoyu chubanshe, 1987), 57.

42   Liang Qichao, 58. The term "aesthetic education" was coined by Cai Yuanpei as a translation of the German concept of *ästhetische erziehung*. See Cai Yuanpei, "Ershiwu nian lai Zhongguo zhi meiyu" (Twenty-five years of aesthetic education in China), in Gao Pingshu, ed., 216.

43   Borthwick, 147.

44   For an informative account of the development of the newspaper and publishing industries in the late Qing and early Republic, see Leo Ou-fan Lee and Andrew J. Nathan, "The Beginnings of Mass Culture: Journalism and Fiction in the Late Ch'ing and Beyond," in David Johnson, Andrew J. Nathan, and Evelyn S. Rawski, eds., *Popular Culture in Late Imperial China* (Berkeley: University of California Press, 1985), 360–98.

45   Wang Yuhe, 28. Unfortunately, it is difficult (if not impossible) to estimate how many of these sorts of songbooks were actually published and sold. Considering that these books were for classroom use, and that the music classes for which they served as primary material were mandatory in primary schools throughout China, the numbers must have been considerable.

46   Isabel K. F. Wong, "*Geming gequ*," 116.

47   The schools in question were the Beijing Women's Normal College (1920), Shanghai Normal College (1920), Shanghai School of Fine Arts (1925), Shanghai Fine Arts University (1925), and the Beijing National Institute of Beaux-Arts (1926). See Wang Yuhe, 67.

48   For an extremely thorough and useful bibliography of these periodicals and their contents, see the Archive of the Institute of Music Research at the Academy of Research on Literature and Art, ed., *Zhongguo yinyue qikan pianmu huilu, 1906–40* (Bibliography of the contents of Chinese music magazines, 1906–49) (Beijing: Wenhua yishu chubanshe, 1990).

49 See Tie Min, "Yinyue de wuli jichu" (The physical basis of music), *Yinyue zazhi* 1 (March 1920).

50 Five such articles appeared in the first six issues, of which the most notable was Xiao Youmei's "Zhongxi yinyue de bijiao yanjiu" (Comparative research on Chinese and Western music), *Yinyue zazhi* 10 (1920).

51 See, for example, Chen Zhongzi, "Guominxing yu guoge" (National character and the national anthem), *Yinyue zazhi* 1 (March 1920).

52 See Chen Zhongzi's two-part article, "Yu guoyue zhi fuxing yi tong xiyue shuo" (An understanding of Western music theory will help effect the renaissance of Chinese music), *Yinyue zazhi* 9 (December 1920/January 1921).

53 Wang Yuhe, 74.

54 For a summary of the *kunqu* revival movement, see Isabel K. F. Wong, "Chinese Musicology in the Twentieth Century," 38–39.

55 For a discussion of major intellectual positions on the relationship of traditional Chinese and Western music, see Wang Yuhe, 68–69.

56 Benjamin Z. N. Ing, "Music Chronicle," *T'ien Hsia Monthly* 1 (January 1937): 54.

57 Chao Mei-pa, 285. See also Zhou Bang, "Sheng de gailiang" (The improvement of the *sheng*), *Yinyue jiaoyu* 4 (April 1936).

58 The only book-length study of this campaign is Hung Chang-tai, *Going to the People: Chinese Intellectuals and Folk Literature, 1918–1937* (Cambridge, Mass.: Harvard University Press, 1985).

59 Isabel K. F. Wong, "Chinese Musicology in the Twentieth Century," 42. For a detailed profile of Liu's life and works, see Wang Yuhe, 95–99.

60 This program for Chinese music is laid out in Zhao's introduction to his first collection of art songs, *Xin geshi ji* (A collection of new song-poetry) (Shanghai: Commercial Press, 1928), as cited in Wang Yuhe, 80. Zhao's experiments in "Sinified harmony" are explained in an article published in the magazine of Liu Tianhua's Society for the Reform and Advancement of Traditional Music, *Yinyue zazhi* (not to be confused with the earlier *Yinyue zazhi*, published by the Beijing University Music Research Group). See "Zhongguo pai hesheng de jige xiao shiyan" (A few small experiments in Chinese-style harmony), *Yinyue zazhi* 4 (October 1928). Zhao's work exerted considerable influence on intellectual youth of the 1920s and 30s, and many of his songs are remembered even today. Perhaps the most popular of his creations, "How Could I Forget Her" (Jiao wo ruhe bu xiang ta), was written in collaboration with Liu Fu. For a discussion of the relationship between linguistic tones and melody in Chinese music, see Zhao's "Geci zhong de guoyin" (The national sound in song lyrics), *Yinyue yuekan* 3 (February 1938). For a later discussion of the same topic in English, see Y. R. Chao, "Tone, Intonation Singing, Chanting, Recitation, Tonal Composition, and Atonal Composition in Chinese," in Morris Halle, ed., *For Roman Jakobson* (The Hague: Mouton, 1956), 52–59.

61 Xiao Youmei, "Guanyu woguo xin yinyue yundong" (On the Chinese new

music movement), *Yinyue yuekan* 4 (February 1938): 74. In the same article, Xiao affirms that to revitalize Chinese music, "all our tools and techniques must come from the West, even as we retain the spirit [of Chinese music] so as to preserve a sense of our own nationality." For Xiao's explanation of the gap that separated Chinese and Western music, see "Zuijin yiqian nian xiyue fazhan zhi xianzhe shishi yu woguo jiuyue buzhen zhi yuanyin" (The obvious truth of Western music's progress in the last thousand years and the reason why traditional music failed to improve), *Yinyue zazhi* 3 (July 1934).

62   Wang Yuhe, 44.

63   For a discussion of the use of *kaipian* in Shanghai's broadcasting industry, see Carlton Benson, "From Teahouse to Radio: Storytelling and the Commercialization of Culture in 1930s Shanghai," Ph.D. dissertation, University of California, Berkeley, 1996.

64   Wang Yuhe, 64.

65   The actual amount seems pitifully small: $2,600. By 1929, however, with swelling enrollments and a new home on Route Pichon in the French concession of Shanghai, the subsidy increased to $5,000 per month. In 1934 the government purchased sixteen acres of prime Shanghai real estate for a new campus and contributed $80,000 toward its construction. For an account of the founding and expansion of the school, see Chao Mei-pa, 276–80.

66   The most prominent of these visitors was the noted Russian composer Alexander Tcherepnin, whose tenure at the conservatory resulted in a *Study on the Pentatonic Scale for Piano Students,* published by Commercial Press. Tcherepnin was unusually interested in and supportive of indigenous musical traditions and sponsored a composition prize in 1930 won by Rodin Ho (He Luting), who later went on to become a fixture in the leftist music scene. For Tcherepnin's own impressions of his time in Shanghai, see his "Music in Modern China," *Musical Quarterly* 4 (October 1935): 391–400.

67   Chao Mei-pa, 280.

68   Wong, "Chinese Musicology in the Twentieth Century," 43.

69   Kraus provides an interesting discussion of the Chinese urban middle class and music. See Kraus, 24–25.

70   Zhang, 214.

71   The school was responsible for the publication of a journal, *Guangzhou Music* (*Guangzhou yinyue*). Ma later went on to conduct the first all-Chinese symphony orchestra at the Central Conservatory of Music in China's wartime capital, Chongqing.

72   See Institute of Music Research at the Academy of Research on Literature and Art, eds., *Zhongguo yinyue qikan pianmu huilu, 1906–49,* 19–36.

73   See Ma Hiao-Ts'iun, 47.

74 See Isabel K. F. Wong, "Chinese Musicology in the Twentieth Century," 44.

75 As cited in Wang Yuhe, 121.

76 See Wang Yuhe's summary of Qingzhu's musical thought, 119–23.

77 See Xiao Youmei, "Yinyue de shili," *Yinyue zazhi* 2 (April 1934); *Yinyue jiaoyu* 3 (March 1934): 9–13; *Yisheng* (September 1936).

78 See the conclusion of Walter Benjamin's "The Work of Art in the Age of Mechanical Reproduction," in *Illuminations* (New York: Schocken Books, 1969), 242.

79 Xiao, 9–10. All references are to the transcript printed in *Yinyue jiaoyu*.

80 The locus classicus of this idea is the *Record of Music* (*Yueji*), which states: "The tones of a well-managed age are peaceful and happy; its government is balanced. The tones of an age of turmoil are bitter and full of anger: the government is perverse. The tones of a ruined state are filled with lament and brooding: its people are in difficulty. The way of sounds and tones communicates with governance." See Stephen Owen, ed., *Readings in Chinese Literary Thought* (Cambridge, Mass.: Harvard University Press, 1992), 52.

81 Xiao, 10–11.

82 See Michel Foucault, *Discipline and Punish: The Birth of the Prison* (New York: Vintage Books, 1979).

83 Xiao, 11.

84 Walter Benjamin, writing around the same time as Xiao Youmei, is sharply aware of the way in which this fascistic vision is produced by new media technologies: "Mass reproduction is aided especially by the reproduction of the masses. In big parades and monster rallies, in sports events, and in war, all of which nowadays are captured by camera and sound recording, the masses are brought face to face with themselves." See Benjamin, *Illuminations*, 251.

85 For a fascinating collection of essays on the relation between fascism and modernist aesthetics, see Richard J. Golsan, ed., *Fascism, Aesthetics, and Culture* (Hanover, N.H.: University Press of New England: 1992). Andrew Hewitt's essay in the same volume on "Fascist Modernism, Futurism, and Post-modernity" is a particularly useful treatment of the link between fascist politics and futurist aesthetics. Susan Sontag's analysis of Leni Riefenstahl's classic 1935 cinematic evocation of Nazi mass rallies, *Triumph of the Will*, is also a good starting point. See Sontag, "Fascinating Fascism," *New York Review of Books*, February 6, 1975.

86 For a description of Chiang's links to Nazi Germany, see William Kirby, *Germany and Republican China* (Princeton, N.J.: Princeton University Press, 1984). For an account of the links between fascist ideology, the Blueshirts, and the New Life Movement, see Jonathan Spence, *The Search for Modern China* (New York: W. W. Norton, 1990), 415–18.

87 See Fu Pei-mei, "Music Chronicle," *T'ien Hsia Monthly* (March 1939): 258.

88   Xiao, 12.
89   Xiao, 13.
90   Xiao, 13.

2. THE GRAMOPHONE IN CHINA

1   The record was recorded in Paris, catalog number 32606, by Pathé-Frères, and titled "Five Men Laughing." The five men in question laugh, chortle, and guffaw throughout the two and a half minutes of the disc. See Li Qing et al., *Guangbo dianshi qiye shi neibu shiliao* (Internal documents on the history of the broadcasting and television industries) (Shanghai: Zhongguo changpian gongsi, 1994), 137. Interestingly, one of the first gramophone records to arrive in India was "The Laughing Song," recorded by Burt Shephard for the Gramophone Company. See G. N. Joshi, "A Concise History of the Phonograph Industry in India," *Popular Music* 7 (May 1988): 148. The same record seems to have been part of the early gramophone listening experience of colonial Africa, too. Wole Soyinka, writing about the records he listened to as a child in a middle-class Nigerian household, recollects, "The voices of Denge, Ayinde Bakare, Ambrose Campbell; a voice which was so deep that I believed it could have only been produced by a special trick of His Master's Voice, but which father assured me belonged to a black man called Paul Robeson. . . . Christmas carols, the songs of Marian Anderson; oddities such as a record in which a man did nothing but laugh throughout. . . ." See Soyinka, *Aké* (London: Arrow, 1983), 108. As cited in Michael Chanan's fascinating study, *Repeated Takes: A Short History of Recording and Its Effects on Music* (London: Verso, 1995), 90.

2   See Roland Gelatt, *The Fabulous Phonograph, 1877–1977* (New York: Macmillan, 1977), 172.

3   See David Harvey, *The Condition of Postmodernity* (Cambridge, Mass.: Basil Blackwell, 1990), 240–41.

4   Jacques Attali, *Noise: The Political Economy of Music* (Minneapolis: University of Minnesota Press, 1985), 95. For Attali, the introduction of recording heralded a transition in the political economy of music from a regime of "representation" to one of "repetition."

5   For a book-length account of the various debates around the issue of mass media and cultural imperialism, see John Tomlinson, *Cultural Imperialism* (Baltimore: Johns Hopkins University Press, 1991).

6   Chanan, "Repeated Takes," 7.

7   Gelatt's study suggests that this emphasis on domesticity was an inportant aspect of the marketing strategy for the phonograph as early as the 1890s (Gelatt, 69); there continued to be a great emphasis on disguising the machine as a piece of domestic furniture by way of "cabinetry and styling" throughout the teens and twenties. See Gelatt, 191.

8   As the 1930 ad copy in a record trade journal indicates, the expansion of the media into private space was essential to the growth of the industry: "In the home . . . New Moon Records are the most elegant and proper sort of leisure product." See *Xinyue ji* 1 (September 1929): 39. Jiang Tie's 1932 consumer guide to the gramophone includes a long section on its "Use in the Home." See Jiang Tie, *Liushengji* (The phonograph) (Shanghai: Commercial Press, 1932). See also Ke Zhenghe, "Liusheng ji de liyong fa" (How to use the phonograph), *Yinyue chao* 1 (December 1927): 7–10, and "Chang-pian de shiyong ji baocun fa" (The use and preservation of records), *Yinyue zazhi* 9 (January 1930).

9   One example is Xu Xu's 1930's novella "Untitled" in which a wealthy Shanghainese love poet issues the following complaint about his disaffected (but beautiful and artistic) wife: "She doesn't even like all the piano records I bought her anymore, hasn't listened to them in months, but when she goes out on the town and starts to discuss music with someone, she'll always brag about all the records we have at home, about how we stay up late together just to listen to them. . . ." See *Xu Xu quanji* (Complete works of Xu Xu), (Taipei: Zhengzhong, 1967), vol. 4, p. 428. A second example, from 1943, is Zhang Ailing's short story "Huadiao" (A withered flower), in which an ironic assessment of the Zheng household's economic situation is offered by way of an inventory of their consumer goods and leisure activities. "It was hard to tell if the Zheng family was rich or poor. A house full of servants at their beck and call, living in a foreign-style building, but only two beds in the whole place, so that their daughters had to carry bedding down to the living room and spread it across the floor every night before they went to sleep. The few sticks of furniture in the living room were actually borrowed from other people. Only the wireless set was their own, and the cabinets of the gramophone were always stuffed full with all the latest popular records. . . ." See Eileen Chang, *Chuanqi* (Romances) (Shanghai: Zhongguo tushu gongsi, 1946), 360. In the 1920s, gramophones (and wireless radios) were more unambiguously playthings of the rich, as indicated in Zhang Henshui's description of the bedroom of a Beijing warlord's pampered concubine in *Fate in Tears and Laughter.* In the concubine Yaqin's own words, as she attempts to overawe the visiting Shen Fengxi: "Sister, I want you to feel at home, so I've invited you into the bedroom. It's not easy for us to get a chance to visit, so don't leave just yet. You can eat here, chat, listen to the talking machine, or I can let you hear the wireless radio. Our wireless isn't the same as the usual kind, because we can hear foreign opera singers sing, so it's just about as new and fresh as can be." See Zhang Henshui, *Tixiao yinyuan* (Fate in tears and laughter) (Taiyuan: Beiyue wenyi chubanshe, 1993), 156.

10 Shui Jing notes that in the 1940s almost every corner store in Shanghai's residential districts was equipped with a radio and a gramophone and that

such spaces became prime sites for popular music consumption. See his *Liuxing gequ cangsang ji* (Record of the odyssey of pop music) (Taipei: Dadi chubanshe, 1981), 8.

11   It is no surprise, given both the industry's emphasis on domesticity and the expansion of musical space, that one frequently finds advertisements for gramophone records and radio equipment in the women's magazines of the period. See, for example, the string of RCA-Victor print ads that ran in the popular wartime journal *Nüsheng* (Women's Voice).

12   Arjun Appadurai, "Disjuncture and Difference in the Global Cultural Economy," in his *Modernity at Large: Cultural Dimensions of Globalization* (Minneapolis: University of Minnesota Press, 1996), 31.

13   Appadurai, "Disjuncture and Difference in the Global Cultural Economy," 30. The phrase "nostalgia for the present" is Fredric Jameson's.

14   Appadurai, "Disjuncture and Difference in the Global Cultural Economy," 47.

15   Appadurai, "Here and Now," 9.

16   See Deanna Campbell Robinson, Elizabeth B. Buck, Marlene Cuthbert, and the International Communication and Youth Consortium, *Music at the Margins: Popular Music and Global Cultural Diversity* (Newbury Park, Calif.: Sage, 1991), 41. The six companies in question are Sony Music (which owns CBS Records, itself a descendant of Columbia Graphophone), Thorn-EMI (a product of the 1931 merger of the Gramophone Company, the Columbia Phonograph Company, and Pathé-Frères), Bertelsmann Music Group (which owns the recording empire of what used to be known as RCA-Victor), WEA (a division of Time-Warner), Polygram Records (a German conglomerate that began international operations as early as the 1910s as the Polyphon Company), and MCA (an American major label recently purchased by the Japanese electronics firm Matsushita). For a brief review of the structure of the global record industry, see René Peron, "The Record Industry," in Armand Mattelart and Seth Siegelaub, *Communication and Class Struggle* (New York: International General, 1979): 292–97. As I write, finally, the record industry seems poised for further consolidation. The new corporate entity forged of the 1999 merger of Time-Warner with America Online has announced plans to purchase EMI as well, thus reducing the global field to a mere five corporations.

17   The authoritative study of this first phase in the evolution of recording technology is Walter L. Welch and Leah Brodbeck Stenzel Burt's *From Tinfoil to Stereo: The Acoustic Years of the Recording Industry, 1877–1929* (Gainesville: University Press of Florida, 1994). For a comprehensive (if less technical) history of the recording industry, see Gelatt, *The Fabulous Phonograph, 1877–1977.*

18   F. W. Gaisberg, *The Music Goes Round* (New York: Macmillan, 1942), 48.

19   Gaisberg, 62.

20   Gaisberg, 63.

21 Gaisberg, 64.

22 As Pekka Gronow notes, this also was true of other national and ethnic groups. Columbia, for instance, was marketing Syrian and Arabian recordings "for the U.S. ethnic market" around the turn of the century. Nor should we forget that the sorts of recordings made in Europe by Gaisberg and others also were targeted at U.S. immigrants of Italian, German, and Russian descent, among others. See "The Record Industry Comes to the Orient," *Ethnomusicology* 2 (May 1981): 261.

23 Gronow, 251. Gronow is perhaps the foremost historian of the global record industry. See also "The Record Industry: the Growth of a Mass Medium," *Popular Music* 3 (1983): 53–76.

24 Heinrich Bumb, "The Great Beka 'Expedition,' 1905–6," *Talking Machine Review* 41 (1976): 731. As cited in Gronow, 251.

25 A. G. Kenwood and A. L. Lougheed, *The Growth of the International Economy, 1820–1960* (London: Allen and Unwin, 1971), 93. An interesting anecdotal testament to the growing importance of the Asian record market is supplied by Claude Lapham, an American arranger and composer who worked as musical director for Columbia Records in Japan in 1935: "For the Japanese are not only avid students of all jazz records but also of all symphonic ones; in fact, during the year of my contract with Columbia Records, more Beethoven symphonies were sold than in all of Europe combined. I also walked into a teashop one day and found a huge stack of every standard symphonic movement and string quartet." See Lapham, "Looking at Japanese Jazz," *Metronome* (June 1936), 14.

26 John F. Perkins, Alan Kelly, and John Ward, "On Gramophone Company Matrix Numbers, 1898 to 1921," *Record Collector* 23 (1976): 57. These sorts of arrangements often followed the familiar pathways of colonial power. Companies tended to be stronger in markets where their own country's colonial interests were best represented. English companies dominated Indian and Egyptian markets, American concerns were strongest in Latin America and the Philippines, and Germans relied on record sales to Turkey and the Dutch East Indies. China, reflecting its partial and multiple colonization at the hands of several countries, was a free-for-all; the Shanghai record industry was financed by English, American, French, German, and Japanese capital.

27 For details and dates, see Gronow, 252–70.

28 The scope of Pathé's operations provides some indicators of this decentralization of the record industry. By 1908 the company already maintained several factories throughout Europe as well as branch offices in Tokyo, Shanghai, Bombay, and Singapore. A factory in Latvia served the Russian market, while its Vienna facility catered to record buyers in the Balkan states, Syria, and Egypt. In Russia alone, recordings were made for nine different linguistic groups, and efforts also were made to break into the Afghan market. In 1914, Pathé opened its first factory in the United

States. The year 1916 brought the first Chinese record factory. Pathé was especially strong in the North African and East African markets because of the French colonial presence in Algeria, Tunisia, Morocco, Somaliland, and Madagascar. The company also produced records for French colonial holdings in Southeast Asia (Indochina) and the Pacific (Tahiti). See Gronow, 263–66.

29   Such was the dominance, both real and imagined, of Pathé that when the hero of a late 1920s Zhou Shoujuan short story, "Phonograph Record" (Liusheng ji pian), wants to record his last words for his lost love in Shanghai, he calls for the manager of the local Pathé branch office, despite the fact that he is living on a fanciful Isle of Regret (Hen dao) situated in the middle of the Pacific! See Fan Boqun, ed., *Yuanqing juzi Zhou Shoujuan* (Master of sorrow: Zhou Shoujuan) (Taipei: Yeqiang chubanshe, 1994): 166–75.

30   Unaffiliated American labels like Brunswick (whose principal business was the manufacture and sale of gramophones) also remained in Shanghai after the merger, but they concentrated on selling imports of American popular music. According to Ke Zhenghe, a contemporary commentator, recordings of the European classical repertoire issued by the German multinational Polydor and the American Columbia Records also were available in Shanghai in the early 1930s, but it is unclear whether these companies actually established agencies in Shanghai. See Ke Zhenghe, "Changpian de piping" (Record criticism), *Yinyue zazhi* 1 (February 1932): 17.

31   Because of the paucity of available trade statistics and sales figures, the ratio of domestic production to imported repertoire can only be estimated. I will, however, venture a few tentative conclusions, based on Pekka Gronow's pioneering research on record export figures as well as estimates of domestic production capacity garnered from materials presented in Li Qing's history of the Chinese record industry. Bear in mind that some of what follows is merely guesswork. As many authors (including Gronow and Gelatt) note, 1929 represented a high-water mark for the transnational record industry in the interwar years. Gronow's figures indicate that total record exports to China in 1929 amounted to 1.1 million records from Germany (887,000 units), the United States (215,000), and France (40,000). If we add to this figure U.S. imports to Hong Kong and Canton (366,000 units) and an estimated 500,000 units from the United Kingdom (a conservative estimate extrapolated from the fact that the U.K. exported more than 600,000 units to India and 483,000 to Java in the same year), we arrive at a total of almost 2 million records. Before the 1930s—which saw the modernization of the Pathé operation following its merger with EMI and the expansion of the RCA-Victor plant—domestic production capacity almost certainly was limited to about the same amount. Thus, it seems clear that imports surpassed domestic production by a considerable margin between 1916 (the year that the first domestic manufacturing facilities were

established in Shanghai) and 1930. In the six years before the Sino-Japanese war, however, it appears that domestic products came to dominate the market. By 1932, domestic production capacity had mushroomed to 5.4 million records per annum, with Pathé-EMI accounting for a whopping 2.7 million records; RCA-Victor, 1.8 million, and Great China, a distant third at 900,000. Although precise figures are unavailable, we also know that substantial numbers of these records were produced for export to overseas Chinese and Southeast Asian markets. Gronow notes that China exported almost 50,000 records to the Dutch East Indies (Indonesia) in 1929 alone. The total figure was certainly much larger. For Gronow's numbers, see 281–84. Estimates of domestic production capacity are extrapolated from Li Qing's description of the facilities maintained by the three majors in Shanghai, 138–41.

32 For a detailed account of these local operations, see Li Qing, 141–43.

33 Other pocketbook companies included Asia Records (Yazhou changpian), National Music Records (Guoyue changpian), Harmony Records (Hesheng changpian), Kunlun Records (Kunlun changpian), Taiping Records (Taiping changpian), and Xingshi Records (Xingshi changpian). The Hong Kong–based New Moon Records (Xinyue liusheng ji changpian gongsi)—to be discussed in more detail for its role in the anticolonial promotion of an indigenous Chinese record industry—also should be included among this group.

34 See *The Commercial Directory of Shanghai* (Shanghai: Commercial Press, 1928), 123–24. For later listings of record companies in Shanghai and their management personnel, refer to the *Guide to China's Foreign Trade: Import and Export Annual 1933* (Shanghai: Bureau of Foreign Trade of the Ministry of Industry, 1933) and *The Shanghai Hong List* (Shanghai: Investigation Bureau of Commerce & Industry, 1940). This state of affairs persisted well after Pathé-EMI's move to Hong Kong in 1949 in the wake of the Communist revolution. Interestingly, Zhang Changfu went on to parlay his position at Pathé into a leading stake in the cinema exhibition business in Shanghai when his newly established organization, the Central Film Company (Zhongyang yingxi gongsi), acquired the chain of movie theaters established in China by the pioneering Spanish film entrepreneur, A. Ramos. See Zheng Junli, "Xiandai Zhongguo dianying shilüe" (A brief history of modern Chinese cinema), in Zhongguo dianying ziliao guan, ed., *Zhongguo wusheng dianying* (Chinese silent cinema) (Beijing: Zhongguo dianying chubanshe, 1996), 1408.

35 Sadly, both EMI and RCA-Victor have long since disposed of the kinds of archival materials that could elucidate exactly how business decisions were carried out in the 1920s and 1930s. Li Qing's work, however, presents a summary of much of this now unavailable material, as culled from documents confiscated from Pathé's offices in Xujiahui after the company left Shanghai for Hong Kong in 1949.

36   Interview with Yao Li in Hong Kong, October 20, 1995. See also Wong
     Kee-chee, "Shanghai Baidai gongsi de yange" (Pathé: the evolution of a
     record company), in Law Kar, ed., *Mandarin Films and Popular Songs, 40s–
     60s*, 91. White Russian women are often portrayed in accounts of the era's
     nightlife as low-class cabaret dancers and prostitutes. See Marc T. Greene,
     "Shanghai Cabaret Girl," *Literary Digest*, October 23, 1923: 25, for example.
     As such an article makes abundantly clear, Russians were seen as the poor
     and distinctly inferior cousins of the American, English, and French colo-
     nizers who dominated political and economic life within the International
     Settlement.

37   The house band at the famous Paramount Ballroom, for instance, was a
     Filipino outfit led by Gloria Andico. For a picture of the band, see the cover
     of *Yinyue shijie* 1 (August 1938).

38   See Li Jinhui, "Wo he Mingyue she" (The Bright Moon ensemble and my-
     self), *Wenhua shiliao* 4 (1986): 240.

39   See Spence, *The Search for Modern China*, 329.

40   I rely here on the account of the company provided by Li Qing, 140–41.

41   See, for instance, Qian Guangren, "Tantan woguo jiben shuchupin yu xin-
     xing gongye" (A discussion of China's basic import-export goods and
     newly emergent industries), *Xinyue ji* 2 (September 1930).

42   For a more recent work on the early Hong Kong film industry's rela-
     tionship with the Mainland and the articulation of a regional identity in
     Cantonese cinema, see Fu Po-shek, "Framing Identity: Mainland Émi-
     grés, Marginal Culture, and Hong Kong Cinema, 1937–1941," unpublished
     manuscript.

43   See, for example, the song "Shouzai paituo" (Shouzai goes dating) re-
     printed in *Xinyue ji* 2 (September 1930). This amusing send-up of middle-
     class courtship, colonial-style, brims with Cantonese neologisms. The song
     was written and accompanied on the piano by Zhao Enrong and sung
     by Huang Shounian, a comedian apparently fluent in several languages.
     Interestingly (and ironically, given the popular and self-consciously colo-
     nial character of the song), the promotional blurb for the record invokes
     Cai Yuanpei's May 4th era dictum of "incorporating East and West" to
     create a new national aesthetic.

44   Guo Moruo, "Liusheng jiqi de huiyin" (The phonograph's echo), in *Moruo
     wenji* (Collection of Moruo's works) (Beijing: Renmin wenxue chubanshe,
     1958), vol. 10, 345.

45   For a month-by-month chronology of Ren's life, see Qin Qiming, *Yinyue
     jia Ren Guang* (The musician Ren Guang) (Hefei: Anhui wenyi chubanshe,
     1988). For a description of Ren's duties, see Qin Qiming, 9.

46   As estimated by Li Qing, 149. Something of the market dominance of non-
     leftist popular songs and traditional music, however, is suggested by the
     fact that these fifty songs represent only 5 percent of Pathé's domestic out-
     put from 1932 until 1949 (which numbered 1,900 titles in all).

47 Li Qing, 148.

48 See Qin Qiming, 31–32.

49 Qin Qiming, 44. Ren Guang, fearing for his life, fled the "Paris of the East" for Paris itself. After a year in exile, he returned to China in 1938 to participate in anti-Japanese resistance efforts. He was killed in action in January 1941, a victim of "friendly fire."

50 See *Xinhua huabao* 2 (January 1937).

51 Indeed, it is "generally considered the most valuable trademark in existence." See Welch and Burt, 134, as cited in Taussig, *Alterity and Mimesis*, 212. Taussig's illuminating study contains two chapters on "colonial phonography" and the appropriation of the HMV logo by the Cuna people of Panama in their textile designs.

3. THE YELLOW MUSIC OF LI JINHUI

1 See Luo Ting, "Guanyu Li Jinhui" (On Li Jinhui), *Yinyue jiaoyu* 2 (December 1934): 35.

2 See Clayton, 76, on performing in Shanghai.

3 See Li Sui, "Li Jinhui bei Jiang Qing zhemo er si" (Li Jinhui tortured to death by Jiang Qing) in Tu Guangqi, ed., *Zhou Xuan de zhenshi gushi* (Zhou Xuan's real story) (Taipei: Zhuanji wenxue she, 1987), 239. In a colonial climate in which imported dance bands from Russia, the Philippines, and the United States were almost always preferred to local musicians, this was no mean feat.

4 The treatment of Li's music and its milieu in Wang Yuhe's authoritative history of modern Chinese music is representative.

> With the failure of the first revolutionary war [in 1927], a white terror gradually engulfed every major city and small town, forcing the revolutionary movement of workers and peasants into retreat. Under these political circumstances, the cultural life of the urban masses also underwent a series of changes, including a resurgence of popular "Mandarin Ducks and Butterflies" fiction, cinematic period pieces and costume dramas, martial arts movies, as well as the popularity of imported musicals and the rapid development of domestic soft entertainment films. With Li Jinhui's New Moon Song and Dance Troupe as their example, all sorts of similar troupes sprang up, spreading a veritable plague of pornographic song and dance numbers like "Drizzle," "Peach Blossom River," "Express Train," and "Darling, I Love You" among the middle to lower classes by way of the stage, radio stations, records, and films, and poisoning the masses with their fleshly and fragrant allure. All of this was in point of fact little different from the reactionary wing of the KMT's attacks on the Red base areas, and the intensification of their fascist control over the cities and towns of the white areas. Indeed, each complemented the other, and

> this music became one of the means whereby the counterrevolutionaries
> attempted to put into effect a reactionary cultural "siege."

Interestingly, the phrase "yellow music" was excised from Wang's 1994 revision of the text. See Wang, 115.

5   See Li Sui, 231–45. Li Sui, who is Li Jinhui's son, attributes his father's death at the hands of Red Guards to a vendetta on the part of Jiang Qing, who had been refused admittance to Li's Bright Moon Song and Dance Troupe when she was a struggling young actress known as Lan Ping in the mid-1930s.

6   This approach is typical of both Wang Yuhe and Li's biographer, Sun Ji'nan. See Sun Ji'nan, *Li Jinhui pingzhuan* (A critical biography of Li Jinhui) (Beijing: Renmin yinyue chubanshe, 1993). As might be expected, this narrative inevitably moves toward a moment of remorse, repentance, and redemption. Disgusted by his own degeneracy, Li quits Shanghai for his native Hunan in 1936, where he once again devotes himself to the education of the common folk as the general secretary of the Chinese Association to Promote Plebeian Education (Zhonghua pingmin jiaoyu cujin hui).

7   Significantly, one of the central figures in the devlopment of modern Japanese popular music shares with Li this sort of ambiguous positioning between the worlds of education and entertainment, nation-building and urban media culture. Sasa Kōka (1886–1961), the composer of one of the first-ever Japanese pop hits, "You Sweetheart" ("Kimi koishi," recorded by Nippon Victor in 1928), began his career "writing words and music for children's musicals"! Sasa later worked as a designer and composer for the multinational Nippon Columbia Records. For a revealing account of early Japanese popular music, see Tōyō Nakamura, "Early Pop Song Writers and Their Backgrounds," *Popular Music* 10, no. 3 (1991): 267–68.

8   I translate the Chinese *genü* as sing-song girl advisedly. As Gail Hershatter notes, high-class Shanghainese courtesans skilled in the arts of song and storytelling were respectfully referred to by their clients as *xiansheng* (literally, master or first-born). The term sing-song girl is thus a clever English-language malapropism based on the Shanghainese pronunication of *xiansheng*. Because of the constant slippage between the notion of singing and selling sexual services and the way in which these stereotypes shaped Republican era critiques of "yellow music," however, I have elected to retain the English word in this context, despite the more limited denotative scope of the original Chinese term. See Gail Hershatter, *Dangerous Pleasures: Prostitution and Modernity in Twentieth-Century China* (Berkeley: University of California Press, 1997), 41.

9   Some classic examples of this sort of criticism include Mao Dun's "Fengjian de xiao shimin de wenyi" (The feudal art and literature of the urban petit bourgeoisie), in *Mao Dun wenji* (Mao Dun's collected writings) (Bei-

jing: Renmin wenxue chubanshe, 1958), and Lu Xun's "Shanghai wenyi zhi yipie" (A look at literature and art in Shanghai), in *Lu Xun quanji* (Beijing: Renmin chubanshe, 1981).

10 See Perry Link, *Mandarin Ducks and Butterflies: Popular Fiction in Early Twentieth-Century Cities* (Berkeley: University of California Press, 1981).

11 See Lydia Liu's insightful discussion of the role of literary criticism in the creation and legitimation of these cultural categories in *Translingual Practice: Literature, National Culture, and Translated Modernity—China, 1900–1937* (Stanford, Calif.: Stanford University Press, 1995), 233.

12 See Perry Link, "Traditional Style Urban Fiction in the Teens and Twenties," in Merle Goldman, ed., *Modern Chinese Literature in the May Fourth Era* (Cambridge, Mass.: Harvard University Press, 1977), 345.

13 See Li Oufan, "Mantan xiandai Zhongguo wenxue zhong de tuifei" (On decadence in modern Chinese literature), *Jintian* 4 (Winter 1993): 46.

14 See Rey Chow, *Woman and Chinese Modernity: The Politics of Reading Between East and West* (Minneapolis: University of Minnesota Press, 1991), 87.

15 Li had seven brothers and two sisters, many of whom went on to prominence in the arts, science, and politics. Some of his more notable siblings included his eldest brother, Li Jinxi (an educator, linguist, and one of the creators of the Bpmf phonetic system for Chinese), Li Jinyao (a geologist), Li Jinming (a left-wing writer and onetime disciple of Lu Xun), Li Jinguang (a songwriter and musical director of Pathé Records from 1936 to 1949), and Li Jinyang (also known as C. Y. Lee, an author whose English novel *The Flower Drum Song* was adapted in 1961 from its Broadway presentation as Hollywood's first and only big-budget Asian-American musical).

16 Mao Zedong was from a neighboring town in Hunan, and the two men attended the same middle school, although they were not (as far as I can ascertain) in the same classes. According to Li Sui, Li Jinhui's eldest brother, Li Jinxi, was Chairman Mao's Chinese teacher during his early years in Changsha.

17 See Li Jinhui, "Wo he Mingyue gewu she" (The Bright Moon society and myself), in *Wenhua shiliao* 3 (May 1982): 94.

18 Li Jinhui, "Wo he Mingyue gewu she," 94. Li responded to these objections with a pair of articles advocating the "reform" of folk material.

19 Zhou's call for a literature of the common people was first published as "Pingmin wenxue" (Literature of the common people), *Meizhou pinglun,* January 19, 1919. Li also was influenced by his brother Jinxi's mentor and fellow Hunanese provincial, Xu Teli, a tireless advocate of "education for the common people" (*pingmin jiaoyu*). This intellectual genealogy is also evident in the manner in which he titled his Mandarin language primer, *Pingmin qianzi keben* (Thousand-character text for the common people) (Shanghai: Zhonghua shuju, 1927). The 1927 edition that I examined was the fifteenth printing of the book, which was originally published several years earlier.

20   See, for example, Li Jinhui, ed., *Geyao* (Folk songs) (Shanghai: Zhonghua shuju, 1924). This compilation comprises eight volumes representing only a fraction of the thousands of songs that Li claimed to have collected.

21   See Sun, 7.

22   See Li Jinhui, *Xin jiaocai jiaokeshu guoyu keben* (New Mandarin primer) (Shanghai: Zhonghua shuju, 1920). The book was published under the pen name Li Junquan.

23   In introducing his early work "The Magpie and the Child," Li takes pains to explain its pedagogical value in some detail. In his own estimation, chief among the virtues of such a form of performance literature is its capacity to stimulate use of the national language. In addition, Li claims that the plays impart knowledge of "literature in the national language, of ethical citizenship, knowledge of nature, painting, handicrafts, music, and sports." Nor does he neglect the realm of experiential learning, that is, the educational value of children actively and collectively producing the play's sets, costumes, and performance. Good spectatorship is the final piece in this pedagogical puzzle, one having less to do with children than the (seemingly benighted) adults who watch their performances. "When most people go to a performance at a school, they arrive with a rather different and more respectful feeling than if the show was at a theater. Thus we can use this opportunity to gradually train the masses in the habit of upholding public order and in how to watch theater in a proper manner (no commotion, no talking and laughing, no eating of snacks). We can also gradually create from scratch a feeling of reverence for art itself within the people." See Li, *Maque yu xiaohai (yi ming juewu de shaonian)* (The magpie and the child, or an awakened youth) (Shanghai: Zhonghua shuju, 1927), 8–10.

24   These discs were advertised as "educational records for school and home." The records sold for one and a half yuan, ten times as much as the books in which they were advertised. See Li Jinhui, *San hudie* (Three butterflies) (Shanghai: Zhonghua shuju, 1926), 99. In some cases a concerted effort seems to have been made to tie the marketing of scripts and gramophone records together. The cover of a three-volume collection, *Collected Songs of Li Jinhui*, for instance, prominently features the logo of Great China Records. See *Li Jinhui gequ ji* (Collected songs of Li Jinhui) (Shanghai: Zhonghua shuju, 1926).

25   For Li's own description of the play, see Li Jinhui, "Wo he Mingyue gewu she," 122. This theme is also struck by Zhou Zuoren in his classic May 4th era essays on children's literature in *Ziji de yuandi* (My own garden) (Beijing: Renmin wenxue chubanshe, 1988).

26   Sun, 81. Sun seems to have drawn the term from the cultural critic Zhu Yingpeng's 1930 article on Li's work. See Zhu Yingpeng, "Guanyu wuhui de hua" (On a dance performance), *Shenbao*, July 27, 1930.

27   Li Jinhui, "Wo he Mingyue gewu she," 121.

28 For a detailed analysis of the song, see Sun, 64–65.

29 Li outlines the various techniques by which Chinese and Western instruments and musical techniques were combined in his "Wo he Mingyue gewu she," 101–2.

30 Qing Qing, "Women de yinyue jie" (Our musical circles), *Kaiming* 4 (1928): 177.

31 At least one commentator did in fact argue that the folk songs from which Li drew his melodic inspiration were lewd by their very nature, irrespective of lyrical content (for further discussion, see last section of this chapter). See Chang Ping, "Shu 'Guanyu yin yue' hou" (After writing "On lewd music"), *Kaiming* 8 (1929): 447–50.

32 Four short films also were made of the troupe's performances; these were produced by Lianhua in 1931 and starred Li Minghui. They were filmed in color (presumably using one of several two-color processes then available) and never released for public consumption because of technical flaws.

33 See, for example, the photograph of children from the Shanghai Jiande Public School on the flyleaf for the script of "Three Butterflies." Other examples can be seen in the collection of photographs printed in Sun Ji'nan's biography.

34 For a study of Takarazuka's history and the gender politics that informed its founding and reception, see Jennifer Robertson, *Takarazuka: Sexual Politics and Popular Culture in Modern Japan* (Berkeley: University of California Press, 1998).

35 See Li Jinhui, " 'Putao xianzi zengding xuanyan" (Manifesto for the revised and expanded version of "The Grape Fairy"), in *Putao xianzi* (The grape fairy) (Shanghai: Zhonghua shuju, 1928), 4.

36 See Katherine Hui-ling Chou, "Nü yanyuan, xieshi zhuyi, "xin nüxing" lunshu: wanqing dao wusi shiqi Zhongguo xiandai juchang zhong de xingbie biaoyan" (Actresses, realism, and the discourse of the "new woman": the performance of gender in modern Chinese theater from the late Qing to the May 4th era), *Jindai Zhongguo funü shi yanjiu* 4 (August 1996): 87–133.

37 Chou, 89. One of the more interesting stories Chou tells about drama in the years directly preceding the May 4th Movement has to do with Zhou Enlai. As a student at Nankai University in Tianjin, Zhou was active in the spoken drama movement and often performed in drag. See Chou, 102.

38 The group's activities included staging plays, translating European drama and dramatic criticism, and promoting spoken drama and Li's children's opera; it featured several actresses, actors, musicians, and directors who would go on to prominence in the film world of the 1930s. The most prominent of these include the directors Maxu Weibang and Cheng Bugao, the leftist actor Gu Menghe, and the dramatist Yan Gongshang. The group was founded and led by Yang Jiuhuan. See Li Jinhui, "Wo he Mingyue gewu she," 112–13.

39   Li Jinhui, "Wo he Mingyue gewu she," 113.

40   See Chou, 117.

41   See Xie Bo, ed., *Wode chengming yu buxing: Wang Renmei huiyi lu* (My success and misfortune: the reminiscences of Wang Renmei) (Shanghai: Shanghai wenyi chubanshe, 1985), 145.

42   Zhu Yingpeng, "Guanyu wuhui de hua."

43   Li Jinhui, "Juantou yu" (Introduction), in *San hudie* (Three butterflies) (Shanghai: Zhonghua shuju, 1926), 4.

44   Li Jinhui, "Juantou yu," 4–5.

45   For a study of the linkage between medical science and nationalist discourse, see Frank Dikötter, *Sex, Culture, and Modernity in China: Medical Science and the Construction of Sexual Identities in the Early Republican Period* (Honolulu: University of Hawaii Press, 1995). For a summary of the discourse of eugenics in Republican China, see Frank Dikötter, *The Discourse of Race in Modern China* (Stanford, Calif.: Stanford University Press, 1992), esp. 164–90. The most prominent Chinese eugenicist was undoubtedly Pan Guangdan, author of numerous articles and books on the subject. As Dikötter and others have documented, this sort of pseudo-scientific discourse was not restricted to Pan's writings; instead, it saturated both the popular and "serious" press of the Republican period.

46   Bi Fen, "Yinyue gewu you jiji tichang de biyao" (Musical drama needs to be actively promoted), *Yingxi zazhi* 1 (July 1930): 43.

47   Sun Yu, "Qingchun de biaoxian" (An expression of youth), *Yingxi zazhi* 1 (July 1931): 42.

48   See Chou, 117–21. Chou's extended metaphor for this process is useful. Drawing on Eileen Chang's celebrated essay on women's fashion, "A Chronicle of Changing Clothes" (Gengyi ji), Chou contends that the *qipao* is emblematic of the double-edged quality of emancipation for women in the May 4th era. The *qipao*, adopted by women in the 1920s as an emblem of gender equality and modernity rapidly becomes the medium by which the society as a whole indulges its scopophilic desire to look at women's bodies. For Chang's essay, see *Liuyan* (Rumors) (Hong Kong: Huangguan, 1994), 67–76. Chang's own translation of the essay into English was published as "Chinese Life and Fashions," *XXth Century* (January 1943): 54–61.

49   See Xie Bo, 43–45.

50   Xie Bo, 44.

51   This dual threat conveys something of the complexity and ambiguity of the colonial situation in Shanghai. With the success of Chiang Kai-shek's Northern Expedition and the KMT's assumption of control of Greater Shanghai in 1927, Li ran afoul of both the colonial authorities (themselves constituted of representatives from several different nations, including the United States, Britain, France, and Japan) in the International Settlement and the new KMT city government. After hanging a Republican flag from the International Settlement building that housed the school, Li (according

to his own account) was interrogated by the Shanghai municipal police, who were incensed by the anti-imperialist message of "The Final Victory" and other anthems that Li had penned in support of China's nation-building effort. At the same time, he came under pressure from KMT authorities angered by his efforts on behalf of an acquaintance slated for execution by Chiang Kai-shek's campaign of white terror. For Li's account of these events, see "Wo he Mingyue gewu she," 127.

52   Li Jinhui, "Wo he Mingyue gewu she," 210. Interestingly, the tour was endorsed by the prominent leftists Tian Han and Zheng Zhenduo, both of whom heartily endorsed Li's nationalist agenda.

53   Li Jinhui, "Wo he Mingyue gewu she," 211. For Wang Renmei's account of the incident, see Xie Bo, 75.

54   Li Jinhui, "Wo he Mingyue gewu she," 208.

55   Li Jinhui, *Jiating aiqing gequ ershiwu zhong* (Twenty-five family love songs) (Shanghai: Shanghai wenming shudian, 1929).

56   Zhang Zhang, "Yinyue yishu wang na'er qu?" (Quo vadis, musical art?), *Yinyue jiaoyu* 8 (August 1936): 84.

57   For a review of their performance in Tianjin, see Qiu Chen, "Mingyue gewu yu kaiming" (Ming Yeoh Musikverein at the Kaiming Theater), *Beiyang huabao*, August 19, 1930, 2.

58   For a sample program, see Li Jinhui, "Wo he Mingyue gewu she," 224.

59   The three songs were "Peach Blossom River," "Express Train," and "Song of the Dancer" (Wuban zhi ge). This last song presents an interesting defense of the value of dance crazes like the fox-trot and the Charleston. For the lyrics of these and other compositions by Li Jinhui, see *Xiandai mingge wubaiqu* (Five hundred modern songs) (Shanghai: Guoguang shudian, 1937).

60   The term will be familiar to fans of Cantonese pop music, which was dominated in the 1990s by four singers collectively known as "the four sky kings."

61   See the Shanghai tong she (Shanghai experts' society), eds., *Shanghai yanjiu ziliao xuji* (Shanghai research materials, vol. 2) (Shanghai: Shanghai shudian, 1984), 717.

62   Interview with Yao Li in Hong Kong, October 20, 1995. See also the broadcasting column in *Yule* (Variety weekly), January 1, 1936, 5. For a summary of the origins of the Plum Blossom Song and Dance Troupe, see Xie Bo, 47.

63   "Shanghai boyin jie gechang tuanti tongji" (Statistics on singing organizations in Shanghai's broadcasting world), *Yule zhoubao* 9 (November 1935): 463.

64   An item in the inaugural issue of *Variety Weekly* commented on this eclipse: "In years past, Li Jinhui made his name through songs like 'Drizzle' and 'Darling, I Love You.' With the rise of wireless broadcasting, these kinds of songs gained many, many more listeners. But at the same time, there were also more and more imitators, on top of which came the talking pic-

tures, each of which includes at least one or two songs, thus stealing away even more of Li's market." See "Li Jinhui ye ruanhua le" (Even Li Jinhui has relented), *Yule zhoubao,* July 7, 1935, 2.

65   Frances Russell, "Hollywood in China," *Vox Magazine,* October 1, 1935. *Vox* was a bilingual pictorial published in Shanghai and known as *Shengse huabao* in Chinese. *The Love Parade* played for more than 200 days in Shanghai and spurred substantial record sales of its screen songs.

66   The review was printed in *Yingxi zazhi* 3 (January 1931). As cited in Wang Wenhe, *Zhongguo dianying yinyue xunzong* (Tracing Chinese film music) (Beijing: Zhongguo guangbo dianshi chubanshe, 1995), 12–13.

67   For commentary on this development, see Sun Yu and Si Kong, "Zhongguo de gewu" (Chinese musical drama), *Yingxi zazhi* 1 (July 1931): 39–40. The troupe was a flop in almost every respect. Besides the shorts films, an abortive stage production of Li Jinguang's anti-imperialist play *The Light of the Nation (Minzu zhi guang,* 1931) was subsequently banned by KMT authorities who were wary of offending the Japanese.

68   The film was produced by the Tianyi Film Company (Unique Photoplay) in 1931; Li provided three songs for the soundtrack. As with so many other films of its era and genre, it appears to be no longer extant. The soundtrack was recorded by American technicians using the Movietone system. For an illustrated advertisement with plot summary and credits, see "Gechang chunse" (The romance of the opera) in *Xin yinxing* 33 (October 1931). The first-ever Chinese talkie, *Sing-song Girl Red Peony (Genü Hong mudan),* was produced in 1930 by the Star Film Studio (Mingxing) and told the story of a traditionally styled sing-song girl; it featured several Peking opera arias. The film used the early and sometimes clumsy sound-on-disc format and could not have been produced without the technical assistance of recording engineers from Pathé Records. The film also was screened in the Philippines and Indonesia. For more on this collaboration between Pathé and Mingxing, see Qin Qiming, 11–12.

69   The magazine *Yule* is probably the best example of this phenomenon because it was expressly formulated as a journalistic guide to modish urban leisure activities (filmgoing, dancing, listening to the wireless, dog racing, and more).

70   Collecting photographs of performers was another important aspect of the star-making machinery and pop fandom in Shanghai; movie magazines often ran advertisements for photo studios selling shots of the stars.

71   Editors of *Gexing huabao,* "Chuangkan ci" (Editor's introduction), *Gexing huabao* 1 (March 1935).

72   Precedents exist in earlier urban tabloids for this kind of "consumer guide" approach to the prostitution trade. Also, many formats and representative strategies adopted by film magazines and tabloids in China were, I suspect, adapted from American magazines and Hollywood celebrity tabloids.

73 See A Han, "Sizi yin" (Four characterizations), *Gexing huabao* 2 (October 1935): 10. See also, for example, Yan Hong, "Nü mingxing chang ge su-xie" (Brief descriptions of female stars singing), *Yisheng* (Music and movie monthly) 3 (August 1935).

74 See *Yisheng* 2 (July 1935): 13.

75 In the *Nightly News Magazine* poll, initiated by editor Cui Wanqiu, Bai Hong came in first with 9,103 ballots, followed by Zhou Xuan (8,876) and Wang Manjie (8,854). See "Dangxuan sanda gexing zhi Zhou Xuan" (Zhou Xuan selected as one of the top three pop stars), *Qingqing dianying* 7 (1941). As cited in Wang Shihui, ed., *Zhou Xuan zishu* (Zhou Xuan in her own words) (Shanghai: Sanlian shudian, 1995), 125–26. Apparently these fig-ures were not unusual. The *Pop Star Pictorial* 1935 contest offered free copies of the magazine to the first 10,000 voters. For a sample ballot, see "Haishang shi da gexing xuanju" (Ten best pop stars in Shanghai contest), *Gexing huabao* 2 (October 1935).

76 See Siegfried Kracauer, *The Mass Ornament: Weimar Essays*, trans. Thomas Y. Levin (Cambridge, Mass.: Harvard University Press, 1995), 76.

77 The best examples of Berkeley's craft can be seen in the Warner Bros. films *Gold Diggers of 1933*, *42nd Street*, and *Footlight Parade*.

78 See Wu Ruifeng, "Zhongguo dianying zuijin zhi xin de qingxiang" (The latest trends in Chinese movies), *Yingmi zhoubao*, November 14, 1934, 130. For photographs of Chinese mass ornaments, as well as a sense of the ex-tent to which the Chinese form was appropriated from Hollywood mod-els, see a magazine photo spread with stills from these films captioned "Gewu zai Zhongguo shi zheyangde, gewu zai Meiguo shi zheyang de" (Musicals in China are like this, musicals in America are like that), in *Shidai dianying* 3 (August 1934).

79 The exodus of talent to the cinema is strikingly illustrated by a two-page photo spread published by *Yingmi zhoubao* in 1934 and titled, "From the musical stage to the movies." The spread features several of Li's protégées, including Zhou Xuan, Bai Hong, Li Lihua, and Jiang Manjie. See "Cong getai dao yinmu" (From the musical stage to the silver screen), *Yingmi zhoubao*, November 14, 1934.

80 Li Jinhui, "Wo he Mingyue gewu she," 240–41.

81 With the proceeds from this and other ventures (as well as extensive re-cording activities for all the major record labels), Li made one more stab at reviving a new (and short-lived) Bright Moon Musical Drama Society (Mingyue geju she), which he abandoned in 1936 after a final tour to Nan-jing.

82 Chang Ping, "Shu 'Guanyu yin yue' hou."

83 Chang Ping, "Shu 'Guanyu yin yue' hou," 447.

84 Chang Ping, "Shu 'Guanyu yin yue' hou," 448.

85 Xie Bo, 58. For Li's own explanation of these techniques, see Li Jinhui, "Wo he Mingyue gewu she," 101.

86   Chang Ping, 449. For a piece in which Li defends his advocacy of music for
     the common people (*pingmin yinyue*), see his two-part essay "Yinyue yu
     shipin" (Music and food), *Yule banyuekan* 2 (July-August 1935). Li's argu-
     ment here is essentially that just as everyone cannot eat expensive meals
     in fancy restaurants, not all audiences will be willing or able to enjoy high-
     brow music. His proposed solution to this dilemma is also couched in
     terms of restaurants: "I read in the paper that someone has opened a 'Com-
     mon People's Canteen' (Pingmin shitang) where a big bowl of rice only
     costs a hundred coppers, tofu and vegetable soup is only thirty, plus ten
     cents for soy milk. Altogether two meals worth of food for less than ten
     cents on a silver dollar. Great! Maybe after another year someone will open
     up a Masses Canteen, add a few more dishes, so that you could eat two
     meals a day for less than a twenty cents. At the same time, they could give
     some thought to cleanliness, to nutritional value, and also pay attention to
     good taste. What a boon that would be for the common people. . . ." See Li
     Jinhui, "Yinyue yu shipin," 27.

87   Xiao, 13.

88   See Anna's brief introductory comments to her translation of Alfredo Ca-
     sella, "Fengmi shijie de jueshi yinyue" (Jazz music is all the rage the world
     over), *Dongfang zazhi* 29, no. 4 (1932): 93. This discourse on jazz-as-primi-
     tive also was reflected in the works of modernist authors like Liu Na'ou.
     His "Youxi" (Games) states: "Suddenly the air rocked with a wave of
     music, a startling cry of sound. A musician in the middle of the bandstand
     held a saxophone—the demon of jazz—and began to blow crazily towards
     the people. And with that came too the palpitating cries of cymbals, drums,
     piano, and strings. This was a memory of Black people of Africa, of the sac-
     rificial rite before the hunt, of the rumble of blood in the veins, a discovery
     of the primitive. . . ." For the original text, see Li Oufan, ed., *Xin ganjue pai
     xiaoshuo xuan* (A selection of new perceptionist fiction) (Taipei: Yonchen
     wenhua, 1988), 320–21. As Shu-mei Shih notes, in order to primitivize
     the music, Liu locates what is a uniquely African *American* musical form
     in a timeless, imaginary "Africa." See Shu-mei Shih, "Gender, Race, and
     Semicolonialism: Liu Na'ou's Urban Shanghai Landscape," *Journal of Asian
     Studies* 55 (November 1996): 944. An interesting critique of this "primitiv-
     ist myth" in discourse about jazz is contained in Ted Gioia's *The Imperfect
     Art: Reflections on Jazz and Modern Culture* (New York: Oxford University
     Press, 1988), 19–49.

89   Clayton, 76.

4. MASS MUSIC AND THE POLITICS OF PHONOGRAPHIC REALISM

1   See Hengtang tuishi, ed., *Tangshi sanbai shou* (Three hundred Tang poems)
     (Beijing: Zhonghua shuju, 1990), 212. In this famous Tang dynasty qua-

train, the sing-song girl performs a sensual popular song called "Flowers in the Courtyard" for her clients, oblivious to the fact that it was composed by the decadent last emperor of the short-lived Chen dynasty (573–88) and was considered by the Tang to symbolize his frivolous (and ultimately fatal) inattention to matters of state.

2 *Xin Shanghai mingge sanbai shou* (Three hundred songs of new Shanghai) (Shanghai: Gequ she, 1935), 43.

3 For Nie Er's account of this expedition, see his "Yige maoxian de sheying gushi: Yi er ba de huiyi" (A photographic adventure story: memories of January 1932), in Zhou Weizhi, ed., *Nie Er quanji* (The complete Nie Er) (Beijing: Wenhua yishu chubanshe, 1985), vol. 2, 35–37.

4 From the March 4, 1932, entry of Nie Er's diary, *Nie Er quanji,* vol. 2, 364 (italicized phrases originally in English).

5 From the March 7, 1932, entry of Nie Er's diary. *Nie Er quanji,* vol. 2, 365 (italicized phrases originally in English).

6 The first of these essays was "Li Jinhui de 'Bajiao ye shang shi' " (Li Jinhui's "Poems on a plantain leaf"), *Dianying shibao,* July 13, 1932. The second, and perhaps the most significant, was "Zhongguo gewu duanlun" (A brief essay on Chinese musicals), *Dianying yishu* 3 (July 1932). See also *Nie Er quanji,* vol. 2, 44–48. Nie Er died in Japan, where he was visiting on the first leg of a projected journey organized by his associates in the Chinese Communist Party that would have taken him to Europe and the Soviet Union.

7 See Guo Moruo, "Liusheng jiqi de huiyin" (The echo of the phonograph), in *Moruo wenji* (Collection of Moruo's works) (Beijing: Renmin wenxue chubanshe, 1958), vol. 10, 345.

8 Guo's initial call for a phonographic realism was published in a 1928 essay, "Yingxiong shu" (The hero tree). Li attacked the excessive and unrealistic degree of objectivity implied by this standard in his "Zenyang jianshe geming wenxue?" (How do we construct a revolutionary literature?). This criticism, in turn, prompted Guo's "Liusheng jiqi de huiyin." A record of the entire debate is provided in *Geming wenxue lunzheng ziliao xuanbian* (An edited selection of materials on the revolutionary literature debate) (Beijing: Renmin wenxue chubanshe, 1981).

9 For an informative and nuanced analysis of this debate, see Marston Anderson, *The Limits of Realism: Chinese Fiction in the Revolutionary Period* (Berkeley: University of California Press, 1990), 46–54.

10 Guo, 345–46. The question of just how new media technologies left their imprint on literary theory and literary works in the late Qing and Republican periods is fascinating but beyond the scope of this study. For a methodologically illuminating monograph on a similar process of mediatization in nineteenth-century Brazil, see Flora Süssekind, *Cinematograph of Words: Literature, Technique, and Modernization in Brazil* (Stanford, Calif.: Stanford University Press, 1997).

11   See Nie Er's diary entry of June 3, 1933, in which he attempts to give theoretical definition to "China's emergent new music." *Nie Er quanji,* vol. 2, 511.

12   See Marston Anderson, "The Morality of Form: Lu Xun and the Modern Chinese Short Story," in Leo Ou-fan Lee, ed., *Lu Xun and His Legacy* (Berkeley: University of California Press, 1985), 32–53.

13   I would like to thank Wen-hsin Yeh for pointing out this crucial point when I presented this chapter to the Berkeley China Seminar in November 1999.

14   Benjamin, *Illuminations,* 251.

15   Denton was a short-lived leftist studio whose pointedly nationalistic claim to fame was the invention and use of the first Chinese-designed and produced sound film apparatus, dubbed the "Three Friends" (Sanyou shi) and featured in the 1934 production *Plunder of Peach and Plum* (*Taoli jie*).

16   The slogan was devised by the Communist cultural theoretician Zhou Yang in 1934. See Zhou Yang, "Guanyu guofang wenxue" (On national defense literature), *Wenxue jie,* June 5, 1936. For a useful overview of the literary criticism of the period, see Kirk Denton, ed., *Modern Chinese Literary Thought: Writings on Literature, 1893–1945* (Stanford, Calif.: Stanford University Press, 1995), 403–8.

17   For a good overview, see Denton's "General Introduction," 2–61. More detailed studies include Tsi-An Hsia's *The Gate of Darkness: Studies on the Leftist Literary Movement in China* (Seattle: University of Washington Press, 1968) and Anderson's *The Limits of Realism.*

18   The classic account of the development of the leftist film movement is that of Cheng Jihua and Li Shaobai, *Zhongguo dianying fazhan shi* (A history of the development of Chinese film) (Beijing: Zhongguo dianying chubanshe, 1963). Cheng's work is flawed, however, by the way it distorts and sometimes flat-out erases aspects of Chinese film history that do not jibe with the official historiography of the Chinese Revolution. Cheng's coverage of entertainment cinema in the 1930s is limited at best, thus obscuring the nature of the larger cinematic field against which leftist auteurs like Tian Han and others were working to differentiate themselves.

19   As cited in Spence, *The Search for Modern China,* 415.

20   As Sue Tuohy notes, many titles of leftist films from this period draw on musical vocabulary and/or musical metaphors. Examples include *Song of the Fisherman* (*Yuguang qu,* Lianhua, 1934), *Sad Song of Life* (*Sheng zhi aige,* Yihua, 1935), *Song of Triumph* (*Kai ge,* Yihua, 1935), *Lianhua Symphony* (*Lianhua jiaoxiang qu,* Lianhua, 1937), *Song at Midnight* (*Yeban gesheng,* Xinhua, 1937), and *The March of Youth* (*Qingnian jinxingqu,* Xinhua, 1937). See Sue Tuohy, "Metropolitan Sounds: Music in Chinese Films of the 1930s," in Yingjin Zhang, ed., *Cinema and Urban Culture in Shanghai, 1922–43* (Stanford, Calif.: Stanford University Press, 1999), 203.

21   I use Pierre Bourdieu's term *prise de position* (position-taking) in the sense suggested by his characterization of the cultural field as an arena "struc-

tured by the distribution of available positions (e.g., consecrated artist vs. striving artist, novel vs. poetry, art for art's sake vs. social art) . . . [and] the struggles between these positions, a struggle often expressed in the conflict between the orthodoxy of established traditions and the heretical challenge of new modes of cultural practice, manifested as *prises de position* or position-takings." See Randal Johnson, "Editor's Introduction," in Pierre Bourdieu, *The Field of Cultural Production: Essays on Art and Literature* (New York: Columbia University Press, 1993), 16–17.

22 For a thoughtful essay on the connection between nationalist discourse and prostitution, see Gail Hershatter's "Modernizing Sex, Sexing Modernity: Prostitution in Early Twentieth-Century Shanghai," in Christina K. Gilmartin, Gail Hershatter, Lisa Rofel, and Tyrene White, eds., *Engendering China: Woman, Culture, and the State* (Cambridge, Mass.: Harvard University Press, 1994), 147–74.

23 Spence, *The Search for Modern China*, 416.

24 According to Fredric Wakeman, the KMT rejected eighty-three film scripts and closed fourteen small film companies in 1934 and 1935 alone. This wave of suppression included the notorious Blueshirt raid on the leftist-identified Yihua Film Studio. See Wakeman, "Licensing Leisure: The Chinese Nationalists' Attempt to Regulate Shanghai, 1927–49," *Journal of Asian Studies* 54 (February 1995): 33. For a study of KMT film censorship policy from 1927 until 1937, see Zhiwei Xiao, "Constructing a New National Film Culture: Film Censorship and the Issues of Cantonese Dialect, Superstition, and Sex in the Nanjing Decade," in Zhang, ed., *Cinema and Urban Culture in Shanghai, 1922–1943*, 183–99.

25 See Nie Er, "Zhongguo gewu duanlun," in *Nie Er quanji*, vol. 2, 44.

26 As defined in the *Ciyuan* (Etymological dictionary) (Hong Kong: Shangwu yinshuguan, 1980).

27 Cheng Maoyun, "Li Jinhui yiliu juqu heyi bixu qudi" (Why the song and dance music of Li Jinhui and his ilk must be eliminated), *Yinyue jiaoyu* 1 (January 1934): 71–73. Cheng is best known for having written the KMT's party anthem.

28 Cheng Maoyun, 71. Given the crypto-fascist bent of the KMT's New Life campaign, it is interesting to note Cheng's use of discursive strategies common to other fascist movements of the era: an apotheosis of the rural "folk" and an idealized national past coupled with a disdain for "degeneracy" and a concomitant drive for tight government restrictions on unorthodox forms of cultural expression.

29 He Luting, "Zhongguo yinyue jie xianzhuang ji women dui yinyue yishu yingyou de renshi" (The present state of China's music world and the attitude we should take toward musical art), *Mingxing banyuekan* 5 (October 1936).

30 Nie Er, "Zhongguo gewu duanlun," *Nie Er quanji*, vol. 2, 48.

31 Ping, "Guanyu jin bo 'Taohua jiang' deng gequ de ji ju hua" (A few words

on the ban on broadcasting "Peach blossom river" and other songs), *Dian-sheng*, June 8, 1934, 416.

32 "Zhengli guangbo jiemu zhi banfa" (Procedures for regulating broadcast programs), *Yule zhoubao*, July 11, 1936, 531.

33 "Zhengli guangbo jiemu zhi banfa," 531.

34 This song was also published in *Music Education*. See the "Yinyue jiaoyu" entry in *Zhongguo yinyue cidian* (Dictionary of Chinese music) (Beijing: Renmin yinyue chubanshe, 1984), 465.

35 Ping, 416.

36 Ping, 416.

37 For a photographic reproduction of the program, see *Nie Er quanji*, vol. 2, 519. The audition included Nie Er's "Graduation Song" (from Yuan Mu-zhi's 1934 film *The Fate of Peach and Plum*) and the "Song of the Great Road" (from Sun Yu's 1935 film *The Great Road*). The program was split into six portions, each featuring a different genre of music in which the record company specialized, including Chinese instrumental and regional musics as well as popular and screen songs (including Li Jinhui's "Fairy Girl on Earth").

38 See "Disan guoji dang de songge" (Song of praise for the Third Interna-tionale), *Xiaoshuo yuebao* 9 (September 1921).

39 See Qu Qiubai, trans., "Guoji ge" (The internationale), *Xin qingnian* 1 (June 1923). For a comprehensive account of the song's trajectory in Chinese, see the "Guoji ge" entry in *Zhongguo yinyue cidian*, 137.

40 See Qiu Shi [Li Weisen], ed., *Geming geji* (Songs of revolution) (Shanghai: Zhongguo qingnian she, 1926).

41 For information on the Zhou Yang translation (which derived from a book on Soviet music published in the United States), see Wang Yuhe, 145. *Music Weekly* was published by the League of Left Musicians on December 14 and 21, 1932, but these two issues seem to be the only ones to have circu-lated. The publication includes anonymous articles on the establishment of a Federation for Proletarian Music in Japan, class struggle and music (translated from Japanese), as well as a piece (translated from English) on avant-garde experimentation in electronic music and the invention of the theremin.

42 For a discussion of the use of Hollywood-style melodrama in 1930s left-ist film, see Paul Pickowicz. "Melodramatic Representation and the 'May Fourth' Tradition of Chinese Cinema," in Ellen Widmer and David Der-wei Wang, eds., *From May Fourth to June Fourth: Fiction and Film in Twentieth-Century China* (Cambridge, Mass.: Harvard University Press, 1993). For commentary on the hybrid nature of leftist film style, see Ma Ning, "The Textual and Critical Difference of Being Radical: Reconstructing Chinese Leftist Films of the 1930s," *Wide Angle* 11 (Spring 1988): 22–31.

43 For more information on the dominance of Hollywood film in the Chinese market, see Marie Cambon, "The Dream Palaces of Shanghai: American

Films in China's Largest Metropolis Prior to 1949," *Asian Cinema* 7 (Winter 1995): 34–45.

44   The term "material unconscious" is borrowed from Bill Brown, *The Material Unconscious: American Amusement, Stephen Crane, and the Economies of Play* (Cambridge, Mass.: Harvard University Press, 1996).

45   Nie Er was not the only dedicated leftist to adopt a foreign name; this practice was almost de rigeur at the time. He Luting, the prominent leftist songwriter who studied under the Russian composer Tcherepnin at the Shanghai Conservatory, styled himself Rodin Ho.

46   For documentation and notation of each song, see *Nie Er quanji*, vol. 1, 15–111.

47   *Nie Er quanji,* vol. 1, 28.

48   For a similar argument issued during the revolutionary literature debate, see Xiang Gu, "Geming de wenxue jia, dao minjian qu" (Revolutionary writers, go to the people!), in *Geming wenxue lunzheng ziliao xuanbian*, 100–107.

49   The film was directed by Xu Xingzhi for the leftist-dominated Denton studio. For the film's scenario, see Chen Bo, ed., *Zhongguo zuoyi dianying yundong* (The Chinese left-wing film movement) (Beijing: Zhongguo dianying chubanshe, 1995), 283–84.

50   For an account of the genesis of the film and the national anthem, see Tian Han, "Fengyun ernü he yiyong jun jinxingqu" (Children of the storm and The march of the vounteers), in Chen Bo, 366–67.

51   Music by Nie Er, words by Xu Xingzhi . In *Xin Shanghai mingge sanbai qu,* 86.

52   In all fairness, however, the singer Wang Renmei portrays the song as "a true-to-life picture of the life of the girls in the Bright Moon Society" in her postrevolutionary memoirs. See Xie Bo, 161.

53   Roland Barthes, *Image-Music-Text* (New York: Hill and Wang, 1977), 179.

54   Personal interview in Hong Kong, October 20, 1995.

55   See Wang Daping [Nie Er], "Yinian lai zhi Zhongguo yinyue" (The past year in Chinese music), *Shenbao,* January 6, 1935. Also reprinted in *Nie Er quanji,* vol. 2, 83.

56   Examples of screen songs featuring male vocalists abound in the classic leftist films of the period, including the 1937 films *Song at Midnight* (music by Xian Xinghai) and *Crossroads* (*Shizi jietou,* music by He Luting).

57   *The Great Road,* premiered in 1935, was directed by Sun Yu and produced by Lianhua (United Photoplay).

58   See Richard Middleton, *Studying Popular Music* (Milton Keynes, Eng.: Open University Press, 1990), 242.

59   Middleton, 242.

60   Ho, 59.

61   Wang Yuhe, 146. This martial metaphor is given concrete expression in the concluding montage of *Children of the Storm.* For a photograph of this event, see *Zhongguo yinyue cidian,* 471.

62 Ruan committed suicide shortly after the film's release.

63 Eisenstein and Pudovkin's theories of montage were well-known to left-
    ist filmmakers. See, for example, Situ Huimin, "Montage yan renren shu"
    (Montage means different things to different people), *Diantong huabao* 11
    (October 1935).

64 DeMille's film, set in the year before the Bolshevik Revolution, was widely
    seen in China and admired by leftist critics as an example (along with
    Frank Borzage's *Seventh Heaven,* F. W. Murnau's *Sunrise,* and Fritz Lang's
    Metropolis) of the progressive political potential of narrative film in China
    in the late 1920s. See Fu Ye, "Dianying de minzhonghua" (The populariza-
    tion of cinema), in Zhongguo dianying ziliao guan, ed., *Zhongguo wusheng
    dianying* (Chinese silent cinema) (Beijing: Zhongguo dianying chubanshe,
    1996), 765.

65 *Nie Er quanji,* vol. 1, 67.

66 Sue Tuohy addresses this use of music as metaphor for mobilization in
    her insightful article on Chinese film music of the 1930s. See Tuohy, 218.
    Andrew Field also provides a detailed analysis of the film in terms of its
    depiction of cabaret culture in his "Selling Souls in Sin City: Shanghai
    Singing and Dancing Hostesses in Print, Film, and Politics, 1920–1949," in
    Zhang, ed., *Cinema and Urban Culture in Shanghai,* 118–22.

67 As Benedict Anderson has pointed out, synchronicity of this sort is an
    essential component in the creation of the sort of imagined community
    that undergirds modern nationalism. Anderson argues that newspaper
    readers participate in a "mass ceremony" in which "each communicant
    is well aware that the ceremony he performs is being replicated simul-
    taneously by thousands (or millions) of others of whose existence he is
    confident, yet of whose identity he has not the slightest notion. Further-
    more, this ceremony is incessantly repeated at daily or half-daily intervals
    throughout the calendar. What more vivid figure for the secular, histori-
    cally clocked, imagined community can be envisioned?" See Anderson,
    Imagined Communities: Reflections on the Origin and Spread of Nationalism
    (New York: Verso, 1991), 35. Yingjin Zhang also reads this film in terms
    of its representation of urban temporality and urban space in *The City in
    Modern Chinese Literature and Film: Configurations of Space, Time, and Gender*
    (Stanford, Calif.: Stanford University Press, 1996).

68 Zhi Er, "Cong 'Malu tianshi' de gequ shuoqi" (On the songs in *Street
    Angel*), *Xinhua huabao* 7 (1937).

69 For lyrics and music, see Chen Bo, 761.

70 Rey Chow has noted a similar tendency in the literary discourse of the era
    in *Woman and Chinese Modernity.* See Chow, 86.

A Han 阿憨. "Sizi yin" 四字吟 (Four characterizations). *Gexing huabao* 2 (October 1935): 10.

A Ying 阿英 [Qian Xingcun 錢杏村]. "Shanghai shibian yu dazhong gequ" 上海事變與大眾歌曲 (Mass songs and the Shanghai incident). In Qian Xingcun, ed., *Xiandai Zhongguo wenxue lun* 現代中國文學論 (Essays on modern Chinese literature). Shanghai: Hezhong shudian, 1933.

Adorno, Theodor, and Max Horkheimer. *Dialectic of Enlightenment.* Trans. John Cumming. New York: Continuum Books, 1988.

All About Shanghai and Environs: A Standard Guide Book. Shanghai: University Press, 1934–35. Reprinted with an introduction by H.J. Lethbridge. Hong Kong: Oxford University Press, 1983.

An E 安娥. "Yuepian duanping" 樂片短評 (Musicals in brief). *Yisheng* 1 (June 1935).

———. "Yuepian duanping" 樂片短評 (Musicals in brief). *Yisheng* 2 (July 1935).

———. "Zhongguo dianying yinyue tan" 中國電影音樂談 (Discussing Chinese film music). Part 1. *Yisheng* 1 (June 1935).

———. "Zhongguo dianying yinyue tan" 中國電影音樂談 (Discussing Chinese film music). Part 2. *Yisheng* 3 (August 1935).

———, and Ren Guang 任光. "Gequ xiao taolun" 歌曲小討論 (A brief discussion of songs). *Dianying huabao* 17 (December 1934).

Anderson, Benedict. *Imagined Communities: Reflections on the Origin and Spread of Nationalism.* Rev. ed. London: Verso, 1991.

Anderson, Marston. *The Limits of Realism: Chinese Fiction in the Revolutionary Period.* Berkeley: University of California Press, 1990.

———. "The Morality of Form: Lu Xun and the Modern Chinese Short Story." In Leo Ou-fan Lee, ed. *Lu Xun and His Legacy.* Berkeley: University of California Press, 1985.

Appadurai, Arjun. *Modernity at Large: Cultural Dimensions of Globalization.* Minneapolis: University of Minnesota Press, 1996.

Atkins, E. Taylor. "The Jazz Frontier: The Japanese Jazz Community in Interwar Shanghai." Unpublished typescript, 1996.

Attali, Jacques. *Noise: The Political Economy of Music.* Trans. Brian Massumi. Minneapolis: University of Minnesota Press, 1985.

Ba Shu 巴淑. "Qingge de yingxiang he shiming" 情歌的影響和使命 (The influence and mission of love songs). *Yinyue jiaoyu* 2 (December 1934): 47–50.

Barlow, Tani. "Colonialism's Career in Postwar China Studies." *Positions* 1 (Spring 1993): 224–67.

———, ed. *Formations of Colonial Modernity.* Durham, N.C.: Duke University Press, 1997.

Barthes, Roland. *Image-Music-Text.* New York: Hill and Wang, 1977.

Baxendale, John. " '. . . Into Another Kind of Life in Which Anything Might Happen . . .': Popular Music and Late Modernity, 1910–1930." *Popular Music* 14, no. 2 (1995): 137–54.

Benjamin, Walter. *Illuminations.* Trans. Harry Zohn. New York: Schocken Books, 1968.

Benson, Carlton. "From Teahouse to Radio: Storytelling and the Commercialization of Culture in 1930s Shanghai." Ph.D. dissertation, University of California, Berkeley, 1996.

Bergère, Marie-Claire. " 'The Other China': Shanghai from 1919 to 1949." In Christopher Howe, ed., *Shanghai: Revolution and Development in an Asian Metropolis.* Cambridge: Cambridge University Press, 1981.

Berlioz, Hector. *Evenings with the Orchestra.* New York: Alfred A. Knopf, 1956.

Bhabha, Homi. *The Location of Culture.* London: Routledge, 1994.

Bi Fen 碧芬. "Yinyue gewu you jiji tichang de biyao" 音樂歌舞有積極提倡的必要 (Musical drama needs to be actively promoted). *Yingxi zazhi* 1 (July 1930): 43.

Borthwick, Sally. *Education and Social Change in China: The Beginnings of the Modern Era.* Stanford, Calif.: Stanford University Press, 1983.

Bourdieu, Pierre. *Distinction: A Social Critique of the Judgment of Taste.* Trans. Richard Nice. Cambridge, Mass.: Harvard University Press, 1984.

———. *The Field of Cultural Production: Essays on Art and Literature.* Trans. Randal Johnson. New York: Columbia University Press, 1993.

Brown, Bill. *The Material Unconscious: American Amusement, Stephen Crane, and the Economies of Play.* Cambridge, Mass.: Harvard University Press, 1996.

Brown, Royal S. *Overtones and Undertones: Reading Film Music.* Berkeley: University of California Press, 1994.

Bumb, Heinrich. "The Great Beka 'Expedition,' 1905–6." *Talking Machine Review* 41 (1976).

Cambon, Marie. "The Dream Palaces of Shanghai: American Films in China's Largest Metropolis Prior to 1949." *Asian Cinema* 7 (Winter 1995): 34–45.

Casella, Alfredo. "Fengmi shijie de jueshi yinyue" 風靡世界的爵士音樂 (Jazz music is all the rage the world over). Trans. Anna 安娜. *Dongfang zazhi* 29, no. 4 (1932): 93–94.

Chanan, Michael. *Musica Practica: The Social Practice of Western Music from Gregorian Chant to Postmodernism.* London: Verso, 1994.

———. *Repeated Takes: A Short History of Recording and Its Effects on Music.* London: Verso, 1995.

Chang, Eileen 張愛玲. "Chinese Life and Fashions." *XXth Century* 4 (January 1943): 54–61.

———. *Chuanqi* 傳奇 (Romances). Rev. ed. Shanghai: Zhongguo tushu gongsi, 1946.

———. *Liuyan* 流言 (Written on water). Hong Kong: Huangguan chubanshe, 1994.

Chang Ping 昌平. "Shu 'Guanyu yin yue' hou" 書《關於淫樂》後 (After writing "On lewd music"). *Kaiming* 8 (1929): 447–50.

———. "Yinyue xiangle yu jingji zhidu" 音樂享樂與經濟制度 (The economic system and the enjoyment of music). *Kaiming* 4 (1928): 167–71.

Chao, Mei-pa 趙梅伯. "The Trend of Modern Chinese Music." *T'ien Hsia Monthly* 4 (March 1937): 269–86.

———. *The Yellow Bell.* Baltimore: Barberry Hill, 1934.

Chao, Yuen-ren. 趙元任. "Geci zhong de guoyin" 歌詞中的國音 (The national sound in song lyrics). *Yinyue yuekan* 3 (February 1938).

———. *Xin geshi ji* 新歌詩集 (A collection of new song-poetry). Shanghai: Commercial Press, 1928.

———. "Tone, Intonation Singing, Chanting, Recitation, Tonal Composition, and Atonal Composition in Chinese." In Morris Halle, ed., *For Roman Jakobson.* The Hague: Mouton, 1956: 52–59.

———. "Zhongguo pai hesheng de jige xiao shiyan" 中國派和聲的几個小試驗 (A few experiments in Chinese-style harmony). *Yinyue zazhi* 4 (October 1928).

Chatterjee, Partha. *The Nation and Its Fragments: Colonial and Postcolonial Histories.* Princeton: N.J.: Princeton University Press, 1993.

———. *Nationalist Discourse and the Colonial World: A Derivative Discourse?* London: Zed Books, 1986.

Chen Bo 陳播, ed. *Zhongguo zuoyi dianying yundong* 中國左翼電影運動

(The Chinese left-wing film movement). Beijing: Zhongguo dianying chubanshe, 1995.

Chen Hong 陳洪. "Jia yang guizi yu Zhongguo xin yinyue" 假洋鬼子與中國新音樂 (Fake foreign devils and China's new music). *Guangzhou yinyue* 2 (March 1934).

Chen Yike 陳伊克, ed. *Dianying mingge ji* 電影名歌集 (Famous screen song collection). Shanghai: Xiandai yinyue yanjiu she, 1940.

Chen Zhongzi 陳仲子. "Guomin xing yu guoge" 國民性與國歌 (National character and the national anthem). *Yinyue zazhi* 1 (March 1920).

———. "Yu guoyue zhi fuxing yi tong xiyue shuo" 欲國樂之復興宜通西樂說 (An understanding of Western music theory will help effect a renaissance of Chinese music). *Yinyue zazhi* 9 (December 1920).

Cheng Jihua 程季華, Li Shaobai 李少白, and Xing Zuwen 邢祖文. *Zhongguo dianying fazhan shi* 中國電影發展史 (A history of the development of Chinese film). 2 vols. Beijing: Zhongguo dianying chubanshe, 1963.

Cheng Maoyun 程懋筠. "Diji wenhua minzu de geyao" 低級文化民族的歌謠 (The folk songs of culturally primitive nations). *Yinyue jiaoyu* 1 (November 1933).

———. "Gailiang Zhongguo yinyue de quyi" 改良中國音樂的芻議 (Modest proposals for the reform of Chinese music). *Yinyue jiaoyu* 1 (April 1933).

———. "Li Jinhui yiliu juqu heyi bixu qudi" 黎錦暉一流劇曲何以必須取締 (Why the song and dance music of Li Jinhui and his ilk must be eliminated). *Yinyue jiaoyu* 1 (January 1934): 71–73.

———. "Nüxing yu yinyue" 女性與音樂 (Women and music). *Yinyue jiaoyu* 2 (April 1934).

Cheng Shi 程詩, Yu Liang 于良, and Jiang Tuo 江沱. "Gechang mingxing sanren xiang" 歌唱明星三人像 (Portraits of three pop stars: Zhou Xuan, Gong Qiuxia, Bai Hong). *Zazhi yuekan* 7 (1943): 181–87.

Ching, Doe. "The Magazines of China." *XXth Century* 4 (April 1943): 276–81.

Chinese Ministry of Information. *China Handbook, 1937–1943*. New York: Macmillan, 1943.

Chou, Katherine Hui-ling 周慧玲. "Nü yanyuan, xieshi zhuyi, 'xin nüxing' lunshu: wanqing dao wusi shiqi Zhongguo xiandai juchang zhong de xingbie biaoyan" 女演員，寫實主義，『新女性』論述－晚清到五四時期中國現代劇場中的性別表演 [Actresses, realism, and the discourse of the "new woman": the performance of gender in modern Chinese theater from the late Qing to the May 4th era]. *Jindai zhongguo funü shi yanjiu* 4 (August 1996): 87–133.

Chow, Rey. *Primitive Passions: Visuality, Sexuality, Ethnography, and Contemporary Chinese Cinema.* New York: Columbia University Press, 1995.

———. *Woman and Chinese Modernity: The Politics of Reading Between East and West.* Minneapolis: University of Minnesota Press, 1991.

"Chuangkan ci" 創刊詞 (Editor's introduction). *Gexing huabao* 1 (March 1935).

Chun Jie 純潔. "Woguo yinyue shuji diaocha lu" 我國音樂書籍調查錄 (A survey of Chinese books about music). *Yinyue shijie* 8 (September 1939): 229–33.

Clark, Paul. *Chinese Cinema: Culture and Politics Since 1949.* New York: Cambridge University Press, 1987.

Clayton, Buck, with Nancy Miller Elliot. *Buck Clayton's Jazz World.* New York: Oxford University Press, 1987.

Commercial Directory of Shanghai. Shanghai: Commercial Press, 1928.

"Cong getai dao yinmu" 從歌台到銀幕 (From the musical stage to the silver screen). *Yingmi zhoubao,* November 14, 1934.

"Dangxuan sanda gexing zhi Zhou Xuan" 當選三大歌星之周璇 (Zhou Xuan selected as one of the top three pop stars). *Qingqing dianying* 7 (1941).

de Barros, Paul. *Jackson Street After Hours: The Roots of Jazz in Seattle.* Seattle: Sasquatch Books, 1993.

De Ren 得人. "Boyin gexing jingxuan jieguo" 播音歌星競選結果 (Broadcasting stars competition results). *Diansheng* 3 (June 1934).

Denton, Kirk A., ed. *Modern Chinese Literary Thought: Writings on Literature, 1893–1945.* Stanford, Calif.: Stanford University Press, 1996.

"Disan guoji dang de songge" 第三國際黨的頌歌 (Song of praise for the Third Internationale). *Xiaoshuo yuebao* 9 (September 1921).

"Diantai texun" 電台特訊 (Special radio station report). *Diansheng,* April 13, 1934, 256.

Dianying xinge ji 電影新歌集 (New screen songs collection). Shanghai: Guoguang shudian, 1938.

Dikötter, Frank. *The Discourse of Race in Modern China.* Stanford, Calif.: Stanford University Press, 1992.

———. *Sex, Culture, and Modernity in China: Medical Science and the Construction of Sexual Identities in the Early Republican Period.* Honolulu: University of Hawaii Press, 1995.

Dissanayake, Wimal, ed. *Colonialism and Nationalism in Asian Cinema.* Bloomington: Indiana University Press, 1994.

Du Yunzhi 杜雲之. *Zhongguo dianying shi* 中國電影史 (A history of Chinese cinema). Taipei: Taiwan shangwu yinshuguan, 1986.

Duara, Prasenjit. *Rescuing History from the Nation: Questioning Narratives of Modern China.* Chicago: University of Chicago Press, 1995.

Du Bois, W. E. B. "China and Japan." *Pittsburgh Courier,* October 23, 1937.

———. "Shanghai." *Pittsburgh Courier,* February 27, 1937.

Fabian, Johannes. *Time and the Other: How Anthropology Makes Its Object.* New York: Columbia University Press, 1983.

Fan Boqun 范伯群, ed. *Yuanqing juzi Zhou Shoujuan* 哀情巨子周瘦鵑 (Master of sorrow: Zhou Shoujuan). Taipei: Yeqiang chubanshe, 1994.

Feng Zikai 豐子愷. "Jueshi yinyue" 爵士音樂 (Jazz music). *Yinyue jiaoyu* 8 (December 1933): 40–41.

Frith, Simon. *Performing Rites: On the Value of Popular Music.* Cambridge, Mass.: Harvard University Press, 1996.

Foreman, Ronald C. "Jazz and Race Records, 1920–32: Their Origins and Their Significance for the Record Industry and Society." Ph.D. dissertation. University of Illinois, 1968.

Foucault, Michel. *Discipline and Punish: The Birth of the Prison.* Trans. Alan Sheridan. New York: Vintage Books, 1979.

Fu, Pei-mei 傅白梅. "Music Chronicle." *T'ien Hsia Monthly* (March 1939), 256–59.

Fu, Po-shek. "Patriotism or Profit: Hong Kong Cinema During the Second World War." In Law Kar 羅卡, ed. *Early Images of Hong Kong and China: Program of the 19th Hong Kong International Film Festival.* Hong Kong: Urban Council, 1995, 73–79.

———. "Struggle to Entertain: The Political Ambivalence of the Shanghai Film Industry Under Japanese Occupation, 1941–45." In Law Kar 羅卡, ed. *Cinema of Two Cities, Hong Kong–Shanghai: The 18th Hong Kong International Film Festival.* Hong Kong: Urban Coucil, 1994, 50–62.

Gabbard, Krin, ed. *Jazz Among the Discourses.* Durham, N.C.: Duke University Press, 1995.

Gaisberg, F. W. *The Music Goes Round.* New York: Macmillan, 1942.

Gálik, Marián. *The Genesis of Modern Chinese Literary Criticism (1917–1930).* London: Curzon Press, 1980.

Gao Pingshu 高平叔, ed. *Cai Yuanpei meiyu lunji* 蔡元培美育論集 (A collection of Cai Yuanpei's essays on aesthetic education). Changsha: Hunan jiaoyu chubanshe, 1987.

Gelatt, Roland. *The Fabulous Phonograph, 1877–1977.* New York: Macmillan, 1977.

Gernet, Jacques. *Daily Life in China on the Eve of the Mongol Invasion, 1250–1276.* Stanford, Calif.: Stanford University Press, 1962.

"Gechang chunse" 歌唱春色 (The romance of the opera). *Xin yinxing* 33 (October 1931).

Geming wenxue lunzheng ziliao xuanbian 革命文學論爭資料選編 (An edited selection of materials on the revolutionary literature debate). 2 vols. Beijing: Renmin wenxue chubanshe, 1981.

"Gewu zai Zhongguo shi zheyangde, gewu zai Meiguo shi zheyang de" 歌舞在中國是這樣的，歌舞在美國是這樣的 (Musicals in China are like this, musicals in America are like that). *Shidai dianying* 3 (August 1934).

Gilmartin, Christina K., Gail Hershatter, Lisa Rofel, and Tyrene White, eds. *Engendering China: Woman, Culture, and the State.* Cambridge, Mass.: Harvard University Press, 1994.

Gioia, Ted. *The Imperfect Art: Reflections on Jazz and Modern Culture.* New York: Oxford University Press, 1988.

Goldman, Merle, ed. *Modern Chinese Literature in the May Fourth Era.* Cambridge, Mass.: Harvard University Press, 1977.

Golsan, Richard J., ed. *Fascism, Aesthetics, and Culture.* Hanover, N.H.: University Press of New England, 1992.

Gould, Randall. "Where Races Mingle but Never Merge." *Christian Science Monitor,* June 24, 1936, 4.

Greenhalgh, Paul. *Ephemeral Vistas: The Expositions Universelles, Great Exhibitions and World's Fairs, 1851–1939.* Manchester: Manchester University Press, 1988.

Gronow, Pekka. "The Record Industry Comes to the Orient." *Ethnomusicology* 2 (May 1981): 251–84.

———. "The Record Industry: The Growth of a Mass Medium." *Popular Music* 3 (1983): 53–76.

———. *The Recording Industry: An Ethnomusicological Approach.* Tampere, Finland: University of Tampere, 1996.

Gu Cangwu 古蒼梧. "Luanshi qihua hua Xianglan" 亂時奇花話香蘭 (A strange flower of turbulent times: on Li Xianglan). *Lianhe wenxue* 105 (July 1993): 96–99.

"Guangbo" 廣播 (Broadcasting). *Yule,* January 1, 1936, 5.

Guide to China's Foreign Trade: Import and Export Annual, 1933. Shanghai: Bureau of Foreign Trade of the Ministry of Industry, 1933.

Gunn, Edward M. *Unwelcome Muse: Chinese Literature in Shanghai and Peking, 1937–45.* New York: Columbia University Press, 1980.

Guo Moruo 郭沫若. *Moruo wenji* 沫若文集 (Collected works of Moruo). 17 vols. Beijing: Renmin wenxue chubanshe, 1957.

"Haishang shi da gexing xuanju" 海上十大歌星選舉 (Ten best pop stars in Shanghai contest). *Gexing huabao* 2 (October 1935).

Hao Ru 浩如. "Yinyue shi fou shuyu teshu jieji de" 音樂是否屬於特殊階級的 (Does music belong to any special class?). *Yinyue zazhi* 2 (September 1934): 44–47.

Harvey, David. *The Condition of Postmodernity.* Cambridge, Mass.: Basil Blackwell, 1990.

Haskell, Harry, ed. *The Attentive Listener: Three Centuries of Music Criticism.* Princeton, N.J.: Princeton University Press, 1996.

Hauser, Ernest O. *Shanghai: City for Sale.* New York: Harcourt Brace, 1940.

He 鶴. "Bu dongting de yuesheng shi diantai boyin shi de da daji" 不動聽的樂聲是電台播音時的大打擊 (Music that doesn't sound good is a big blow for radio stations during broadcasts). *Diansheng,* February 23, 1934, 118.

———. "Chongzheng qigu hou de Li Jinhui you xiang zai guangbo jie fazhan" 重整旗鼓後的黎錦暉又想在廣播界發展 (Having set up shop once again, Li Jinhui wants to move forward in broadcasting). *Diansheng,* April 20, 1934, 276.

He Luting 賀綠汀 [Luo Ting 羅亭]. "Guanyu Li Jinhui" 關於黎錦暉 (About Li Jinhui). *Yinyue jiaoyu* 2 (December 1934): 32–34.

———. *He Luting yinyue lunwen xuan ji* 賀綠汀音樂論文選集 (Selections from He Luting's writings on music). 2 vols. Shanghai: Shanghai yinyue chubanshe, 1981.

———. "Zhongguo yinyue jie xianzhuang ji women dui yinyue yishu yingyou de renshi" 中國音樂界現狀及我們對音樂藝術應有的認識 (The present state of China's music world and the attitude we should take toward musical art). *Mingxing banyuekan* 5 (October 1936).

Hengtang tuishi 蘅堂退士, ed. *Tangshi sanbai shou* 唐詩三百首 (Three hundred Tang poems). Beijing: Zhonghua shuju, 1990.

Hershatter, Gail. *Dangerous Pleasures: Prostitution and Modernity in Twentieth-Century China.* Berkeley: University of California Press, 1997.

———. "Modernizing Sex, Sexing Modernity: Prostitution in Early Twentieth-Century Shanghai." In Christina K. Gilmartin, Gail Hershatter, Lisa Rofel, and Tyrene White, eds. *Engendering China: Woman,*

Culture, and the State. Cambridge, Mass.: Harvard University Press, 1994: 147–74.

Ho, Sam. "The Songstress, the Farmer's Daughter, the Mambo Girl, and the Songstress Again." In Law Kar, ed., *Mandarin Films and Popular Songs, 40s–60s: Catalog of the 17th Hong Kong International Film Festival.* Hong Kong: Urban Council, 1993.

Hsia, Tsi-an. *The Gate of Darkness: Studies on the Leftist Literary Movement in China.* Seattle: University of Washington Press, 1968.

Hughes, Langston. *I Wonder as I Wander: An Autobiographical Journey.* New York: Rinehart, 1956.

Hung, Chang-tai. *Going to the People: Chinese Intellectuals and Folk Literature, 1918–1937.* Cambridge, Mass.: Harvard University Press, 1985.

———. *War and Popular Culture: Resistance in Modern China, 1937–1945.* Berkeley: University of California Press, 1994.

Ing, Benjamin Z. N. 應尚能. "Music Chronicle." *T'ien Hsia Monthly* 4 (January 1937).

Iriye, Akira, ed. *The Chinese and the Japanese: Essays in Political and Cultural Interactions.* Princeton, N.J.: Princeton University Press, 1980.

Jarocinski, Stefan. *Debussy: Impressionism and Symbolism.* London: Eulenberg Books, 1976.

Jiang Tie 江鐵. *Liusheng ji* 留聲機 (The phonograph). Shanghai: Commercial Press, 1932.

Jiao Xiongping 焦雄屏, ed. *Malu tianshi* 馬路天使 (Street angel). Taipei: Wanxiang, 1990.

"Jingren xiaoxi" 驚人消息 (Shocking news). *Shanghai yingxun,* August 23, 1941, 31.

Johnson, David, Andrew Nathan, and Evelyn S. Rawski, eds. *Popular Culture in Late Imperial China.* Berkeley: University of California Press, 1985.

Jones, Andrew F. *Like a Knife: Ideology and Genre in Contemporary Chinese Popular Music.* Ithaca, N.Y.: Cornell East Asia Series, 1992.

Jusdanis, Gregory. *Belated Modernity and Aesthetic Culture: Inventing National Literature.* Minneapolis: University of Minnesota Press, 1991.

Joshi, G. N. "A Concise History of the Phonograph Industry in India." *Popular Music* 7 (May 1988): 147–56.

Kahn, Douglas, and Gregory Whitehead, eds. *Wireless Imagination: Sound, Radio, and the Avant-Garde.* Cambridge, Mass.: MIT Press, 1992.

Kenwood, A. G., and A. L. Lougheed. *The Growth of the International Economy, 1820–1960.* London: Allen and Unwin, 1971.

Ke Zhenghe 柯政和. "Changpian de piping" 唱片的批評 (Record criticism). *Yinyue zazhi* 1 (February 1932): 17.

———. "Changpian de shiyong ji baocun fa" 唱片的使用及保存法 (The use and preservation of records). *Yinyue zazhi* 9 (January 1930).

———. "Liusheng ji de faming jiqi yuanli" 留聲機的發明及其原理 (The invention of the phonograph and its mechanical principles). *Yinyue chao* 2 (March 1928).

———. "Liusheng ji de liyong fa" 留聲機的利用法 (How to use the phonograph). *Yinyue chao* 1 (December 1927): 7–10.

———. "Shengli gongsi yu Radio Copulation [*sic*] of America hebing" 勝利公司與 Radio Copulation [*sic*] of America 合并 (Victor to merge with the Radio Copulation [*sic*] of America). *Yinyue chao* 2 (July 1929).

———. "Wudao yinyue" 舞蹈音樂 (Dance music). *Yinyue chao* 2 (July 1929).

———. "Xin yinyue" 新音樂 (New music). *Yinyue chao* 2 (July 1929).

———. "Zhazi yinyue" 扎茲音樂 (Jazz music). *Yinyue chao* 5 (December 1927).

———. "Zhazi yinyue de chanye hua" 扎茲音樂的產業化 (The industrialization of jazz music). *Yinyue zazhi* 10 (February 1932).

Kirby, William. *Germany and Republican China.* Princeton, N.J.: Princeton University Press, 1984.

Kittler, Friedrich. *Gramophone, Film, Typewriter.* Stanford, Calif.: Stanford University Press, 1999.

Kracauer, Siegfried. *The Mass Ornament: Weimar Essays.* Trans. Thomas Y. Levin. Cambridge, Mass.: Harvard University Press, 1995.

Kraus, Richard. *Pianos and Politics in China: Middle-Class Ambitions and the Struggle Over Western Music.* New York: Oxford University Press, 1989.

Laing, Dave. "A Voice Without a Face: Popular Music and the Phonograph in the 1890s." *Popular Music* 10 (January 1991): 1–9.

Lao She 老舍. "Kangzhan geyao" 抗戰歌謠 (Anthems for the war of resistance). *Yuzhou feng,* May 16, 1939.

Lapham, Claude. "China Needs American Bands." *Metronome* (July 1936): 13.

———. "If You Must Go To Japan." *Metronome* (October 1936): 16.

———. "Looking at Japanese Jazz." *Metronome* (June 1936): 14.

———. "More Jobs in the Orient." *Metronome* (November 1936): 17.

Latourette, Kenneth S. *A History of Christian Missions in China.* New York: Macmillan, 1929.

Law Kar 羅卡, ed. *Mandarin Films and Popular Songs, 40s–60s: Program of the*

17th Hong Kong International Film Festival. Hong Kong: Urban Council, 1993.

Lee, Leo Ou-fan 李歐梵, ed. *Lu Xun and His Legacy.* Berkeley: University of California Press, 1985.

———. "Mantan Zhongguo xiandai wenxue zhong de 'tuifei' " 漫談現代中國文學中的頹廢 (On decadence in modern Chinese literature). *Jintian* 4 (Winter 1993): 26–51.

———. *The Romantic Generation of Modern Chinese Writers.* Cambridge, Mass.: Harvard University Press, 1973.

———. *Shanghai Modern: The Flowering of a New Urban Culture in China, 1930–1945.* Cambridge, Mass.: Harvard University Press, 1999.

———, ed. *Xin ganjue pai xiaoshuo xuan* 新感覺派小說選 (A selection of new perceptionist fiction). Taipei: Yunchen wenhua, 1988.

———, and Andrew Nathan. "The Beginnings of Mass Culture: Journalism and Fiction in the Late Ch'ing and Beyond." In David Johnson, Andrew Nathan, and Evelyn S. Rawski, eds. *Popular Culture in Late Imperial China.* Berkeley: University of California Press, 1985.

Leung Ping-kwan 梁秉鈞, ed. *Xianggang de liuxing wenhua* 香港的流行文化 (Hong Kong popular culture). Hong Kong: Joint Publishing, 1993.

Leung, Paul 梁寶耳. "Dianying shi shidai qu zhi dansheng wenchuang" 電影是時代曲之誕生溫床 (Mandarin movies and mandarin pop). In Law Kar 羅卡, ed., *Mandarin Films and Popular Songs, 40s–60s: Program of the 17th Hong Kong International Film Festival.* Hong Kong: Urban Council, 1993: 43–46.

Leyda, Jay. *Dianying, Electric Shadows: An Account of Films and the Film Audience in China.* Cambridge, Mass.: MIT Press, 1972.

Li Jinhui 黎錦暉. *Aiguo gequ* 愛國歌曲 (Patriotic songs). Shanghai: Shanghai wenming shudian, 1932.

———. *Chuntian de kuaile* 春天的快樂 (The happiness of spring). Shanghai: Zhonghua shuju, 1928.

———. *Dazhong yinyue keben* 大眾音樂課本 (Music textbook for the masses). Shanghai: Shanghai dazhong shuju, 1933.

———. *Gewu biaoyan qu* 歌舞表演曲 (Song and dance performance pieces). 20 vols. Shanghai: Zhonghua shuju, 1929.

———, ed. *Geyao* 歌謠 (Folk songs). 8 vols. Shanghai: Zhonghua shuju, 1924.

———. *Jiating aiqing gequ ershiwu zhong* 家庭愛情歌曲二十五種 (Twenty-five family love songs). Shanghai: Shanghai wenming shudian, 1929.

———. *Li Jinhui gequ ji* 黎錦暉歌曲集 (Collected songs of Li Jinhui). 3 vols. Shanghai: Zhonghua shuju, 1926.

———. *Maque yu xiaohai (yi ming juewu de shaonian)* 麻雀與小孩 (一名覺悟的少年) (The magpie and the child, or an awakened youth). Shanghai: Zhonghua shuju, 1927.

———. *Pingmin qianzi keben* 平民千字課本 (Thousand-character text for the common people). Shanghai: Zhonghua shuju, 1927.

———. *Putao xianzi* 葡萄仙子 (The grape fairy). Shanghai: Zhonghua shuju, 1923.

———. *San hudie* 三蝴蝶 (Three butterflies). Shanghai: Zhonghua shuju, 1926.

———. *Tebie kuaiche* 特別快車 (Express train). Shanghai: Shanghai dazhong shuju, 1928.

———. "Wo he Mingyue gewu she" 我和明月社 (The Bright Moon ensemble and myself). *Wenhua shiliao* 3, no. 4 (1985–86).

———. *Xiao Lida zhi si* 小利達之死 (The death of little Lida). Shanghai: Zhonghua shuju, 1928.

———. *Xin jiaocai jiaokeshu guoyu keben* 新教材教課書國語課本 (New Mandarin primer). Shanghai: Zhonghua shuju, 1920.

———. *Xique yu xiaohai* 喜雀與小孩 (The magpie and the child). Beijing: Beijing chubanshe, 1957.

———. "Yinyue yu shipin" 音樂與食品 (Music and food). *Yule banyuekan* 2 (July-August 1935).

———. *Yue ming zhi ye* 月明之夜 (Night of bright moonlight). Shanghai: Zhonghua shuju, 1926.

"Li Jinhui ye ruanhua le" 黎錦暉也軟化了 (Even Li Jinhui has relented). *Yule zhoubao,* July 7, 1935, 2.

Li Lili 黎莉莉. "Ge chang li de zhen" 歌唱裡的真 (The truth in singing). *Yisheng* 3 (August 1935).

———, ed. *Tian ge yida* 甜歌一打 (A dozen sweet songs). Shanghai: Shanghai dazhong shuju, 1933.

Li Qing 李青, et al. *Guangbo dianshi qiye shi neibu shiliao* 廣播電視企業史內部史料 (Internal historical documents on the history of the broadcasting and television industries). Shanghai: Zhongguo changpian gongsi, 1994.

Li Shaobai 李少白. *Dianying lishi ji lilun* 電影歷史及理論 (Film history and theory). Beijing: Wenhua yishu chubanshe, 1991.

Li Sui 黎遂. "Li Jinhui bei Jiang Qing zhemo er si" 黎錦暉被江青折磨而死 (Li Jinhui tortured to death by Jiang Qing). In Tu Guangqi 屠光啟, ed.

Zhou Xuan de zhenshi gushi 周璇的真實故事 (Zhou Xuan's real story).
Taipei: Zhuanji wenxue she, 1987: 231–45.

Liang Maochun 梁茂春. "Dui woguo liuxing yinyue lishi de sikao" 對我
國流行音樂歷史的思考 (Thoughts on the history of Chinese popular
music). *Renmin yinyue* 7 (1988): 32–34.

Liang Qichao 梁啟超. *Yinbing shi heji* 飲冰室合集 (Collected works from
the ice drinker's studio). Shanghai: Zhonghua shuju, 1936.

———. *Yinbing shi shihua* 飲冰室詩話 (Poetry talk from the ice drinker's
studio). Beijing: Renmin wenxue chubanshe, 1982.

Liang, Sung-ling 梁松齡. "Music Chronicle." *T'ien Hsia Monthly*, 11
(October-November 1940): 174–77.

Liao Fushu 廖輔叔. "Ji zuoqu jia Liu Xue'an 記作曲家劉雪庵
(Remembering the composer Liu Xue'an). *Wenhua shiliao* 7 (July 1983):
151–57.

Link, Perry. *Mandarin Ducks and Butterflies: Popular Fiction in Early
Twentieth-Century Chinese Cities.* Berkeley: University of California
Press, 1981.

———. "Traditional Style Popular Urban Fiction in the Teens and Twenties." In Merle Goldman, ed., *Modern Chinese Literature in the May Fourth
Era.* Cambridge, Mass.: Harvard University Press, 1977.

Liu, Lydia H. *Translingual Practice: Literature, National Culture, and Translated Modernity—China, 1900–1937.* Stanford, Calif.: Stanford University
Press, 1995.

Liu Na'ou 劉吶鷗. "Dianying xingshi mei de tanqiu" 電影形式美的探求
(The pursuit of formal beauty in the cinema). *Wanxiang* 1 (May 1934).

Liu Xue'an 劉雪庵. "Zenyang cai neng chedi qudi Li Jinhui yi liu zhi juqu"
怎樣才能徹底取締黎錦暉一流劇曲 (What must be done before we
will be able to thoroughly eliminate the music of Li Jinhui and his ilk).
Yinyue zazhi 3 (July 1934).

Lu Ji 呂驥. "Zhongguo xin yinyue de zhanwang" 中國新音樂的展望 (The
prospects for China's new music). *Guangming* 1, no. 5 (1936).

Ma, Hiao-Ts'iun. *La Musique Chinoise de Style Européen.* Paris: Jouve, 1941.

Ma Ning. "The Textual and Critical Difference of Being Radical: Reconstructing Chinese Leftist Films of the 1930s." *Wide Angle* 11 (Spring
1988): 22–31.

Manuel, Peter. *Popular Musics of the Non-Western World: An Introductory
Survey.* New York: Columbia University Press, 1988.

Mao Dun 茅盾. "Fengjian de xiao shimin wenyi" 封建的小市民文藝

(The feudal culture of the urban petit bourgeoisie). *Dongfang zazhi,* February 1, 1933.

——. *Mao Dun wenji* 茅盾文集 (Selected writings of Mao Dun). Beijing: Renmin chubanshe, 1963.

——. *Mao Dun zixuan sanwen ji* 茅盾自選散文集 (Collected essays written and selected by Mao Dun). Hong Kong: Xiandai wenjiao she, 1954.

Mao Zedong 毛澤東. *Selected Works of Mao Tse-tung.* Beijing: Foreign Languages Press, 1967. 4 vols.

Mattelart, Armand. *Mapping World Communication: War, Progress, Culture.* Minneapolis: University of Minnesota Press, 1994.

——. and Seth Siegelaub, eds. *Communication and Class Struggle.* New York: International General, 1979.

May, Elizabeth. *The Influence of the Meiji Period on Japanese Children's Music.* Berkeley: University of California Press, 1963.

McClary, Susan, and Richard Leppert, eds. *Music and Society: The Politics of Composition, Performance, and Reception.* Cambridge: Cambridge University Press, 1987.

Middleton, Richard. *Studying Popular Music.* Milton Keynes, Eng.: Open University Press, 1990.

Modleski, Tania, ed. *Studies in Entertainment: Critical Approaches to Mass Culture.* Bloomington: Indiana University Press, 1986.

Nakamura, Tōyō. "Early Pop Song Writers and Their Backgrounds." *Popular Music* 10, no. 3 (1991): 263–82.

"Naliang hui ji" 納涼會記 (Transcript of an al fresco gathering). *Zazhi yuekan* 8 (1945).

Nattiez, Jean-Jacques. *Music and Discourse: Toward a Semiology of Music.* Trans. Carolyn Abbate. Princeton, N.J.: Princeton University Press, 1990.

Needham, Joseph. *Science and Civilization in China.* 4 vols. Cambridge: Cambridge University Press, 1962.

Nettl, Bruno. *The Western Impact on World Music.* New York: Schirmer Books, 1985.

Ng Ho 吳昊. "Tianya genü qing" 天涯歌女情 (Songstresses of the world). In Law Kar 羅卡, ed., *Mandarin Films and Popular Songs, 40s–60s: Program of the 17th Hong Kong International Film Festival.* Hong Kong: Urban Council, 1993: 21–23.

Ou Manlang 歐漫郎. "Kelian de jueshi" 可憐的爵士 (Pitiable jazz). *Guangzhou yinyue* 3 (December 1934).

Owen, Stephen, ed. *Readings in Chinese Literary Thought.* Cambridge, Mass.: Harvard University Press, 1992.

Pan, Ling. *In Search of Old Shanghai.* Hong Kong: Joint Publishing, 1991.

Perkins, John F., Alan Kelly, and John Ward. "On Gramophone Company Matrix Numbers, 1898 to 1921." *Record Collector* 23 (1976).

Pickowicz, Paul. "Melodramatic Representation and the 'May Fourth' Tradition of Chinese Cinema." In Ellen Widmer and David Derwei Wang, eds., *From May Fourth to June Fourth: Fiction and Film in Twentieth-Century China.* Cambridge, Mass.: Harvard University Press, 1993.

Pietz, William. "The Phonograph in Africa: International Phonocentrism from Stanley to Sarnoff." In Derek Attridge, Geoff Bennington, and Robert Young, eds., *Post-structuralism and the Question of History.* Cambridge: Cambridge University Press, 1987: 263–85.

Ping 萍. "Guanyu jin bo 'Taohua jiang' deng gequ de ji ju hua" 關於禁播桃花江等歌曲的幾句話 (A few words on the ban on broadcasting "Peach blossom river" and other songs). *Diansheng* 3 (June 1934): 416.

Qian Guangren 錢廣仁. "Ben gongsi wunian yilai jingyu lüeli" 本公司五年以來經遇略曆 (Brief résumé of the New Moon record company's experiences in the last five years). *Xinyue ji* 1 (September 1929): 11–13.

———. "Chunran maoyi shi de changpian shiye bu neng chijiu" 純然貿易式的唱片事業不能持久 (A purely commercial record industry can't survive for long). *Xinyue ji* 1 (September 1929): 46.

———. "Cong wuxian dian boyin yingxiang changpian shiye de fada shuodao yousheng dianying yu changpian de guanxi" 從無線播音影響唱片事業的發達說到有聲電影與唱片的關係 (From the influence of wireless broadcasting on the development of the record industry to the relationship of sound films and records). *Xinyue ji* 2 (September 1930).

———. "Jinggao gebu rexin tichang guohuo tongzhi" 警告各埠熱心提倡國貨同志 (A warning to those in every city who are enthusiastic about promoting domestic goods). *Xinyue ji* 1 (September 1929).

———. "Tantan woguo jiben shuchupin yu xinxing gongye" 談談我國基本輸出品與新興工業 (A discussion of China's basic import-export goods and newly emergent industries). *Xinyue ji* 2 (September 1930).

———. "Yinyue yu ganqing" 音樂與感情 (Music and emotion). *Xinyue ji* 3 (August 1931).

Qin Qiming 秦啟明, ed. *Yinyue jia Ren Guang* 音樂家任光 (Musician Ren Guang). Hefei: Anhui wenyi chubanshe, 1988.

Qing Qing 青青. "Women de yinyue jie" 我們的音樂界 (Our musical circles). *Kaiming* 4 (1928).

Qiu Chen 秋塵. "Mingyue gewu yu kaiming" 明月歌舞於開明 (Ming Yeoh Musikverein at the Kaiming Theater). *Beiyang huabao,* August 19, 1930, 2.

Qu Qiubai 瞿秋白, trans. "Guoji ge" 國際歌 (The Internationale). *Xin qingnian* 1 (June 1923).

Radio Corporation of America. *Annual Reports, 1927–1945.*

Rasula, Jed. "The Media of Memory: The Seductive Menace of Records in Jazz History." In Krin Gabbard, ed., *Jazz Among the Discourses.* Durham, N.C.: Duke University Press, 1995: 134–64.

Rayns, Tony. "Missing Links: Chinese Cinema in Shanghai and Hong Kong from the 1930s to the 1940s." In Law Kar 羅卡, ed. *Early Images of Hong Kong and China: The 19th Hong Kong International Film Festival.* Hong Kong: Urban Council, 1995: 105–11.

Robertson, Jennifer. "Gender-bending in Paradise: Doing 'Female' and 'Male' in Japan." *Genders* 5 (Summer 1989): 50–69.

———. *Takarazuka: Sexual Politics and Popular Culture in Modern Japan.* Berkeley: University of California Press, 1998.

Robinson, Deanna Campbell, Elizabeth B. Buck, Marlene Cuthbert, and the International Communication and Youth Consortium. *Music at the Margins: Popular Music and Global Cultural Diversity.* Newbury Park, Calif.: Sage Publications, 1991.

Russell, Frances. "Hollywood in China." *Vox Magazine* (October 1935).

Scott, A. C. *Literature and the Arts in Twentieth Century China.* New York: Anchor Books, 1963.

Sergeant, Harriet. *Shanghai: Collision Point of Cultures, 1918–1939.* New York: Crown, 1990.

"Shanghai boyin jie gechang tuanti tongji" 上海播音界歌唱團體統計 (Statistics on singing organizations in Shanghai's broadcasting world). *Yule zhoubao,* November 9, 1935, 463.

Shanghai Hong List 上海市工商行名錄. Shanghai: Investigation Bureau of Commerce & Industry, 1940.

Shanghai tong she 上海通社, eds. *Shanghai yanjiu ziliao xuji* 上海研究資料

續集 (Shanghai research materials, vol. 2). Shanghai: Shanghai shudian, 1984.

Shanghai Municipal Police Files. Microfilms from the National Archives.

Shen Ji 沈寂. *Yidai gexing Zhou Xuan* 一代歌星周璇 (Zhou Xuan: greatest star of an era). Xi'an: Shaanxi renmin chubanshe, 1986.

Shen Ziyi 沈子宜. "Duiyu guochan dianying shuo ji ju ni er de hua" 對於國產電影說幾句逆耳的話 (A few contrary words about domestic films). *Dianying yuebao* 7 (1932): 1–4.

Shepherd, John. *Music as Social Text*. Cambridge, Mass.: Polity Press, 1991.

Shi Zhongxing 史中興. *He Luting zhuan* 賀綠汀傳 (A biography of He Luting). Shanghai: Shanghai wenyi chubanshe, 1992.

Shih, Shu-mei. "Gender, Race, and Semicolonialism: Liu Na'ou's Urban Shanghai Landscape." *Journal of Asian Studies* 55 (November 1996): 934–56.

Shidai xiaodiao yiqian zhong 時代小調一千種 (One thousand modern folk tunes). Shanghai: Guoguang shudian, 1936.

"Shouzai paituo" 壽仔拍拖 (Shouzai goes dating). *Xinyue ji* 1 (September 1929).

Shui Jing 水晶. *Liuxing gequ cangsang ji* 流行歌曲滄桑記 (A record of the vicissitudes of popular song). Taipei: Dadi chubanshe, 1985.

Situ Huimin 司徒慧敏. "Montage yan renren shu" Montage 言人人殊 (Montage means different things to different people). *Diantong* 11 (October 1935).

Song Shouchang 宋壽昌. "Yinyue jiaoyu yu xiandai Zhongguo" 音樂教育與現代中國 (Music education and modern China). *Yinyue jiaoshi de liangyou* 1 (May 1926).

Sontag, Susan. "Fascinating Fascism." *New York Review of Books*, February 6, 1975.

Spence, Jonathan. *The Memory Palace of Matteo Ricci*. New York: Viking Penguin, 1984.

———. *The Search for Modern China*. New York: W. W. Norton, 1990.

Staley, S. James. "Is It True What They Say About China?" *Metronome* (December 1936): 12.

Sternberg, Josef von. *Fun in a Chinese Laundry*. London: Columbus Books, 1965.

Stock, Jonathan. "Reconsidering the Past: Zhou Xuan and the Rehabilitation of Early Twentieth-century Popular Music." *Asian Music* 26 (spring/summer 1995): 119–35.

Sun Ji'nan 孫繼南. *Li Jinhui pingzhuan* 黎錦暉評傳 [A critical biography of Li Jinhui]. Beijing: Renmin yinyue chubanshe, 1993.

Sun Yu 孫瑜. "Qingchun de biaoxian" 青春的表現 (Manifestation of youth). *Yingxi zazhi* 1 (July 1931): 42.

———, and Si Kong 司空. "Zhongguo de gewu" 中國的歌舞 (Chinese musicals). *Yingxi zazhi* 1 (July 1931): 39–40.

Süssekind, Flora. *Cinematograph of Words: Literature, Technique, and Modernization in Brazil.* Trans. Paulo Henriques Britto. Stanford, Calif.: Stanford University Press, 1997.

Tagg, Philip. "Analysing Popular Music: Theory, Method, Practice." *Popular Music* 2 (1982): 37–67.

Tam, Yue-him. "Meiji Japan and the Educational and Language Reforms in Late Ch'ing China." In James W. White, Michio Umegaki, and Thomas R. H. Havens, eds., *The Ambivalence of Nationalism: Modern Japan Between East and West.* Lanham, Md.: University Press of America, 1990, 61–78.

Tang Kaijin 唐開錦. "Tingdao er fasheng de ganxiang" 聽到而發生的感想 (Reflections upon listening to the radio). *Yinyue shijie* 8 (September 1939): 227.

Taussig, Michael. *Alterity and Mimesis: A Particular History of the Senses.* New York: Routledge, 1993.

Tcherepnine, Alexander. "Music in Modern China." *Musical Quarterly* 4 (October 1935): 391–400.

Teo, Stephen. "The Shanghai Hangover: The Early Years of Mandarin Cinema in Hong Kong." In Law Kar 羅卡, ed. *Mandarin Films and Popular Songs, 40s–60s: Program of the 17th Hong Kong International Film Festival.* Hong Kong: Urban Council, 1993: 17–25.

Thomas, Nicholas. *Colonialism's Culture: Anthropology, Travel, and Government.* Princeton, N.J.: Princeton University Press, 1994.

Tian Ren 天人. "Li Jinhui bai ri zhi meng" 黎錦暉白日之夢 (Li Jinhui's daydream). *Dianying xinwen,* August 18, 1935.

Tie Min 鐵民. "Yinyue de wuli jichu" 音樂的物理基礎 (The physical basis of music). *Yinyue zazhi* 1 (March 1920).

Tu Guangqi 屠光啟. *Zhou Xuan de zhenshi gushi* 周璇的真實故事 (Zhou Xuan's real story). Taipei: Zhuanji wenxue she, 1987.

Tu, Heng 杜衡. "Cinema Chronicle." *T'ien Hsia Monthly* 7 (October 1938): 291–94.

———. "Cinema Chronicle." *T'ien Hsia Monthly* 9 (November 1939): 383–86.

Vianna, Hermano. *The Mystery of Samba: Popular Music and National Iden-

tity in Brazil. Trans. John Charles Chasteen. Chapel Hill: University of North Carolina Press, 1999.

Wakeman, Frederic, Jr. "Licensing Leisure: The Chinese Nationalists' Attempt to Regulate Shanghai, 1927–1949." *Journal of Asian Studies* 54 (February 1995): 19–42.

Wang Dingjiu 王定九. *Shanghai menjing* 上海門徑 (Guide to Shanghai). Shanghai: Zhongyang shuju, 1932.

Wang Shihui 汪士薈, ed. *Zhou Xuan zishu* 周璇自述 (Zhou Xuan in her own words). Shanghai: Sanlian shudian, 1995.

Wang Wenhe 王文和. *Zhongguo dianying yinyue xunzong* 中國電影音樂尋蹤 (Tracing Chinese film music). Beijing: Zhongguo guangbo dianshi chubanshe, 1995.

Wang Yizhi 王懿之. *Nie Er zhuan* 聶耳傳 (A biography of Nie Er). Shanghai: Shanghai yinyue chubanshe, 1992.

Wang Yuhe 王毓和. *Zhongguo jinxiandai yinyue shi* 中國近現代音樂史 (A history of modern Chinese music). Beijing: Beijing renmin chubanshe, 1984.

Weber, Max. *The Rational and Social Foundations of Music.* London: Feffer and Sims, 1977.

Welch, Walter L. and Leah Brodbeck Stenzel Burt. *From Tinfoil to Stereo: The Acoustic Years of the Recording Industry, 1877–1929.* Gainesville: University Press of Florida, 1994.

Williams, Raymond. *Marxism and Literature.* Oxford: Oxford University Press. 1977.

Wong, Isabel, K. F. "Chinese Musicology in the Twentieth Century." In Bruno Nettl and Philip V. Bohlman, eds., *Comparative Musicology and Anthropology of Music.* Chicago: University of Chicago Press, 1991, 37–55.

———. "*Geming gequ:* Songs for the Education of the Masses." In Bonnie Macdougal, ed., *Popular Chinese Culture and Performing Arts in the People's Republic of China, 1949–1979.* Berkeley: University of California Press, 1984.

Wong, Kee-chee 黃奇智. "Shanghai Baidai gongsi de yange" 上海百代公司之沿革 (Pathé: the evolution of a record company). In Law Kar 羅卡, ed., *Mandarin Films and Popular Songs, 40s–60s: Program of the 17th Hong Kong International Film Festival.* Hong Kong: Urban Council, 1993: 91.

———. "Shidai gequ er san shi" 時代歌曲二三事 (Two or three things about mandarin pop). In Law Kar 羅卡, ed., *Mandarin Films and Popular*

Songs, 40s–60s: Program of the 17th Hong Kong International Film Festival.
Hong Kong: Urban Council, 1993: 12–17.

———, ed. *Shidai qu de luiguang suiyue* 時代曲的流光歲月 (The age of
Shanghainese pops, 1930–1970). Hong Kong: Joint Publishing, 2000.

———. *Shidai qu zonglun* 時代曲綜論 (A comprehensive study of modern songs). Hong Kong: Chinese University of Hong Kong Extension
School and RTHK, 1978.

Wu Ruifeng 吳瑞豐. "Zhongguo dianying zuijin zhi xin qingxiang"
中國電影最近之新傾向 (The latest trends in Chinese movies). *Yingmi
zhoubao,* November 14, 1934, 130.

Xiandai liushui xingyun qu 現代流水行雲曲 (Modern popular songs).
Shanghai: Shidai yinyue yanjiu she, 1936.

Xiandai mingge wubai qu 現代名歌五百曲 (Five hundred famous modern
songs). Shanghai: Guoguang shudian, 1937.

Xiao Min 小民. "Wuxiandian boyin jiemu wo jian" 無線電播音節目我見
(My views on wireless radio programs). *Diansheng,* July 14, 1934, 516.

Xiao Youmei 蕭友梅. "Fakan ci" 發刊詞 (Editor's introduction). *Yinyue
yuekan* 1 (November 1937).

———. "Guanyu woguo xin yinyue yundong" 關於我國新音樂運動 (On
the Chinese new music movement). *Yinyue yuekan* 4 (February 1938).

———. "Shenme shi yinyue?" 甚麼是音樂 (What is music?). *Yinyue zazhi*
1 (May 1920).

———. "Shinian lai yinyue jie zhi chengji" 十年來音樂界之成績 (The
achievements of music professionals in the last ten years). *Yinyue
yuekan* 2 (December 1937): 25–30.

———. "Weishenme yinyue zai Zhongguo bu wei yiban ren suo
zhongshi" 為甚麼音樂在中國不為一般人所重視 (Why isn't music taken
seriously by most people in China?). *Yinyue zazhi* 4 (June 1934): 1–3.

———. "Yinyue de shili" 音樂的勢力 (The power of music). *Yinyue jiaoyu*
3 (March 1934): 9–13. Reprinted in *Yinyue zazhi* 2 (April 1934) and
Yisheng 4 (September 1936).

———. "Yinyue zhi yanjin" 音樂之演進 (The evolution of music). *Dazhong*
3 (January 1934): 6–7.

———. "Zhongxi yinyue de bijiao yanjiu" 中西音樂的比較研究 (Comparative research on Chinese and Western music). *Yinyue zazhi* 10
(1920).

———. "Zuijin yiqian nian xiyue fazhan zhi xianzhe shishi yu
woguo jiuyue buzhen zhi yuanyin"
最近一千年來西樂發展之顯著事實與我國舊樂不振之原因 (The obvious

truth of Western music's progress in the last thousand years and the reason why traditional music failed to improve). *Yinyue zazhi* 3 (July 1934).

Xie Bo 解波, ed. *Wode chengming yu buxing: Wang Renmei huiyi lu* 我的成名與不幸—王人美回憶錄 (My success and misfortune: the reminiscences of Wang Renmei). Shanghai: Shanghai wenyi chubanshe, 1985.

Xin Shanghai mingge sanbai qu 新上海名歌三百曲 (Three hundred popular songs of new Shanghai). Shanghai: Shanghai gequ she, 1935.

Xu Gongmei 徐公美. *Dianying fada shi* 電影發達史 (History of the rise of cinema). Shanghai: Shangwu, 1938.

Xu Xu 徐訏. *Xu Xu quanji* 徐訏全集 (Complete works of Xu Xu). 15 vols. Taipei: Zhengzhong, 1967.

Yamaguchi, Yoshiko 山口淑子 [Li Xianglan 李香蘭]. *Zai Zhongguo de rizi* 在中國的日子 (My days in China). Trans. Jin Ruojing 金若靜. Taipei: Linbai chubanshe, 1989.

Yan Hong 燕虹. "Nü mingxing chang ge suxie" 女明星唱歌速寫 (Brief descriptions of female stars singing). *Yisheng* 3 (August 1935).

Yan Ru 宴如. "Dianying gequ yinggai zhuyi de wenti" 電影歌曲應該注意的問題 (Problems to do with screen songs). *Yisheng* 2 (July 1935).

Yao, Hsin-nung 姚莘農. "Chinese Movies." *T'ien Hsia Monthly* 4 (April 1937): 393–400.

Yeh, Wen-Hsin, and Frederic Wakeman, eds. *Shanghai Sojourners.* Berkeley, Calif.: Institute of East Asian Studies, 1992.

"Yinyue zuotan hui" 音樂座談會 (A roundtable discussion of music). *Zazhi yuekan* 7 (1944): 37–45.

Yuan Jin 袁進. *Yuanyang hudie pai* 鴛鴦蝴蝶派 (The mandarin duck and butterfly school). Shanghai: Shanghai shudian, 1994.

"Zai tingbudao Zhou Xuan de yuanyin gesheng le" 再聽不到周璇的原音歌聲了 (We'll never hear Zhou Xuan's original recordings again). *Yangcheng wanbao,* April 8, 1999.

Zha, Jianying. *China Pop: How Soap Operas, Tabloids, and Bestsellers Are Transforming a Culture.* New York: New Press, 1995.

Zhang Henshui 張恨水. *Tixiao yinyuan* 啼笑因緣 (Fate in tears and laughter). Taiyuan: Beiyue wenyi chubanshe, 1993.

Zhang Xichen 章錫琛. "Liushengji zhi guoqu xianzai ji weilai" 留聲機之過去現在及未來 (The past, present, and future of the phonograph). *Dongfang zazhi* 12 (November 1915, December 1915): 14–18, 1–6.

Zhang, Yingjin. *The City in Modern Chinese Literature and Film: Configura-*

tions of Space, Time, and Gender. Stanford, Calif.: Stanford University Press, 1996.

———, ed. *Cinema and Urban Culture in Shanghai, 1922–1943.* Stanford, Calif.: Stanford University Press, 1999.

Zhang Zhang 章杖. "1936 nian xin yinyue fazhan de jiantao" 1936 年新音樂發展的檢討 (An examination of new musical developments in 1936). *Yinyue jiaoyu* 5 (January 1937): 73–86.

———. "Gechang yishu de fuxing" 歌唱藝術的復興 (The renaissance of the art of singing). *Yinyue jiaoyu* 5 (April 1937): 11–15.

———. "Yinyue yishu wang na'er qu?" 音樂藝術往哪兒去? (Quo vadis, musical art?). *Yinyue jiaoyu* 8 (August 1936): 19–40.

———. "Yinyue zhen gaoyu yiqie ma?" 音樂真高於一切麼? (Is music really transcendent?). *Yinyue jiaoyu* 5 (March 1937).

Zhang Zhaowei 張釗維. "Liuxing geyao ciqu zuojia da shi ji chugao" 流行歌謠詞曲家大事記初稿 (A preliminary chronology of popular song composers). *Lianhe wenxue* 82 (August 1991): 130–51.

Zheng Daoyue 鄭導樂. "Xin yinyue fazhan de qingxiang" 新音樂發展的傾向 (The direction of new musical development). *Xiju yu yinyue* 1 (January 1931).

Zheng Junli 鄭君里. "Xiandai Zhongguo dianying shilüe" 現代中國電影史略 (A brief history of modern Chinese cinema). In Zhongguo dianying ziliao guan 中國電影資料館, ed., *Zhongguo wusheng dianying* 中國無聲電影 (Chinese silent cinema). Beijing: Zhongguo dianying chubanshe, 1996: 1385–1432.

"Zhengli guangbo jiemu zhi banfa" 整理廣播節目之辦法 (Procedures for regulating broadcast programs). *Yule zhoubao,* July 11, 1936, 531.

Zhi 芝. "Wuxiandian bosong de gequ he xiaodiao" 無線電播送的歌曲和小調 (Songs and folk tunes broadcast on the wireless). *Diansheng,* January 19, 1934, 38.

Zhi Er 之爾. "Cong 'Malu tianshi' de gequ shuoqi" 從《馬路天使》的歌曲說起 (On the songs in *Street Angel*). *Xinhua huabao* 7 (1937).

Zhongguo yinyue cidian 中國音樂詞典 (Dictionary of Chinese music). Beijing: Renmin yinyue chubanshe, 1984.

Zhongguo yinyue qikan pianmu huilu, 1906–49 中國音樂期刊篇目匯錄 (Bibliography of the contents of Chinese music magazines, 1906–49). Beijing: Wenhua yishu chubanshe, 1990.

Zhou Bang 周邦. "Sheng de gailiang" 笙的改良 (The improvement of the *sheng*). *Yinyue jiaoyu* 4 (April 1936).

Zhou Wei 周偉, with Chang Jing 常晶. *Wode mama Zhou Xuan*

我的媽媽周璇 (My mother Zhou Xuan). Taiyuan: Shanxi renmin chubanshe, 1987.

Zhou Weizhi 周巍峙, ed. *Nie Er quanji* 聶耳全集 (The complete Nie Er). 2 vols. Beijing: Wenhua yishu chubanshe, 1985.

Zhou Yang 周揚. "Guanyu guofang wenxue" 關於國防文學 (On national defense literature). *Wenxue jie,* June 5, 1936.

Zhou Zuoren 周作人. "Pingmin wenxue" 平民文學 (Literature of the common people). *Meizhou pinglun,* January 19, 1919.

———. *Ziji de yuandi* 自己的園地 (My own garden). Beijing: Renmin wenxue chubanshe, 1988.

Zhu Ying 朱英. "Zhongguo yinyue de chulu" 中國音樂的出路 (The way out for Chinese music). *Yinyue yuekan* 1 (November 1937): 11–14.

Zhu Yingpeng 朱應鵬. "Guanyu wuhui de hua" 關於舞會的話 (On a dance performance). *Shenbao,* July 27, 1930.

———, et al. *Yishu sanjia yan* 藝術三家言 (Three artists on art). Shanghai: Liangyou, 1928.

Zui xin zhongwai mingge ji 最新中外名歌集 (Latest songs from China and the West). Shanghai: Guoguang shudian, 1940.

Chinese-language Periodicals

Beiyang huabao 北洋畫報 (North China pictorial)
Diansheng 電聲 (Movietone)
Diantong huabao 電通畫報 (Denton pictorial)
Dianying huabao 電影畫報 (Screen pictorial)
Dianying yishu 電影藝術 (Film art)
Dianying yuebao 電影月報 (Film monthly)
Dongfang zazhi 東方雜誌 (Eastern miscellany)
Gexing huabao 歌星畫報 (Pop star pictorial)
Guangzhou yinyue 廣州音樂 (Guangzhou music)
Kaiming 開明 (Enlightenment)
Liangyou huabao 良友畫報 (The young companion)
Meiyu 美育 (Aesthetic education)
Meizhou pinglun 每週評論 (The weekly review)
Mingxing banyuekan 明星半月刊 (Star biweekly)
Nüsheng yuekan 女聲月刊 (Women's voice)
Qingqing dianying 青青電影 (Chin-chin movie magazine)
Shanghai shenghuo 上海生活 (Shanghai life)
Shanghai yingxun 上海影訊 (Shanghai film update)

Shenbao 申報 (Shanghai news)
Shengse huabao 聲色畫報 (Vox magazine)
Shidai dianying 時代電影 (Modern cinema)
Wanxiang 萬象 (Phenomena)
Xiao pengyou 小朋友 (Little friend)
Xiaoshuo yuebao 小說月報 (Short story monthly)
Xiju yu yinyue 戲劇與音樂 (Drama and music)
Xin qingnian 新青年 (New youth)
Xin yinxing 新銀星 (Silverland)
Xinyue ji 新月集 (New moon collection)
Xinhua huabao 新華畫報 (New China pictorial)
Yingmi zhoubao 影迷週報 (Film fan weekly news)
Yingxi zazhi 影戲雜誌 (The film magazine)
Yinyue chao 音樂潮 (Music wave)
Yinyue jikan 音樂季刊 (Music quarterly)
Yinyue jiaoshi de liangyou 音樂教師的良友 (The music teacher's companion)
Yinyue jiaoyu 音樂教育 (Music education)
Yinyue jie 音樂界 (Musician's world)
Yinyue shijie 音樂世界 (Music world)
Yinyue yuekan 音樂月刊 (Music monthly)
Yinyue zazhi 音樂雜誌 (Music magazine)
Yisheng 藝聲 (Art sound: Film and music monthly)
Yule zhoubao 娛樂週報 (Variety weekly)
Yuzhou feng 宇宙風 (Cosmic wind)
Zazhi yuekan 雜誌月刊 (Miscellany monthly)

Andrew F. Jones is Assistant Professor in the Department of East Asian Languages and Cultures at the University of California, Berkeley. He is the author of *Like a Knife: Ideology and Genre in Contemporary Chinese Popular Music* and translator of Yu Hua, *The Past and the Punishments.*

Library of Congress Cataloging-in-Publication Data
Jones, Andrew F.
Yellow music : media culture and colonial modernity in the Chinese jazz age /
Andrew F. Jones.
p. cm.
Includes bibliographical references (p.   ) and index.
ISBN 0-8223-2685-x (cloth : alk. paper) —
ISBN 0-8223-2694-9 (pbk. : alk. paper)
1. Popular music—China—History and criticism.   I. Title.
ML3502.C5 J63   2001
781.64'0951—dc21   2001017335